ONE NATION UNDER FEAR

FEAR MONGERS AND SCAREDY CATS IN THE HOME OF THE BRAVE
(AND WHAT YOU CAN DO ABOUT IT)

by Bob Cesca

ONE NATION UNDER FEAR

FEAR MONGERS AND SCAREDY CATS IN THE HOME OF THE BRAVE
(AND WHAT YOU CAN DO ABOUT IT)

by Bob Cesca

S&R
PUBLISHERS

STERLING & ROSS PUBLISHERS
NEW YORK § TORONTO

Published by
Sterling & Ross Publishers
New York, NY 10001
www.sterlingandross.com

Library of Congress Cataloging-in-Publication Data

Cesca, Bob.
  One nation under fear : scaredy cats and fear-mongers in the home of the brave (and what you can do about it) / by Bob Cesca.
    p. cm.
  ISBN 978-0-9814535-0-7 (paperback : alk. paper)
  1. United States--Politics and government--2001- I. Title.
  JK275.C38 2008
  320.60973--dc22
                                        2008034047

Cover design by Bob Cesca and Shulamit Ponet.
Composition/typography by Rachel Trusheim.

10 9 8 7 6 5 4 3 2 1

Printed in the United States of America.

For Tara

Table of Contents

Ignorance and prejudice
and fear walk hand in hand.

−RUSH, "Witch Hunt"

FOREWORD

Fear—specifically the right wing's masterful manipulation of it—is now dominating American politics.

And when it comes to scaring the American people, the Bush administration is in a league of its own—the equivalent of the 1927 New York Yankees, the Steel Curtain Pittsburgh Steelers, or the Showtime-era Lakers of Magic, Kareem, and James Worthy. Everywhere you turn, there is another Alarmist All-Star.

Bush, Cheney, Rice, Rummy, Rove. Over the last five years, this Murderers' Row of lethal bat-swingers has already guaranteed itself a place in the Fear Mongering Hall of Shame with Ruthian blasts of pulse-quickening, anxiety-inducing red alert rhetoric. Call them the Sultans of Cold Sweat.

Then-National Security Advisor Condi Rice made herself a surefire first ballot inductee back in 2003 with her ominous prewar warning about Saddam: "There will always be some uncertainty about how quickly he can acquire nuclear weapons. But we don't want the smoking gun to be a mushroom cloud."

Cheney ensured his enshrinement during the 2004 vice presidential debate: "The biggest threat we face today is the possibility of terrorists smuggling a nuclear weapon or a biological agent into one of our own cities and threatening the lives of hundreds of thousands of Americans."

And who'll ever forget Bush's classic 2003 State of the Union performance? Thumping every panic button in sight, he reeled off all the ways Saddam could rain death and destruction on us, including: "biological weapons sufficient to produce over 25,000 liters of anthrax—enough doses to kill several million people"; "more than 38,000 liters of botulinum toxin—enough to subject millions of people to death by respiratory failure"; "as much as 500 tons of sarin, mustard and VX nerve agent. In such quantities, these chemical agents could also kill untold thousands."

But despite these legendary fear-inducing feats, Team Terror has never been content to take a breather on the bench. We are always being reminded of the terrorists' imminent arrival just before an election.

The president's chat with Matt Lauer on the fifth anniversary of 9/11, less than two months before the 2006 midterm election, was a shoo-in Hall of Shame performance.

Here was his up-close-and-extremely-personal response to Lauer's questions about torture: "Matt, I'm just telling you, what this government has done is to take steps necessary to protect you and your family... We're at war. This is people that want to come and kill your families... This isn't make-believe." Gulp.

As if that weren't ominous enough, the president followed up with this leap into the dread end zone at a press conference later that week: "It's a dangerous world. I wish it wasn't that way. I wish I could tell the American people, don't worry about it, they're not coming again. But they are coming again."

Not to be outdone, the always cheerful Cheney cleared the bases two days later on *Meet the Press*, trotting out one of his patented "what if" scenarios of mass murder: "The real threat is the possibility of a cell of al-Qaeda in the midst of one of our own cities with a nuclear weapon, or a biological agent. In that case, you'd be dealing—for example, if on 9/11 they'd had a nuke instead of an airplane, you'd have been looking at a casualty toll that would rival all the deaths in all the wars fought by Americans in 230 years." And if Dick Cheney had rocket-powered wheels instead of legs, he'd be the fastest man alive.

Then, just two weeks before the 2006 election, with the polls heavily skewing Democratic, the administration's panic-button pushers brought out the big guns, including an ad featuring Osama bin Laden saying that 9/11 was "nothing compared to what you will see next," the specter of colossal tax raises, Dick Cheney repeatedly mentioning the possibility of "mass death in the United States," and even that old race-baiting favorite, the fear of black men lusting after southern white women.

The despicable Republican National Committee ad featured bin Laden's right-hand man Ayman al-Zawahiri, a ticking clock, a nuclear, explosion, and the tag line: "These are the stakes. Vote November 7th." What a contemptible piece of work. This collage of horror prompted Keith Olbermann to deliver an acid-tongued response. Here's a taste:

The dictionary definition of the word "terrorize" is simple and not open to misinterpretation: "To fill or overpower with terror; terrify. To coerce by intimidation or fear." ... By this definition, the leading terrorist group in this world right now is al Qaeda. But the leading terrorist group in this country right now is the Republican Party.

Eleven presidents ago, a chief executive reassured us that "we have nothing to fear but fear itself." His distant successor has wasted his administration insisting that there is nothing we can have but fear itself. Not content with scaring the bejesus out of voters with the equivalent of a GOP-financed al Qaeda recruitment video, the RNC also produced an ad that made the unfounded claim, "If Democrats take over Congress, they will raise taxes by 2.4 trillion dollars to keep up with their reckless spending." Excuse me? "Their reckless spending"? Did I miss something?

Then there was a blast-from-the-Jim-Crow-past use of race-based fear, in the form of a slimy RNC ad that accused Harold Ford, who was threatening to take a Republican Senate seat in Tennessee, of accepting donations from pornographers and featured a scantily clad blonde who claimed to have met Ford at a Playboy party winking and saying "Harold, call me." It was a mudslinging twofer: at once sleazy and laced with racist overtones.

You can be sure that John McCain and the Right will continue to play the fear card in 2008 because that's all that's left in their deck. And that's why it's incredibly important that Democrats take back national security as an issue from the Republicans.

We've had enough of spineless, fear-driven, walking-on-eggshells would-be leaders. Enough of Beltway versions of the Cowardly Lion of Oz, driven by the fear of saying the wrong thing (wouldn't want to give the other side ammo for the inevitable attack ad), of offending someone (anyone!), of going out on a limb, and, above all, of losing.

It is time for our leaders to stand up and refuse to be cowed or give an inch when the hate-mongers try to appeal to voters' lizard brains by raising the specter of madrassa schools, foreign-sounding middle names, missing lapel pins, fulminating preachers, or terrorists celebrating over the election of a specific candidate.

Arianna Huffington

PREFACE

THIS IS A DARK RIDE

So here we are. The end of the Bush administration: or what I like to call "the dark ride." At various carnivals and amusement parks, you might recall the signs posted at the entrance to haunted houses and the like, warning customers who dared to enter the attraction: THIS IS A DARK RIDE. John Larroquette, on his classic (and underrated) television series once joked that these signs ought to be posted at the end of the human birth canal.

But I don't think anyone expected that the Bush administration was going to be quite *this* dark. Despite the insanity of the 2000 election, the first nine months of the Bush presidency appeared to level off into what might become a mostly nothing administration. Another one-term Bushie. Rather than a "dark ride," it'd be more like a "dork ride." I remember trying to make the best of the Bush-Cheney election theft by thinking, screw it, he doesn't have a mandate to do anything, and, besides, we can make fun of his special-needs gaffes for a while longer. Then, I figured, Al Gore would run again in 2004 and win. It'll all be over like *that*.

I missed the signs.

Little did I know that the Bush regime would dramatically mutate into what became arguably the most deceptive and incompetent executive regime in American history. The stops along this dark ride included scenes of torture; war; dead soldiers; dead children; the destruction of liberty; the rewriting of science books; the dumping of toxins into our air and water; news graphics of animated airplanes exploding over the ocean; dead bodies washing their way down flooded American streets; and the near collapse of our national economy. And the Bush Republicans were able to get away with all of it largely due to their unprecedented campaign to exploit our darkest fears.

I wrote this book as a reaction to this criminal conspiracy of fear-mongering and what I perceive to be a trend toward a fully realized authoritarian America, guided by manipulative cowards who have proved their utter disregard for the freedoms, liberties and fearlessness that ought to dominate our national character.

Our generation has been tasked with recording the history of this regime now, before time and nostalgia smoothes over the insanity of it all. And, for my part in that effort, this book is intended to be, much like my blog entries for the *Huffington Post*, a series of essays that aim to debunk and ridicule (I'm a snarky blogger, after all) some of the more twisted or hubristic episodes of fear-mongering from this dark ride. It's not entirely comprehensive, of course. For that, I'd have to kill way too many trees. That said, you'll find that these essays will suffice as an adequate tour through the darkness.

My hope is that, by the end of this book, you're so sick and bloody tired of the Bush Republican fear-mongering—all of their cowardice and their scare tactics—that you'll want to perhaps help out some of your fellow Americans in their efforts to achieve something truly heroic.

In the meantime, fasten your safety harness, keep your hands and feet inside the car at all times and enjoy the ride.

Bob Cesca
On the summit of Little Round Top
Gettysburg, Pennsylvania
April 26, 2008

ARGUMENTUM IN TERROREM

Fear is the foundation of most governments;
but it is so sordid and brutal a passion, and renders
men in whose breasts it predominates so stupid and miserable,
that Americans will not be likely to approve of
any political institution that is founded on it.

–John Adams
Thoughts on Government (1776)

Aboard this dark ride at the bloody start of this fourth American century, the most manly, warhawking, right-wing testostonauts among us—those Americans who condemn the French, bash the gays and accuse the Democrats of being effete—are also the most easily frightened into submission by the scare tactics and cowardice of the Bush Republicans. They are, as John Adams wrote, "stupid and miserable" with fear.

According to conventional wisdom, Bush Republican politicians and pundits are allegedly the ones who "take the fight to the enemy." They involuntarily blurt out plainspoken things like "shoot first and ask questions later" and "bring 'em on" and "these colors don't run." They possess what I like to call Hillbilly Defiance: an ability to literally take pride in how much money they burn per diem pumping gasoline into their Hummers and SUVs. Gay jokes are hilarious and gay marriage is an abomination. They shoot their friends in the face and then, by the power of their awesome manliness, somehow convince *the wounded friend* to apologize on national television.

So why, then, if they're so tough and manly, are the Bush Republicans the first ones to enable and orchestrate the dismantling of our Constitution and American ideals? The answer is remarkably simple. They're mostly cowards. Misguided, reactionary cowards who are wholly accustomed to submitting to the will of their authoritarian masters.[1] They are, at best, easily spooked fainting sheep and, at worst, willfully ignorant, myopic halfwits who are simply too lazy to read the facts and accept basic truths—be they scientific, political, ideological or miscellaneous. It's a group that includes President Bush, Vice President Cheney, Senator John McCain, Rudy Giuliani, Karl Rove, Newt Gingrich, Joe Lieberman, the Project for the New American Century (PNAC) neoconservatives including William Kristol, and other congressional and bureaucratic far-right political leaders who have dominated and exaggerated the terrorism issue—especially since the September 11 attacks—for the sake of consolidating their political and financial power. They're supported by corporate media propagandists like Bill O'Reilly, Ann Coulter, Rush Limbaugh, Michelle Malkin, Sean Hannity, G. Gordon Liddy and the rest of the well-known talkers, bloggers and FOX News Channel personalities.

And, collectively, they're exploiting fear and terror at the ex-

---

1   See the chapter "The Ultimate Fear Bomb" for more about epithets and name-calling in politics… unless you're chicken.

pense of our liberty and national character.

The pejorative term "fear-mongering" is the colloquial form of a logical fallacy known as Argumentum in Terrorem, or an "appeal to fear." The most widely regarded species of fear-monger systematically demagogues the threat of terrorist attacks; the threat of God's wrath; or the specter of "menacing" brown people as a means of manipulating citizens, voters, other leaders and the media into supporting the fear-monger as the great protector, the one who can best save us and our so-called American ideals from being destroyed by these evildoers.

By now, we know the lines practically by rote. *If you don't support the Bush administration or the McCain campaign, then the terrorists win… or the next attack will come in the form of mushroom cloud… the terrorists are a threat to your children… or there will be race wars… or you will burn in eternal hellfire,* and so on and so on.[2] In some instances, fear-mongers such as Vice President Cheney have claimed that victories for Democrats are victories for "al-Qaeda types."[3] Most recently, an attempt has been made to scare the less educated, racist and gullible portions of the American electorate with a rumor that Senator Barack Obama is an Islamic terrorist.

Fear-mongers seek authoritarian control and, in order to secure this level of domination, they openly threaten us with warn-

2   During a May 21, 2007 press conference, President Bush confronted NBC News reporter David "Stretch" Gregory over the issue of Iraq. By the end of the exchange, the president was so worked up in a lathery feargasm that he injected Gregory's children into the debate: "These people attacked us before we were in Iraq. They viciously attacked us before we were in Iraq, and they've been attacking ever since. They are a threat to your children, David, and whoever is in that Oval Office better understand it and take measures necessary to protect the American people."

3   See the chapter "Bottled Liquids are Banned from this Chapter"… unless you're chicken.

ings of berserker toe-monsters lurking under our beds, waiting to reach out and bite our feet as we dash for the safety of our covers. Political thinkers and social scientists have differentiated modern fear-mongering, Bush-Cheney-McCain-style authoritarian conservatives into two distinct subgroups: Leaders, also described as Social Dominators, and Followers of Right-Wing Authoritarianism.

John Dean, former Nixon White House special counsel, author of *Conservatives Without Conscience* and present-day critic of the Bush administration (see the chapter "Paruresis" about Dean's nemesis, G. Gordon Liddy), picked up on the work of psychologist Dr. Robert Altemeyer, who developed and popularized the theory of Right-Wing Authoritarianism. Dean, expanding on Dr. Altemeyer's work, described our current authoritarian conservative Leaders, like so:

> ...manipulative and cunning personalities, who are typically men: dominating, opposes equality, desirous of personal power, amoral, intimidating and bullying, faintly hedonistic, vengeful, pitiless, exploitive, manipulative, dishonest, cheats to win, highly prejudiced (racist, sexist, homophobic), mean-spirited, militant, nationalistic, tells others what they want to hear, takes advantage of "suckers," specializes in creating false images to sell self, may or may not be religious, usually politically and economically conservative/Republican.[4]

I would only expand this list with one important addition: many of the Leaders are also, themselves, cowards. These authoritarian conservative Leaders fear a wide variety of toe-monsters, but they fear *We the People* almost as much as they do

---

4   http://writ.news.findlaw.com/dean/20070921.html

any sort of terrorist threat or attack.

They fear participatory American democracy because it's an obstacle in their ascent to permanent rule. They fear voter participation, they fear a well-educated populace, and they fear our constitutionally guaranteed rights and liberties because they distrust the people. They attempt to suppress voters and rig elections because high voter turnout has traditionally benefited more liberal candidates.[5] They use fear to intimidate the electorate. They tell us that a vote for their opponent is a vote for the terrorists. They attempt to dumb down education both in terms of funding and content because educated people are better equipped to see through their propaganda and faith-based, jingoistic far-right worldview. They attempt to censor and control free thought, speech and expression as a means to limit dissent—the sworn enemy of the authoritarian. They buy up newspapers, radio stations and television networks to limit and regulate the distribution of information while attempting to force legislation that would give corporations preferential access to the Internet.

And then there are Dr. Altemeyer's equally cowardly Right-Wing Authoritarian Followers, who John Dean described like so:

> ...highly religious, moderate to little education, trust untrustworthy authorities, prejudiced (particularly against homosexuals, women, and followers of religions other than their own), mean-spirited, narrow-minded, intolerant, bullying, zealous, dogmatic, uncritical toward their chosen authority, hypocritical, inconsistent and contra-

---

5   This is conventional wisdom. For example, if turnout is higher than usual, it implies a larger than normal turnout among younger people, women and minorities, all of whom are more inclined to vote Democratic than Republican.

dictory, prone to panic easily, highly self-righteous, moralistic, strict disciplinarian, severely punitive, demands
loyalty and returns it, little self-awareness, usually politically and economically conservative/Republican.

Generally, this describes anyone who has enabled the Bush-
Cheney-McCain Republicans over the years—simply put, that
remaining 30 percent who believe that, despite all proof to the
contrary, President Bush has done a heck of a job. Conservative
pundits, talk-show hosts and bloggers, like the screeching half-
real-half-ghost Nazgûl from *Lord of the Rings*, exist in both the
realm of the Leaders and the Followers. As Leaders, they help to
demagogue and propagandize the will of the political Leaders
and shape the debate into bite-sized morsels for consumption by
their dittohead Followers. As Followers themselves, they aren't always privy to the truth behind the fear-mongering and are therefore subjected to the will of their authoritarian political Leaders.
Consequently, they possess the twice-as-dangerous personality
traits of both, which makes them super-authoritarians, super-
cowards and super-fear-mongers who possess the combined psy-
cho-strength of both groups. In a way, these media Nazgûl are
more powerful than the political Leaders in that they aren't subject to the checks and balances found in America's constitutional
form of government and, consequently, are much more prone to
lying and flagrantly manipulative statements. For example, it's
much easier for Bill O'Reilly and Sean Hannity to deliberately
mislead the public. When O'Reilly falsely accused American soldiers of killing Nazi prisoners at Malmedy during World War
II (the exact opposite was true), no one at FOX News Channel
convened any committee hearings at which O'Reilly would've
been forced to back up his claims under oath. The only means of

accountability were MSNBC's Keith Olbermann, who reported extensively on O'Reilly's gaffe, and the independent watchdog group Media Matters for America. Irrespective of both investigations, O'Reilly never apologized or corrected this statement, and his viewers, who very likely are *not* Olbermann viewers, were none the wiser. The result? Bill O'Reilly and his ilk have fear-mongering latitude far beyond that of their Leaders. For now.

The truth is that despite the backwards marketing of the modern conservative movement, the progressive and liberal voices of post-September 11 America have displayed far more bravery and patriotism in the face of terrorism than any far-right talk-show host, blogger, activist, politician or voter who insists that a false sense of security takes precedent over our liberties and freedom. We're experiencing a revival of that for which liberalism used to stand before the post-Goldwater conservative movement hijacked the discourse and, with unwitting support from the left, managed to inaccurately define liberalism as somehow cowardly and foppish. Prior to the rise of the modern conservative movement within the establishment and its subsequent re-branding of liberalism, it was an undisputed fact that liberals helped to defeat the Nazis, Imperial Japan and Fascist Italy. Liberals freed the slaves and desegregated the South. Liberals and progressives established trade unions and invented the middle class despite attacks from conservative corporate barons and money interests. Liberals defeated McCarthyism; they stood up against an unjust war in Vietnam; and they exposed a cancer in the Nixon White House even though they were attacked as unpatriotic subversives. Classical liberal revolutionaries, the evolutionary ancestors of modern progressives, created the Constitution and the Bill of Rights. These were radical free-thinkers who rebelled against a unitary executive in King George and dared to confront a superpower in the fields and forests of the new world. Prior to the American Revolution, the truth is that the Boston Tea Party was, in fact, a radical liberal protest against a corporate tax cut.[6] The Patriots who organized against the British Empire were men of the Age of the Enlightenment:[7] a progressive movement that sought to evolve beyond religious dogma and political tyranny, and you can bet that if they existed today, the Enlightenment would be mislabeled by the far-right as somehow "faggy." Yet none of these liberals could ever reasonably be accused of being weak or ineffectual.

So it's with significant necessity that this tradition of unwavering fearlessness and audacious defiance against both terrorism and far-right fear-mongering has been reinvigorated in our time.

Conversely, Bush Republicanism is the exact opposite of how it's been popularly mythologized. The truth is that the Republican Party has been hijacked by an endless cycle of cowardly yet self-proclaimed manly-men happily feeding the goals of equally cowardly fear-mongers. In the last eight years, we've witnessed

---

6   The Tea Act of 1773 eliminated the import duty, also known as the Tea Tax paid by the massive British East India Company. The Tea Act allowed the East India Company to severely undercut tea prices offered by smaller colonial merchants. Don't let Bush-Cheney-McCain Republicans co-opt this one. The Boston Tea Party was a progressive/liberal protest and one of the most patriotic events in our nation's history.

7   The ridiculous yet earnest Conservapedia.com, which is intended to be a right-wing alternative to Wikipedia.com (as Stephen Colbert says, "Reality has a well-known liberal bias."), lists a very-short Enlightenment entry including the following paraphrased observation: "According to researcher Rodney Stark, the The 'Enlightenment' [was] conceived initially as a propaganda ploy by militant atheists and humanists who attempted to claim credit for the rise of science [through promulgating] the falsehood that science required the defeat of religion." In other words, the Enlightenment was a conspiracy by secular progressives. America, then, was founded by secular progressive conspirators. Thanks for the assist, Conservapedia!

the enabling of a slow but systematic destruction of American principals by easily frightened authoritarian Followers, a group that is more than eager to succumb under the duress of fear-mongers who, in turn, are selling-out our history, traditions and posterity for political and financial advantage. Yet very few in our very serious corporate media have taken up the task of correcting the presently inaccurate national ideological dynamic. No task is more important. The price of ignoring the truth is the continued smothering of the Constitution under the suffocating pressure of a thousand false statements about *this* or *that* threat.

While necessity dictates that you and I remain strong in our defense of American liberty, it's okay to be afraid of terrorism. In fact, it's perfectly natural to fear all sorts of things, whether it's terrorism or cancer or foreclosure or fecal coliform bacteria in our beef or Suze Orman's huge nagging mouth biting me on the head like that freakish half-human, half-alien mutant at the end of *Alien: Resurrection*.[8] As Barry Glassner wrote in *The Culture of Fear*:

> Valid fears have their place; they cue us to danger. False and overdrawn fears only cause hardship.

And how we react to that fear, whether valid or overdrawn, separates cowards from heroes; it separates Americans of character from spineless reactionaries who rush to war and trample our liberties along the way. The difference is whether we allow our collective fears to paralyze us into supporting radical authoritarianism. In other words, while it's okay to fear a terrorist attack, it's the worst kind of cowardice to willingly hand over our rights

---

8   It might appear as if I have an irrational fear of financial guru Suze Orman. I don't really fear Suze Orman, but I'll understand if you do.

in order to prevent one. It's even more egregious to exploit this fear as part of a sinister plot to, as Senator Obama says, "scare up votes."

This will read as cliché, but throughout the last six or seven years, I will occasionally contrast for whoever is within range of my gesticulating arms the striking difference between modern Republicans and that lone Chinese man who stood in front of the tanks in Tiananmen Square. He risked either being killed on the spot or surely dying in a variety of ways in a Chinese prison. He risked his life in order to attain something unheard of in communist China. Something you and I take for granted.

On the other side of the world, more than ten years later, the faction of America that carries itself with balls-out Reagan-ish toughness can't run fast enough from even our most basic liberties in order to cobble together even a nominal level of additional safety and security. I can't think of a species of American less patriotic. You and I are un-American because we don't have a flag on our lapels, but the Bush Republicans are considered to be true patriots simply because they supported something called the U.S.A. Patriot Act. There are few things in this world or the next that are more backwards.

Dittoheads and the like hear from their fear-mongering man-ly-men that the only way to catch a terrorist is to have the power to literally *disappear* American citizens without legal recourse, so they go along with it. They hear that the only way to keep us safe is to support illegal invasion and indefinite occupation of another nation without a strategy for withdrawal, so they support that, too. They probably don't know nor care what habeas corpus is, so that's gone. Illegal searches under the president's bastardization of the Foreign Intelligence Surveillance Act (FISA)? Amnesty for the telecommunications corporations when they illegally turn over your phone records to the administration? Awesome, as long as they're sufficiently tricked into believing they're safe from the toe-biting evildoers lurking under their beds.

These Bush Republican cowards are far too full of piss and vinegar to stop repeating Rush Limbaugh's fantastical rhetoric and to begin to grasp that the price of doing business in our constitutional democracy is that our liberty makes us vulnerable to a certain level of danger. Freedom has a price. Sorry.

They don't understand that the endgame in their slow acquiescence to fear-mongering is to finally give oligarchy and authoritarianism a shot. We'll start with removing our shoes and belts at the airport, eliminating habeas corpus and authorizing illegal searches. Check, check and check. We'll move on to a government-controlled press. FOX News Channel is practically there already. Then move up to the government tracking your whereabouts with national IDs and GPS devices; maybe a secret police force kidnapping dissenters in the middle of the night; fencing off our borders just like Soviet Berlin; and suddenly ethnic groups with funny names are rounded up and imprisoned. Hey—anything to keep us safe, right? Whatever it takes, right? After all, the evildoers are *RIGHT BEHIND YOU! DROP YOUR FREEDOM AND RUN, GODDAMN IT!*

Instead of standing defiantly against it, as that lone Chinese protester did so many years ago, the self-proclaimed "most patriotic" among us have run away from our Constitution with greater zeal than Brave Sir Robin in *Monty Python's Holy Grail*. In doing so, they have abandoned that famous ultimatum of Patrick Henry, "Give me liberty or give me death," and subsequently adopted the maxim, "Give me liberty or the evildoer under my bed is gonna bite my toes! Zoinks!"

In a May 2006 Gallup Poll, Americans were asked about President Bush's illegal wiretapping program (see the chapter "The FISA Feargasm"),[9] as well as the administration's unconstitutional seizing of phone records from the major telecommunications companies as part of a massive plot to violate both the Fourth Amendment of the Constitution as well as FISA.[10] Nevertheless, of the 43 percent who were frightened into supporting the program, 69 percent said that they support violating civil liberties if it means fighting the terrorists. Gallup noted in its summary:

> Republicans are also more willing than Democrats to say
> the government should take whatever steps are necessary
> to prevent future acts of terrorism even if basic civil liber-
> ties are violated.

When it comes to terrorism, Republicans talk about civil liberties with the same condescending tone as when they talk about their "black friends" just prior to telling a horribly racist joke. They begrudgingly refer to civil liberties in a way that initially lets them off the hook, and then they uncork an authoritarian fear-mongering doozy. Senator Pat Roberts (R-KS), once said:

> I am a strong supporter of the First Amendment, the
> Fourth Amendment and civil liberties. But you have no

---

9   http://www.gallup.com/poll/5263/Civil-Liberties.aspx

10   The Fourth Amendment to the Constitution: "The right of the people to be secure in their persons, houses, papers, and effects, against unreasonable searches and seizures, shall not be violated, and no Warrants shall issue, but upon probable cause, supported by Oath or affirmation, and particularly describing the place to be searched, and the persons or things to be seized."

civil liberties if you are dead.[11]

Senator Roberts wasn't alone. Here's Senator Jeff Sessions (R-AL):

> Over 3,000 Americans have no civil rights because they are no longer with us.

And Senator "Big" John Cornyn (R-TX):

> None of your civil liberties matter much after you're dead.[12]

Rush Limbaugh, with urine dribbling down his ridiculous Excellence In Broadcasting golf slacks, once said on his radio program:

> Our civil liberties are worthless if we are dead! If you are dead and pushing up daisies, if you're sucking dirt inside a casket, do you know what your civil liberties are worth? Zilch, zero, nada. You aren't even here! Ask the families, ask the people who were in the World Trade Center towers right before they were attacked if they are more concerned with the loss of their civil liberties than the loss of their lives. They can't sue Saddam Hussein for loss of civil liberties because they're dead. How can you sue somebody for your civil liberties being taken away when they killed you first?[13]

Nevermind that one can't "suck dirt" if they're dead, either. But I'll let that one slide because it was a figure of speech and

---

11   http://www2.ljworld.com/blogs/kansas_congress/2006/may/19/roberts/

12   http://www.perrspectives.com/blog/archives/000319.htm

13   http://www.freerepublic.com/focus/f-news/1543669/posts

because Limbaugh was probably stoned on hillbilly heroin at the time and likely hallucinated a trio of dirt-sucking zombies in the studio named Zilch, Zero and Nada. Never mind that Rush Limbaugh, even in December of 2005, continued to insist that Saddam Hussein orchestrated the terrorist attacks of September 11, 2001. Never mind that none of the people who were killed in those attacks—attacks which, I might add, occurred on the watch of a tough-guy Republican mayor, a tough-guy Republican Congress and a tough-guy Republican president—will never have a chance to respond to Rush Limbaugh's anti-constitutional rant one way or another. And, anyway, I'm too busy trying to forget that upwards of twenty million dittoheads across the nation heard this cowardly speech, this hillbilly heroin-induced hallucination of his.

Elsewhere, in late 2006, former Speaker of the House Newt Gingrich specifically talked about limiting free speech in order to fight terrorists. If you disagree with Gingrich, you're probably an elitist, effete liberal.

My view is that either before we lose a city, or if we are truly stupid after we lose a city, we will adopt rules of engagement that we use every technology we can find to break up their capacity to use the Internet, to break up their capacity to use free speech, and to go after people who want to kill us...

Yep. See again the John Adams quote at the beginning of this chapter, re: "stupid and miserable" fear-mongers. Outrageously enough, Gingrich delivered these remarks as the keynote speaker at the Nackey S. Loeb First Amendment Awards Dinner held in Manchester, New Hampshire: a state that boasts as its motto the famous General John Stark ultimatum from 1809:

Live free or die. Death is not the worst of evils.

As recently as June 2008, when the U.S. Supreme Court ruled in favor of due process and the restoration of habeas corpus, Mr. Gingrich reemerged and belched a huge chunk of fear-mongering all over Bob Schieffer's desk on *Face the Nation*:

> I will say, the recent Supreme Court decision to turn over to a local district judge decisions of national security and life and death that should be made by the president and the Congress is the most extraordinarily arrogant and destructive decision the Supreme Court has made in its history... Worse than Dred Scott...
>
> The problem with Obama is he's wrong. It's not that he's inexperienced, it's that his policies are wrong. He applauded this court decision. This court decision is a disaster which could cost us a city. And the debate ought to be over whether or not you're prepared to risk losing an American city on behalf of five lawyers...[14]

By Gingrich's logic, restricting constitutional liberties is the smart thing to do. Defending the Constitution, however, is really stupid and not very serious and cities will be destroyed because of such lunacy.

Cowardly Republicans like Mr. Gingrich suggest that liberals and progressives are helping the terrorists simply because liberals insist upon protecting our constitutional liberties. Too many representatives of the far-right insist that the Bush administration's policies—the torture, the wiretapping, the suspension of habeas corpus and all the rest of it, are designed solely to target

---

14   http://www.crooksandliars.com/2008/06/15/face-the-nation-gingrich-thinks-scotus-gitmo-decision-could-cost-us-a-city/

terrorists and not the American people. When we oppose these measures, they say that we're emboldening the enemy.

What they fail to realize, while caught in the throes of a debilitating feargasm, is that there's often no distinction between an American citizen and a terrorist. Unlike conventional warfare, terrorists don't wear colorful helmets and matching striped pantaloons. So the only way to smoke 'em out is to cast a really wide net, which, invariably, ensnares honest, law-abiding Americans. You and me. But more importantly, once similar laws are passed, there are no legal restrictions against government deliberately turning these unconstitutional weapons against you and me. This is precisely why we freak out when it's revealed that the president and his cohorts have been engaged in such things as surveillance and data mining against American citizens, regardless of whom the fear-mongers claim is their actual target.

I have no great desire to embrace anyone who aims to kill me or my family, but I do have a strong desire to make sure that your cowardice doesn't crush my right to remain secure in my person, house, papers and effects against unreasonable searches and seizures; or my right to demand a court-approved warrant if any of those things are to be seized by the government; or my right to have a phone conversation without the government spying on me; or my right to know why I've been arrested and detained by federal authorities; or my right to speak freely; to peaceably assemble, to vote in elections, and all the rest of it.

Courage isn't about, as President Bush said on September 11, 2001, "[doing] whatever is necessary to protect America and Americans."[15] True courage is protecting America against both

---

15   http://www.whitehouse.gov/news/releases/2001/09/20010911-1.html

our enemies and the cowardly, "stupid and miserable" mob that demands security above all else. There's nothing effete or dandy-ish about liberals who are fighting to make especially sure that the collective fear of the people doesn't intrude upon an individual's constitutional rights.

Contrary to the security doctrine of Bush and McCain Republicanism—heretofore referred to as McBush Republicanism—our elected officials have quite literally sworn an oath to do whatever is necessary to protect the Constitution first, and subsequently, as is mandated within the bounds of that founding document, to "provide for the national defense." But as this dark ride has proved, McBush Republicans have failed miserably to correctly prioritize these very basic and fundamentally American ideas.

Congressman Silvestre Reyes (D-TX) said it best in a letter he wrote to President Bush, dated February 14, 2008:

> I, for one, do not intend to back down—not to the terrorists and not to anyone, including a president, who wants Americans to cower in fear.
>
> We are a strong nation. We cannot allow ourselves to be scared into suspending the Constitution. If we do that, we might as well call the terrorists and tell them that they have won.[16]

You tell me which approach is more patriotic, or more American: rising up against fear, or acquiescing in the face of it.

---

16   http://wwwc.house.gov/reyes/news_detail.asp?id=1370

ENDLESS WAR

In order to stand up against McBush Republican fear-mongering, we should probably accept the idea that there will, unfortunately, always be terrorism. As soon as this simple idea is drilled into the heads of our elected representatives, they will finally be able to put an end to this far-right conspiracy to wage an endless and futile ground war against it.

Late in Senator John Kerry's 2004 campaign, the Bush team descended upon the senator like a brigade of hyperkinetic spider monkeys armed with giant cartoon mallets, thwacking Senator Kerry about the head and neck for a solid two weeks simply because he suggested that (*WHOOPS!*) there will always be terrorists and terrorism:

> We have to get back to the place we were, where terrorists are not the focus of our lives, but they're a nuisance...
> As a former law enforcement person, I know we're never going to end prostitution. We're never going to end illegal gambling. But we're going to reduce it, organized crime, to a level where it isn't on the rise. It isn't threatening people's lives every day, and fundamentally, it's something that you continue to fight, but it's not threatening

the fabric of your life.[1]

In the preceding decade, President Clinton used law enforcement to bring the Oklahoma City bomber, Timothy McVeigh, to justice. Law enforcement, under President Clinton, successfully captured and convicted Mohammad Salameh, Ahmad Ajaj, Mahmud Abouhalima, Nidal Ayyad and Ramzi Youssef, the individuals who carried out the first World Trade Center bombing. How dare Senator Kerry tell the truth about using law enforcement to successfully prosecute terrorists. I suppose the truth is too... um, French.

The Bush campaign destroyed Senator Kerry with this quote, twisting the meaning and inaccurately claiming the senator suggested that terrorism is simply annoying but not dangerous or life threatening. Several weeks later, President Bush was re-elected by more than three million votes because he lied to his base and told them that if they didn't vote for him, gays and terrorists will destroy America. Yet during these intervening four years of the president's second term, a National Intelligence Estimate confirmed that al-Qaeda has actually gained strength.[2] Heckuva job, Mr. President.

As long as human beings are able to experience fear, terrorist leaders and their apparently bottomless cup of "number twos" will come and go; new terrorists will replace the old ones and generation after generation will lurk in the dark corners of the world, waiting to trigger our most primal instincts. One day, a million years from now when humans have evolved into freakish,

---

1   http://edition.cnn.com/2004/ALLPOLITICS/10/10/bush.kerry.terror/

2   According to the *National Intelligence Estimate* dated July 12, 2007 titled "Al-Qaeda better positioned to strike the West."

rubbery cyborgs that resemble Charles Krauthammer, fear will become irrelevant and, with it, terrorism.

Until then, terrorist attacks will continue to be carried out by relatively small groups of militant extremists in order to use fear and violence as a means of retaliating against political, regional and religious enemies, or to merely subvert governments and economies by violently targeting strategic interests and civilians.

Sure, it won't always and forever be synonymous with an Islamic fundamentalist group called al-Qaeda, but then again al-Qaeda represents only one terrorist group out of hundreds in existence today including, for example, God's Army, Hamas, the Animal Liberation Front and Hans Gruber from *Die Hard*. Gruber isn't real, but as terrorists go, he was pretty awesome.

Al-Qaeda, or as President Bush calls it: "the evildoers," "Islamofascists," "the terrrsts" and "them folks," are just the latest and most infamous group on the world stage.[3] Its leader, Osama bin Laden, whom President Bush doesn't spend much time on, is just the latest boogeyman in a long line of socio-political villains.[4]

No one in the very serious corporate media wants to stare into your living room with a very serious corporate logo emblazoned just above the lower-third ticker and speak the truth like Senator Kerry did four years ago. No corporate-owned network anchor would ever risk being attacked, crushed and fired because he or she admitted on TV: *Terrorism will never be defeated because terror and fear will always exist and therefore will always be exploited. So fighting a conventional war against it can't possibly end it now*

---

3   I'll be using the word "evildoer" throughout this book in order to mock and bait the McBush Republicans. I might also occasionally replace "Islamofascists" with "Filet-o-fascists" because both are equally as ridiculous.

4   http://www.whitehouse.gov/news/releases/2002/03/20020313-8.html

and will only succeed in producing exponentially more terrorists in the future. We'll back after this word from Flomax.

Your corporate media also has no intention of ever telling you that many of your elected leaders are often accomplices in carrying out an agenda that terrorists themselves could never possibly achieve alone.

The evildoers, however dangerous and psychotic, have no chance whatsoever of single-handedly overthrowing the American government or any other Western government for that matter—ever. No, sir. Not a chance in hell. It doesn't matter how severe the attack; terrorist groups like al-Qaeda simply don't have the manpower or sophistication necessary to achieve anything more than a contained attack. Even the most frightening kind of attack possible—a nuclear attack—doesn't stand a chance in hell of somehow collapsing our government.[5]

In order to overthrow governments, terrorists require the after-the-fact assistance of manipulative leaders with authoritarian tendencies who, despite their public face as the self-proclaimed sworn enemies of terrorists, serve to elevate and expand the long-term goals of terrorism. In terms of the United States, these leaders seek to manufacture the illusion of increased safety when in fact they aim to either rearrange, at best, or dismantle, at worst, the Constitution, our American principles, our dignity

---

5   In the summer of 2002, the Bush White House outed CIA operative Valerie Plame-Wilson. Before her cover was blown by I. Lewis "Scooter" Libby and Karl Rove as part of an effort to build a case for invading Iraq, Plame-Wilson's role with the CIA was to track what are called "loose nukes." Loose nukes are nuclear material that is smuggled onto the black market and potentially sold to terrorists. Plame-Wilson's role in the Agency's effort to track this stray nuclear material ended when Robert Novak published a column exposing her as a CIA operative. Clearly political vengeance against Plame-Wilson's husband, Ambassador Joe Wilson, was more important to the Bush Republicans than preventing a dirty-bomb attack.

as a nation and our ability to self-determine the course of our future. To these fear-mongering McBush Republicans, terrorism is a convenient political weapon. A campaign strategy. The September 11 attacks were simply the fortuitously timed "Pearl Harbor events" they needed in order to fight their endless, financially profitable wars in the Middle East and their politically profitable war against…us.[6]

No one's arguing with the fact that there exist religious fundamentalists who have sworn an oath to kill Americans—not as many as we've been tricked into believing exist, but ones who have increased in numbers since President Bush invaded and occupied Iraq (see the chapter "The No Attacks Mythology"). So we should, especially since the president has raised innumerable armies of new extremists, support an effort to defend ourselves against any potential attack. The operative term being "defend." That certainly doesn't mean that we should go around engaging in ground wars using conventional forces against a tactic, an abstraction called "terror."

Imagine if President Lincoln had engaged in a war not against the Confederacy, but against flank marches, sharpshooters and gigantic itchy mustaches. If that had been the case, historians would still be shaking their heads and wringing their hands about that war, and our Confederate neighbors would still be laughing out loud from behind their gigantic itchy mustaches.

Yet, in the most precise language possible, if someone at-

---

6   From Section 5 of the PNAC report titled "Rebuilding America's Defenses": "Further, the process of transformation [in the Middle East], even if it brings revolutionary change, is likely to be a long one, absent some catastrophic and catalyzing event—like a new Pearl Harbor." This report was authored by Thomas Donnelly, with contributions by more well-known neocons like William Kristol, Paul Wolfowitz, and someone named Scooter Libby. http://www.newamericancentury.org/RebuildingAmericasDefenses.pdf

tempts to attack our cities, landmarks or citizens, it's important to use our defense and intelligence apparatus to stop them. Just like we always have.

But fear-mongers need this war against terrorism precisely because terrorism can never be defeated, therefore protracting the war effort indefinitely. It's what General John Abizaid called the "long war."[7] Their perpetual war. Because, simply stated, a government's power over its people rests in its ability to wage war. Endless war, endless power. Everything in such a conflict depends entirely upon the mission being ambiguous and infinite.

To that point, James Madison exactly summarized what we've witnessed in the first decade of the twenty-first century:

> Of all the enemies to public liberty, war is, perhaps, the most to be dreaded, because it comprises and develops the germ of every other. War is the parent of armies; from these proceed debts and taxes; and armies, and debts, and taxes are the known instruments for bringing the many under the domination of the few.

> In war, too, the discretionary power of the Executive is extended; its influence in dealing out offices, honors, and emoluments is multiplied; and all the means of seducing the minds are added to those of subduing the force of the people.

> The same malignant aspect in Republicanism may be traced in the inequality of fortunes and the opportunities of fraud growing out of a state of war, and in the degeneracy of manners and of morals engendered by

---

7   http://www.washingtonpost.com/wp-dyn/content/article/2006/02/02/AR2006020202242.html

both. No nation could reserve its freedom in the midst of continual warfare.[8]

Throughout the Bush years, we've witnessed the rise of war and the destruction of "public liberty." Our national debt has ballooned to record levels as we're preparing to spend more than a trillion dollars on an unnecessary and continual war. The Executive has been "extended" beyond its normal degree of power as enumerated by the Constitution (co-authored by Madison). President Bush has paid "emoluments" to far-right talk-radio hosts—inviting them to the White House for roundtable meetings, and, in the case of pundits like Armstrong Williams, paying them taxpayer cash in order to promote administration policies on the radio. "Fortunes" are more lopsided than ever as massive corporations including the mercenaries at Blackwater and the profiteers at Kellogg-Brown & Root are prospering while middle-class Americans are paying record-high prices for gasoline and food. There's rampant "fraud" as billions of dollars in reconstruction cash disappears into thin Iraqi air. And the "degeneracy" of manners and morals has given rise to White House sanctioned "enhanced interrogation techniques" inside American torture chambers.

With Madison's words as the rule, it goes without saying that Senator McCain's now infamous declaration of "continual warfare" in Iraq was more than a little bit alarming:

> Q: President Bush has talked about our staying in Iraq
> for fifty years — [cut off by McCain]

---

8   James Madison "Political Observations" April 20, 1795, as published in Lance Banning's *Liberty and Order: The First American Party Struggle* [1787]

MCCAIN: Make it a hundred.

Q: Is that ... [cut off]

MCCAIN: We've been in South Korea ... we've been in Japan for sixty years. We've been in South Korea fifty years or so. That would be fine with me. As long as Americans—[9]

This last part is another in a series of deliberate falsehoods handed down by Senator McCain to his supporters who can't wait to repeat it, even though they tend to sound like idiots when they do. After World War II, Japan and Germany didn't have insurgencies that were attacking our forces every day, inflicting casualties in the tens of thousands. These nations didn't have three warring sectarian groups that have clashed throughout history to the point at which a previous imperial power, Great Britain, had entirely abandoned the effort. Senator McCain continued:

> ... As long as Americans are not being injured or harmed
> or wounded or killed. That's fine with me, I hope that
> would be fine with you, if we maintain a presence in a
> very volatile part of the world where al-Qaeda is train-
> ing and equipping and recruiting and motivating people
> every single day.[10]

The logical explanation for why Americans continue to be "harmed or wounded or killed" is quite simply because we're *there*; and because people like Senator McCain have pledged to be *there* forever. Well, forever is a strong word. David Corn re-

---

9   http://thinkprogress.org/2008/01/04/mccain-100-years/

10   http://www.motherjones.com/mojoblog/archives/2008/01/6735_
mccain_in_nh_wo.html

ported on a follow-up conversation with the senator:

> After the event ended, I asked McCain about his "hundred years" comment, and he reaffirmed the remark, excitedly declaring that U.S. troops could be in Iraq for "a thousand years" or "a million years," as far as he was concerned.

A million years isn't technically "forever" but it's a long time.[11] And James Madison just threw up into his own severely decomposed mouth. For shits and giggles, how much would it cost for America to stay in Iraq for a million years? If we calculate based on the Congressional Budget Office's estimate of 275 million dollars per day, it will ultimately cost America $100,375,000,000,000,000. That's 100 quadrillion, 375 trillion dollars. Not factoring for inflation. Put into perspective, if you had 100 quadrillion dollars and you were to donate one quadrillion dollars to me, you'd still have 99 quadrillion.

Now to be fair, it's possible that Senator McCain was exaggerating, but it's crystal clear that he has no intention of withdrawing from Iraq and would probably endeavor to establish those permanent bases everyone has been arguing about. Permanent American bases in a region where there has already been thousands of years of sectarian violence. Permanent American bases in a region considered holy by men such as Osama bin Laden who, when we previously had occupied military bases in Saudi Arabia, retaliated by attacking New York and Washington, D.C. with hijacked passenger airliners.

---

11   I considered a too-easy "McCain is soooo old" joke here, but he's not so old. CNN's John King, however, once observed that Senator McCain is "older than President Reagan," which would make the senator ninety-eight years old. Senator McCain is, in fact, a youthful seventy-one.

So how might Senator McCain achieve these succeeding goals of first defeating Senator Obama in November, and, second, establishing continual warfare in Iraq? During a February 17, 2008 edition of the satirical weekend comedy show, *FOX News Sunday*, cast member William Kristol accurately predicted a McCain fear-mongering campaign:

> ... at the end of the day it'll be McCain against Obama in a national security election. The Democrats can say Nancy Pelosi's fond of quoting Franklin Roosevelt, "We have nothing to fear but fear itself." We do have something to fear but fear itself. We have terrorists to fear and we have people who want to kill Americans to fear. And people who totally want to destabilize the Middle East to fear. And I think that's a pretty good argument for McCain to make against Obama.

Kristol has been wrong about everything, including the invasion of Iraq, which he helped to mastermind. One could make a pretty strong case that William Kristol was one of a select few neocons who, as he put it, destabilized the Middle East. But Kristol was right (unfortunately) about Senator McCain's use of endless fear-mongering in preparation for his proposed endless war. Last June, Senator McCain's chief strategist, the Washington lobbyist Charlie Black, remarked that another terrorist attack would be most-excellent for the McCain campaign:

> The assassination of Benazir Bhutto in December was an "unfortunate event," says Black. "But [McCain's] knowledge and ability to talk about it reemphasized that this is the guy who's ready to be commander-in-chief. And it helped us." As would, Black concedes with startling candor after we raise the issue, another terrorist attack on

U.S. soil. "Certainly it would be a big advantage to him,"
says Black.[12]

Awful fear-mongering aside, I would argue that such a hy-
pothetical attack would be *terrible* for the McBush Republicans.
It'd be yet another attack on their watch, despite all of the unconstitutional and illegal policies of the last seven years. I seriously
doubt a shocked and shaken American voter would reward that
degree of incompetence, and especially with the botched handling of Katrina looming large in the rear-view mirror. Nevertheless, Black proved Kristol right. Meanwhile, Senator McCain
attempted to apologize by saying:

> I cannot imagine why he would say it. It's not true. I've
> worked tirelessly since 9/11 to prevent another attack on
> the United States of America.[13]

The classic McCain non-apology apology. The very serious
corporate media played this as a denunciation of Black's remarks,
but you'll notice that Senator McCain absolutely *did not* de-
nounce Black's tasteless conflation of the elections and an attack,
or how such a coupling might signal to the terrorists that they
can influence our elections. What Senator McCain condemned
was the *idea of an attack*—period. And, naturally, while he ex-
pressed his outrage, he threw in some fear-mongering (the in-
vocation of the September 11 attacks) just to make sure we're
paying attention.

So, there it is. For the first time in a decade (or more), Wil-

---

12   http://money.cnn.com/2008/06/20/magazines/fortune/Evolu-
tion_McCain_Whitford.fortune/

13   http://blog.washingtonpost.com/the-trail/2008/06/23/mccain_
denounces_top_aides_com.html?hpid=topnews&hpid=topnews

liam Kristol was right about something. Yay.

The case against Senator Obama, Kristol predicted, is that the honor, dignity and courage that President Roosevelt urged in his first inaugural address are completely irrelevant if they get in the way of electing another McBush Republican to the White House. Fear-mongering, Kristol says, is a "pretty good case" against Senator Obama who, in addition to possessing an entirely opposite presence as Senator McCain, has offered an equally opposite prospect for hope, rationality and an end to the endless war.

There will always be terrorism and terrorist attacks. Nevertheless, fear-mongers can't be allowed to continue on, knowingly or unwittingly helping the evildoers in their mission against America. Senator Kerry was exactly right and history will remember him favorably when he said that we have to continue to reduce the number of terrorist attacks but that they'll never entirely go away; and history will be kind to us if we continue to reduce terrorism with our dignity, liberties and values intact. As James Madison's posterity, we have no choice but to stand against fear and endless war or be consumed by it. We have to be willing to forego airtight security rather than to allow our founding principals to be dismantled by radical leaders who exploit fear and endless war to secure not our cities, airports and citizens, but their own uncontested authoritarian power over the nation.

Fear is the fuel for the endless war, and the endless war fuels the political and financial strength of fear-mongers who, in turn, fuel the fear. Trapped on the surface of this Mobius Loop of madness—"minds seduced and people subdued," as Madison wrote—no nation can remain free.

3

THE NO ATTACKS MYTHOLOGY

Every time you state your case,
the more I'd like to punch your face.

–The Flaming Lips
"Haven't Got A Clue"

The McBush Republican refrain "we haven't been attacked in [*fill in the blank*] years" remains a popular applause line delivered by all varieties of fear-mongers, from Vice President Cheney, who boasts that "it's no accident," to Senator McCain, whose shriveled, Grinchy heart is only slightly larger and less cybernetic than Cheney's. Here's Senator McCain on a particularly hilarious episode of the weekend comedy show, *FOX News Sunday*:

> But look, the fact that there has not been an attack on the United States in four years is an indicator of some success. That doesn't mean there isn't going to be an attack tomorrow and that we must be on our guard. But after 9/11, if you said, well, we're going to be able to go four years without an attack, then I think a lot of people would have been surprised. So let's give the president

and this administration some credit for that.[1]

While completely misrepresenting the absence of an attack, notice how the senator once again crow-barred some legitimate fear-mongering into his ridiculous kudos to the administration: *there might be an attack... tomorrow!* Just like the day before a major snowstorm, I imagined panicked hoards of cowardly Bush Republicans across the nation hearing this news and bolting for the grocery store to stock up on bread, milk, toilet paper and, of course, adult diapers.[2] Imagine their relief when, the next day, Monday, January 23, 2006, there was definitely *not* another terrorist attack.[3] Luckily for a disappointed Rudy Giuliani he saved his receipts and was able to return the festive party hats, fruit punch and duct tape.

And then there's Vice President Cheney who loves to repeat this no-attack-since-September-11 myth. Here's the vice president during an interview with WDAY Radio on October 24, 2006:

> I think the basic proposition is, of course, that we've gone more than five years now without another attack inside the homeland. On the day after that attack back in '01, if somebody had put that proposition to you, I don't think anybody would have been willing to bet we could go five years without an attack.[4]

The implication is that the Bush administration's doctrine

---

1   http://www.foxnews.com/story/0,2933,182434,00.html

2   Talk radio host Bill Cunningham only.

3   There wasn't another terrorist attack that day—on American soil, that is. There were, however, nine attacks in Iraq.

4   http://www.whitehouse.gov/news/releases/2006/10/20061024-7.html

of illegal invasions, illegal eavesdropping, illegal torturing and unconstitutional suspension of habeas corpus—not to mention the illegal outing of an undercover CIA agent tasked with tracking loose nukes—have collectively prevented further terrorist attacks. Without these policies, the fear-mongers suggest, the terrorists surely would've attacked again. So we ought to support their authoritarian trampling of the Constitution…or else.

In March of 2008, Congress tried to pass legislation that explicitly prohibits CIA interrogators from torturing prisoners of war. By way of background, this anti-torture provision was stricken from the now famously ineffectual Detainee Treatment Act, also known as the McCain Amendment, back in December of 2005. You might recall that there was, what I consider to be, a staged battle between Senator McCain and the White House over the senator's desire to, with the amendment, codify the anti-torture language of the U.S. Army Field Manual for Human Intelligence Collector Operations, and apply its rules to all United States personnel dealing with detainees in Guantanamo Bay and elsewhere. Vice President Cheney personally lobbied against the amendment and Senator McCain apparently cut a deal with the vice president so that the Field Manual rules would not apply to CIA interrogators. Naturally, the president overruled the entire amendment with one of his signing statements. But we don't torture, right? So why the signing statement?

More than three years later, in March of 2008, Congress passed a bill that would finally ban the CIA's use of torture. Senator McCain, the anti-torture maverick he is, voted *against* the bill—effectively voting in favor of the use of American torture chambers. And, of course, the president vetoed the bill anyway. The president's excuse?

Because of their hard work, and the efforts of many across all levels of government, we have not suffered another attack on our soil since September the 11th, 2001.[5]

While we're here, it's worth noting the president's knee-jerk fear-mongering on the anti-torture bill:

If we were to shut down this program and restrict the CIA to methods in the Field Manual, we could lose vital information from senior al-Qaeda terrorists, and that could cost American lives.

The truth is that there *have* been additional terrorist attacks on American soil—"inside the homeland," as Vice President Cheney calls it. There have been numerous additional terrorist attacks against American citizens since September 11. There have been literally thousands of terrorist attacks elsewhere since September 11. All of this despite the fear-mongering; despite the syllabus of crimes perpetrated by the Bush administration; despite this overpriced, bloody and misappropriated war on terrorism.

Yet there exists this "we haven't been attacked since..." delusion—what I call the No Attacks Mythology—which serves to artificially enhance the cataclysmic McBush national security record. Perhaps the McBushies continue to beat this mythology to death, and their supporters continue to repeat it, because no one I'm aware of in the very serious corporate media has directly challenged Senator McCain or Vice President Cheney or President Bush on its veracity. It's not difficult to nail them on this one, after all, because out of all of their obvious lies, this one is

---

5   President's Weekly Radio Address, March 8, 2008. http://www.whitehouse.gov/news/releases/2008/03/20080308.html

pock-marked with semantic holes large enough to fit Ann Coulter's bulbous Adam's apple. In the course of seven years of recent history, the *only* media figure who has ever come close to challenging the No Attacks Mythology has been Jon Stewart who, once again, illustrated his courageous proficiency for taking-up questions the traditional news media are afraid to ask when he confronted Lynn Cheney after she repeated the No Attacks Mythology on an October 2007 edition of the *Daily Show*.

> LYNN CHENEY: You know I think when the history books are written, we will look back on this period of time, and we will say on 9/11 we really thought within six months we would be attacked again. Even six weeks. It's been more than six years and that is not an accident. I think this administration, my husband and the president deserve a lot of credit for that.

> JON STEWART: Okay. Well. Alright. There were—I mean there was the anthrax thing. And there was—and you know the first time they bombed the World Trade Center, it was eight years until we got attacked again—

> LYNN CHENEY: Well yes, but there were many attacks between 1993 and the World Trade Centers coming down in 2001! Remember the USS Cole, for example? There were worldwide bombing going on. The bombings at the embassies in Africa.

> JON STEWART: Right.

> LYNN CHENEY: So the terrorists weren't—uh—weren't reluctant to damage American interests and kill Americans. [pregnant pause] Friends?

JON STEWART: Friends. You know they have been doing that all these past six years. I mean you know the Spanish bombings, the English bombings, and then all the bombs in Iraq.

LYNN CHENEY: Yes, yes, but we're talking about American interests.

JON STEWART: Aren't we interested in—I had assumed they were our allies, but alright.[6]

As I watched Lynn Cheney attempting to dismiss and parse Stewart's counterpoints, I wished for Comedy Central to give the *Daily Show* an extra twenty minutes of airtime in which Stewart could keep going. But there wasn't enough time to fully expose the game Cheney was playing: to mix up the locations and targets until the issue was reduced to a confusing semantic M.C. Escher painting.

And, just as with her husband and Senator McCain and other like-minded fear mongers, she exhibited an ultimately self-refuting level of arrogance by accelerating down this mythological road in the first place. But she threw it out there anyway because she believed that no one would dare challenge *her*—the very smart and very serious second lady and American Enterprise Institute wizard—on such a flimsily constructed fairy tale. They have to know that while this plays to their mouth-breathing base, it's extraordinarily easy to rip apart. Nevertheless, they roll it out to this day because they're just that cynical about their people; they peg their supporters as automatons who will blindly repeat the No Attacks Mythology despite the blindingly obvious

---

6   http://thinkprogress.org/2007/10/11/lynne-cheney-stewart/

truth to the contrary.

The truth is that during the eight years of the Clinton administration there were just four Islamic terrorist attacks against America and, as Lynn Cheney put it, "American interests." Four.

- The first World Trade Center bombing occurred on February 23, 1993, a little more than one month into the Bill Clinton administration. *Casualties:* Six Americans killed and 1,040 wounded.

- Five and a half years later, on August 7, 1998, al-Qaeda car bombers hit the United States embassies in Dar es Salaam, Tanzania and Nairobi, Kenya. *Casualties:* Two hundred and twelve killed, four thousand wounded in Kenya. Eleven killed and eighty-five wounded in Tanzania. Most are African civilians.

- On October 12, 2000, a suicide bomber attacked the USS Cole docked in Yemen. *Casualties:* Seventeen Americans killed, thirty-nine wounded.

It's both factual and intellectually honest to suggest that President Clinton presided over almost eight full years without an Islamic terrorist attack *on American soil.* He did so without torturing. He did so without illegally invading and occupying a nation for illegitimate reasons. He did so without gathering your phone records from the telecommunications companies. He did so without suspending habeas corpus and leaning on the orange-alert panic button. And he did so as a member of the Democratic Party.

However, yes, there were several other attacks in which Americans were senselessly murdered. To be sure, President Clinton's record isn't spotless on terrorism. But it's a statistical and empirical fact that President Clinton's record is exponentially better than the collective record of these fear-mongering braggarts, these authoritarian criminals and cowards.

Throughout this dark ride between September 11 and today, there have been numerous terrorist attacks on American interests, Mrs. Cheney. There have been numerous attacks on American soil, Senator McCain. There have been thousands of Americans killed and thousands of American allies killed in overseas attacks, Mr. Vice President.

It goes without saying that Jon Stewart was dead right to mention the anthrax attacks. Five Americans were killed by the toxic letters mailed by, as we were told at the time, the terrorists, though everyone in the corporate media seem to have forgotten about these letters and the subsequent fatalities—perhaps because there wasn't dramatic videotape.[7] It remains unmentioned in the context of the televised reporting of the administration's so-called No Attacks record that NBC News, CBS News, ABC News, the *New York Post* and the *National Enquirer* were targets of the anthrax attacks. Seriously, you'd at least think the very serious haircuts who run these outfits would remind us every damn day about how they were assaulted with so-called Iraqi anthrax letters. In an age of fear-mongering for ratings gold, it's a potential Nielsen bonanza to utter *terrorism* and *anthrax* in the same sentence.

Nevertheless, knowing that NBC News had been sent a letter containing anthrax, the late Tim Russert allowed Vice Presi-

---

7   While new information in this cold case has implicated—though not confirmed—a government scientist named Bruce E. Ivins, who committed suicide in August 2008, numerous administration officials, as well as Senator McCain on the *Late Show with David Letterman*, told us that the anthrax might have originated from Iraq.

dent Cheney to repeat the following on a September 10, 2006 edition of *Meet the Press*:

> But the fact of the matter is: I think we've done a pretty good job. And I don't know how you can explain five years of no attacks, five years of successful disruption of attacks, five years of, of defeating the efforts of al-Qaeda to come back and kill more Americans.[8]

With all due respect, and based on the information about the anthrax attacks at that time, Russert failed to remind the vice president about these *other* forgotten attacks, even though Russert was best known for catching people like Cheney in various misstatements and contradictions. In this case, Russert could've held up a copy of the NBC anthrax letter between his thumb and index finger just like he used to whenever he would nail a public official to the wall. But he didn't for some reason. The anthrax attacks were entirely ignored.

Of course, Cheney and the rest of his regime of fear-mongers always seem to conveniently forget about the anthrax attacks when they're discussing their awesome terrorist-fighting skills. They conveniently forget about the attacks...until, that is, they needed to make a case for invading Iraq:

> VICE PRES. CHENEY: It's the fact that we've also seen [Saddam Hussein] in these other areas, in chemicals, but also especially in biological weapons, increase his capacity to produce and deliver these weapons upon his enemies.
>
> MR. RUSSERT: But if he ever did that, would we not

8　　September 10, 2006. http://www.msnbc.msn.com/id/14720480/page/5/

wipe him off the face of the earth?

VICE PRES. CHENEY: Who did the anthrax attack last fall, Tim? We don't know.

MR. RUSSERT: Could it have been Saddam?

VICE PRES. CHENEY: I don't know... But, like I say, I point out the anthrax example just to remind everybody that it is very hard sometimes, especially when we're dealing with something like a biological weapon that could conceivably be misconstrued, at least for some period, as a naturally occurring event, that we may not know who launches the next attack.[9]

Scary! We just don't know when or where! I imagine this is why, as he watched at home, Sean Hannity's testicles permanently retracted into his body cavity.[10]

Clearly, the vice president was running through the same semantic trick popularized by the administration to make their case for invading Iraq: the coupling of September 11 and Saddam Hussein. If you read the various statements, they don't specifically marry the two topics as *A-to-B*, cause-and-effect relationships, but they include them in the same sentence to form a devilishly clever inference. For instance, I could say, "Vice President Cheney doesn't eat adorable baby orangutans, but you've never seen him *not* eating one, so... you tell me." Now I didn't specifically say that the vice president eats adorable baby orangutans, but I'm sure

---

9   September 8, 2002. http://www.mtholyoke.edu/acad/intrel/bush/meet.htm

10   I have no idea the actual status of Hannity's testicles. For that, you'll need to ask Mr. Colmes.

you gathered the inference that, yes, the vice president eats those fuckers on toast. So in the case of his anthrax statement on *Meet the Press*, he obviously intended to conflate anthrax, terrorism and Iraq without explicitly making that connection, even though anyone with functioning brain tissue knew what he meant: the anthrax attacks were acts of terrorism carried out by Iraqi terrorists. Meanwhile, the anthrax attacks are conspicuously missing from his terrorist-attack arsenal when the No Attack Mythology swings into action.

And then there's the series of terrorist attacks that everyone has almost entirely forgotten about. Everyone, that is, except for the families and friends of those Americans who were killed.

The terrorists were nicknamed the Beltway Snipers, or the D.C. Snipers.

While a distracted Bush administration were scaring the piss out of Americans in order to coerce enough support for their manifest invasion of Iraq, two Islamic extremists named John Allen Muhammed and Lee Boyd Malvo killed sixteen people during the late summer and early autumn of 2002 in and around the Capital Beltway and Interstate 95. Muhammed and Malvo had engaged in similar attacks in several other states, and their ultimate plan was to recruit more jihadists to carry out further sniper attacks across the country.

For two months, Americans in Virginia, Maryland and the District of Columbia were afraid to commute along one of the most heavily trafficked highways on the eastern seaboard. The snipers received non-stop, panic-button press coverage for much of September and October of 2002. After all, every major American news outlet has at least one bureau within walking distance of the kill zone.

Now it's easy to suggest that, compared with September 11, these attacks were small-time or insignificant compared to other terrorist attacks against American citizens. It's easy to suggest that the D.C. Sniper shootings don't count as major-league-evildoer terror strikes. The deadly truth is that by the time law enforcement officials finally captured Malvo and Muhammed, they had killed more Americans (sixteen) than had been killed in the first World Trade Center bombing of 1993 (six). Almost as many Americans were killed by the D.C. Snipers as were killed in the USS Cole attack (seventeen).

But there haven't been any attacks on American soil since September 11, 2001, right?

Senator McCain: "... there has not been an attack on the United States." Not true.

Lynn Cheney: "It's been more than six years and that is not an accident." Lie.

Vice President Cheney: "We've gone more than five years now without another attack inside the homeland," and, "I don't know how you can explain five years of no attacks." You *can't* explain it other than to say it's a lie; it's a wholesale fraud perpetrated on the American people.

And if Senator McCain, Vice President Cheney and Lynn "Well yes, but there were many attacks between 1993 and the World Trade Centers coming down in 2001!" Cheney are going to indict President Clinton on the overseas terrorist attacks of the 1990s as a means of besmirching the Democratic record on terrorism, then we have no choice but to compare these relatively few Clinton-era attacks with the endless list of overseas terrorist attacks against Americans, American allies and American interests during the George W. Bush administration.

To begin, I'll be a good sport and give Lynn Cheney the benefit of the doubt on the bombings in Madrid (191 killed, 600 wounded) and London (56 killed, 700 wounded). I'll also strike from the list the 2003 al-Qaeda bombing in Tunisia (15 killed, 20 wounded); the Istanbul attacks in November (53 killed, 750 wounded); the 2002 attack on an American tanker in Yemen (1 killed, 12 wounded, 90,000 barrels of oil spilled); and the 2004 bombing at a Marriot in Islamabad where U.S. diplomats were staying (9 wounded). We'll strike these from the list because Mrs. Cheney disputed these as attacks against America when Jon Stewart mentioned them. And because I'm a good sport.

Let's start with Iraq, which I think we can more or less agree is probably the most notable "American interest," as Mrs. Cheney put it, in the world right now.

This first set of terrorist attacks can specifically be attributed to al-Qaeda in Iraq. According to a September 2007 study by the Center for American Progress:

> Al-Qaeda in Iraq has been responsible for a large number of the attacks within Iraq: The group has claimed more than two hundred incidents causing almost two thousand fatalities. The group was led by Abu Mus'ab al-Zarqawi, who professed loyalty to Osama bin Laden, until his death in a U.S. airstrike on June 7, 2006. Zarqawi saw the group as the center of jihadist activities in Iraq, and it is mostly supported by Sunni Arabs. Tactics range from suicide attacks to kidnappings and smaller raids.[11]

Two hundred al-Qaeda attacks since the 2003 invasion. Nearly two thousand fatalities attributed specifically to al-Qaeda

11   http://www.americanprogress.org/issues/2007/09/alqaeda_map.html

alone (the Center for American Progress doesn't list those who were wounded, which, in Iraq, have numbered around ten times the total killed—in action).

What makes this especially alarming is that al-Qaeda in Iraq only counts for around 2 percent of "the enemy" there. The other 98 percent of the so-called enemy in Iraq—insurgents and militia groups and such—have been routinely nicknamed "terrorists" by President Bush. How many times in the last seven years have we heard the president name Iraq as the "central front in the war on terror"? How many times have we heard the president suggest that if we withdraw or redeploy we'll be emboldening the terrorists? During a June 2005 address designed to reaffirm his commitment to the war, President Bush said:

> There is only one course of action against them: to defeat them abroad before they attack us at home... Our mission in Iraq is clear. **We are hunting down the terrorists.**[12]

Surely he didn't mean that our mission is to fight only 2 percent of the enemy there. He's talking about all of the enemy groups. So an additional 3,970 Americans have been killed and 29,080 Americans have been wounded while fighting an enemy that the president himself has labeled as "terrorists."

A non-profit think tank called the Memorial Institute for Prevention of Terrorism (MIPT)[13] has been maintaining an online Terrorism Knowledge Base since the middle 1990s. In it, they report that between September 11, 2001 and March 2008,

---

12   *New York Times*, June 29, 2006. http://www.nytimes.com/2005/06/29/politics/29ptext.html?_r=1&pagewanted=print&oref=slogin

13   http://www.mipt.org

there have been 9,675 terrorist attacks in Iraq, accumulating 46,271 injuries and 26,161 deaths. In Afghanistan—that *other* American interest—there have been 1,069 terrorist attacks in which 2,323 people were injured and 1,809 people were killed.

Just to recap: from 1993 to 2001, there were four terrorist attacks against Americans and American interests. From 2001 to 2008 there have been, by the accounting of conservative groups and the military, literally tens of thousands of terrorist attacks against Americans and American interests.

And there's more.

Late last year, the popular far-right blogger Michelle Malkin posted a link and widget that was created by a website called Islam: The Religion of Peace.[14] When I saw the widget hosted by Malkin, I was more than a little alarmed by the statistic it had been tracking.[15]

It listed, at the time, 9,995 deadly terrorist attacks by "Islamic Terrorists" since September 11, 2001. As I write this chapter in March of 2008, their fear-mongering toteboard has climbed up to 10,606 deadly terrorist attacks.

The anonymous coward who runs the Religion of Peace website has no love for the Muslim religion to be sure, but it also appears as if he or she is equally as insensitive and cruel to the victims of suicide bombers, evidenced by their front page above-the-fold Picture of the Week for the week of February 17-23, 2008. It was a photograph of a cat dressed up like a suicide bomber: Middle Eastern regalia and fake explosives strapped around its stomach. I'm not making this up. The caption read:

---

14   http://michellemalkin.com/2007/11/15/a-grim-milestone-ignored/

15   http://www.thereligionofpeace.com/

"Nine lives adds up to...a *lot* of virgins."

Wow. Get it? The suicide bomber cat has nine...lives, so. Yeah. I don't even know what else to say about that other than it forms a crazy trifecta: 1) far-right McBush Republicanism, 2) suicide bombers and, 3) people who dress up their animals in human clothing.

Elsewhere on this Malkin-endorsed site, they list an additional ten terrorist attacks on American soil that occurred *after* the D.C. Sniper shootings,[16] including a December 2003 "attack" in which "a Muslim doctor deliberately allows a Jewish patient to die from an easily treatable condition." However awful that might be, I think we can agree that it's hardly an attack.

All of these additional attacks, whether legitimate or not, have occurred on President Bush's and Vice President Cheney's watch since September 11, 2001. Along with Senator McCain, they cannot be permitted to repeat this obviously untrue No Attacks Mythology without being called on it. They cannot

16   http://www.thereligionofpeace.com/Pages/AmericanAttacks.htm

continue to tell us that there haven't been any attacks since September 11 when their own statistics and their own noise-makers refute every last word. They have failed in their pledge to keep America safe at all costs. Our president has given up on finding bin Laden. Our ports aren't secured. At the airport, our security officials are unable to effectively determine the difference between a Capri Sun and liquid explosives (see the next chapter "Bottled Liquids are Banned from this Chapter"). And our first responders continue to operate without the proper funding and hardware.

The truth behind the No Attacks Mythology is that the war on terror has been entirely ineffectual. The authoritarian crimes orchestrated by the Bush Republicans have been achieved by injecting overwhelming amounts of propagandized fear into a nation already lousy with cowards in an effort to further subjugate the American people—to break their will to resist—by waging an unrelenting assault on reason. It's no wonder why the administration has gotten away with so much; they've simply confounded logic to the point of total exasperation (see Jon Stewart with Lynn Cheney). According to their propaganda, there have either been many terrorist attacks and we need to "stay on the offensive" (at the expense of our national reputation and dignity, by the way), or there haven't been any terrorist attacks since September 11, and we need to shower the McBush Republicans with kudos and votes and patriotic lapel pins for their awesome post-September 11 national security record. Senator McCain and Vice President Cheney and all of their cowardly supporters need to get their stories straight because their contradictory bullshit is showing.

The wrong approach against terrorism—the McBush approach—has made things much, much worse. A July 12, 2007 National Intelligence Estimate determined that the policies of the Bush administration, supported by Senator McCain, have literally created all new generations of al-Qaeda terrorists.[17] The *Washington Post* reported:

> Al-Qaeda has reestablished its central organization, training infrastructure and lines of global communication over the past two years, putting the United States in a "heightened threat environment" despite expanded worldwide counterterrorism efforts, according to a new intelligence estimate.

> Intelligence officials attributed the al-Qaeda gains primarily to its establishment of a safe haven in ungoverned areas of northwestern Pakistan. Its affiliation with the Sunni insurgent group al-Qaeda in Iraq, the report said, has helped it to "energize" extremists elsewhere and has aided Osama bin Laden's recruitment and funding. [18][16]

Heckuva job, McBushies!

Lynn Cheney told Jon Stewart that it's "no accident" we haven't been attacked again. Based on this evidence and with this regime in charge…it absolutely has been.

---

17   *National Intelligence Estimate* dated July 12, 2007 titled "Al-Qaeda better positioned to strike the West."

18   *Washington Post*, July 18, 2007. http://www.washingtonpost.com/wp-dyn/content/article/2007/07/17/AR2007071700099.html?hpid=topnews

BOTTLED LIQUIDS
ARE BANNED FROM
THIS CHAPTER

Keith Olbermann has been one of a very few corporate-media heroes during this dark ride. His prime-time cablecasts on MSNBC are required viewing and even though the blogosphere is often better equipped for reporting on events as they happen, *Countdown with Keith Olbermann*, night after night, manages to set the agenda and prioritize the news for those of us following along on the Internet tubes.

Reviewing the soul-crushing, backwards events of this decade, it's difficult to imagine not having Olbermann on television each night setting the record straight, in the same way it's difficult to imagine the cancellation of *Real Time with Bill Maher*, the *Daily Show* or the *Colbert Report*—each being an oasis in a televised world of crapola. But there was a moment when Olbermann was in danger of being fired by then-MSNBC President Rick Kaplan at a time when the truth was considered to be at odds with, you know, patriotism. After Olbermann delivered his very first ever Special Comment about a gruesome details of a personal cancer scare, Kaplan accused him of being "out of control" and that his judgment was "not to be trusted."[1] He was accused of driving away viewers, which, in television, is usually an executive battle cry before a show is summarily set ablaze. In this case and at that time, it's reasonable to assume that executives were grasping for any and all excuses to sack truth-tellers from their networks. But "out of control" and "not to be trusted" are strong words considering Pat Buchanan's declaration on MSNBC that removing Terry Schiavo's feeding tube was a Nazi "crime against humanity."[2] Unless I missed the news, I don't recall Rick Kaplan having coronary over Buchanan's unhinged, high-pitched, Nazi remark.

Three years later, in 2008, Olbermann is rumored to be practically running the network. It turns out the truth can be successful—and patriotic.

Keith Olbermann has also successfully trumped countless authors and graduate students who might have otherwise published various scholarly theses documenting the eerie coincidences between the reporting of bad news for the Bush administration and the issuance of Homeland Security terrorism alerts. In addition to Olbermann's historically important Special Comment segments and his nightly Worst Person in the World feature, *Countdown* is best known for its on-going terror alert compendium known as the Nexus of Politics and Terror.

In total, *Countdown* has reported thirteen occurrences, since

---

1   *New York Daily News*. August 10, 2005

2   According to Media Matters for America, March 22, 2005 (http://mediamatters.org/items/200503220003):

> BUCHANAN: When the German doctors committed those crimes in the 1930s, even before World War II, they were put on trial for crimes against humanity…
> JOE SCARBOROUGH (host): Pat, are you comparing Terri Schiavo's husband to a Nazi?
> BUCHANAN: I'm comparing that judge's decision to a crime against humanity.

September 11, 2001, in which the administration has apparently engaged in carefully calculated and deliberate deception, and issuing, more often than not, unfounded terror warnings in and around bad or embarrassing news breaking against the White House. In other words, when there's bad news for the White House or good news for the Democratic Party, there has been a reasonably solid chance of a terrorism scare and an elevation in the terror-alert level precisely during or immediately following such news.

For instance, when the alarming Presidential Daily Briefing (PDB) titled "Bin Laden Determined to Strike in U.S." was released to the public, and Americans were rightfully outraged that President Bush was warned about a possible attack one month before September 11, the FBI, two days later, warned of several new terror threats and the news cycle shifted from the PDB to worries about whether terrorists were targeting the Brooklyn Bridge, the Statue of Liberty and various railroads. Fast-forward to 2004 when Senator Kerry accepted his party's nomination for president at the Democratic National Convention, news broke three days later that terrorists were targeting "financial centers in New York, New Jersey and Washington."

This pattern repeats over and over and over. And there will be many more of these "alerts" as long as the McBush Republicans maintain any degree of power in Washington. For instance, watch for a bin Laden tape to surface just before Election Day. Or if Senator Obama flummoxes Senator McCain in a televised debate this fall, watch for the announcement of the thwarting of another terror plot to, I don't know, deploy suicide-bomber kittens inside shopping mall pet stores (see the previous chapter). Or if Senator McCain erupts in a fit of rage and jujitsu kicks a baby in the throat while calling the kid a "trollop," expect everyone in Washington with a lapel pin to lose bowel control over a bogus terrorist plot to make Republicans in Washington simultaneously lose bowel control.[3]

Now this might all be coincidence. Olbermann's penchant for telling the truth applies to his own reporting, and, as such, each time he adds to the Nexus he wraps by noting the potential for all of this to be merely speculative. Yet, in his words, "it underscores the need for questions to be asked, and asked continually in this country; questions about what is prudence and what is just fear-mongering."

Taking up that challenge, I have a question that hasn't been asked often enough. It's a question about one of the most ridiculous and most seriously flawed terror warnings to be dumped into the understandably urine-stained laps of the American people. Each time Olbermann airs an updated version of *Countdown's* Nexus of Politics and Terror, he reminds us of:

> Number 11, a sequence of events in August 2006 best understood now in chronological order. As the month begins, the controversy over domestic surveillance without legal warrants in this country crashes. Then, on August 9, the day after the Connecticut Democratic Senatorial primary, Vice President Cheney says the victory of challenger Ned Lamont over incumbent Joe Lieberman is a positive for the, quote, "al-Qaeda types," who he says, quote, "clearly are betting on the proposition that ultimately they break the will of the American people in terms of our ability to stay in the fight."

---

3   Thanks to Cliff Schecter, author of *The Real McCain*, we're treated to a true story about how Senator McCain once called his wife, Cindy, a "trollop" and a "cunt" in public.

The next day, British authorities arrest twenty-four suspects in an alleged imminent plot to blow up U.S.-bound aircraft using liquid explosives smuggled on board in sports drink bottles. Domestic air travel is thrown into chaos as carry-on liquids are suddenly banned. On August 14, British intelligence reveals it did not think the plot was imminent, only the U.S. did, and our authorities pressed to make the arrests. Eleven of the twenty-four suspects are later released. And in the months to come, the carry-on liquids ban is repeatedly relaxed.

According to some very smart people in our government, liquid explosives are possibly, but not *imminently*, determined to be a new weapon against airplanes by U.S. and British authorities. For the purposes of underscoring the unnecessary hysteria this alert generated, Olbermann slyly included during the various Nexus rundowns the following news animation of a fleet of computer-generated passenger airplanes repeatedly exploding over the Atlantic Ocean:

The Bush administration counts on the news media for these awesome representations of hundreds of people aboard a series of cartoon aircraft exploding in fiery terrorist conflagrations at thirty thousand feet. After all, graphics and animations don't require people to read anything, or to even pay attention to the words. *Exploding airplanes?! Must lose bowel control, then vote Republican!*

But there's one visual element to this particular story that's broadcast during Olbermann's Nexus reports that always makes me scream at my television. Not at Olbermann, of course, but at the Bush administration for deliberately deceiving airline passengers, the American people and, hell, anyone who's paying attention.

The liquid explosives thing might have *some* validity to it. Though, as Olbermann noted, the British intelligence wasn't so sure. Be that as it may, the administration's reaction to the intelligence turned out to be anything but intelligent. Before I spell it out, take a look at this screen grab from the NBC News footage, known as "b-roll," which Olbermann included during one of his Nexus reports:

That's an actual Transportation Safety Administration (TSA) official at an actual security gate inside an actual airport. In this NBC News b-roll footage, we see this particular TSA official confiscating bottled liquids from airline passengers as the passengers are sluiced through the airport security labyrinths. She appears to be taking the bottles of *potentially explosive liquid* and... tossing them into a garbage bin:

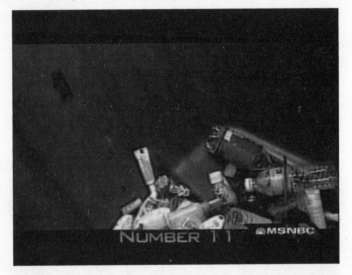

That's right. This TSA official is throwing multiple bottles of *potentially explosive liquid* into a garbage bin...right in front of a crowd of Americans gathered en masse in a small, confined space. The *New York Times* reported:

> A bulletin issued Thursday by the F.B.I. about the plot gave details of some of the properties of liquid-peroxide-based explosives. It noted that they are sensitive to "heat, shock and friction."[4]

4   *New York Times*, August 10, 2006. http://www.nytimes.com/2006/08/11/world/europe/11plot.html?_r=1&oref=slogin

Shock and friction. You mean, like, exactly what happens when an explosive is tossed into a goddamn garbage can? So if one of those bottles contained the volatile chemical known as Hexamethylene triperoxide diamine (HMTD), which officials claimed the terrorists might have been planning to use, would not the action of carelessly chucking such a chemical into a trash can cause that highly sensitive liquid to, you know, blow up? Or let's say the liquid explosives in one of those bottles could be detonated using a cell phone or another electronic device. Wouldn't that be a dangerous location in which to contain such material—right in front of hundreds of people?

All across the nation that August, Americans were told about the scary news. The Homeland Security threat level was raised to Code Red for the first and only time. Red, by the way, means "Severe risk of a terrorist attack." The president then rolled out one of his greatest fear-mongering performances:

> This plot is further evidence that the terrorists we face
> are sophisticated, and constantly changing their tactics.

And we're clearly responding with equally sophisticated garbage cans.

> On September the 11th, 2001, they used box cutters to
> hijack airplanes and kill thousands of innocent people.
> This time, we believe they planned to use liquid explo-
> sives to blow-up planes in mid-air. In response, we've ad-
> justed our security precautions by temporarily banning
> most liquids as carry-on items on planes. ... This week's
> experience reminds us of a hard fact: The terrorists have
> to succeed only once to achieve their goal of mass mur-
> der, while we have to succeed every time to stop them.

Here's a funny part in which he acknowledges the fear-mongering:

> Unfortunately, some have suggested recently that the terrorist threat is being used for partisan political advantage. We can have legitimate disagreements about the best way to fight the terrorists, yet there should be no disagreement about the dangers we face.

Then back to more scary talk:

> America is fighting a tough war against an enemy whose ruthlessness is clear for all to see. The terrorists attempt to bring down airplanes full of innocent men, women, and children. They kill civilians and American servicemen in Iraq and Afghanistan. … They're seeking to take over countries like Afghanistan and Iraq so they can establish safe havens from which to attack free nations.[5]

Before having their water bottles wrestled away by TSA officials, passengers were instructed to preemptively dump their liquids into garbage cans located adjacent to the security line. For days we watched television news b-roll and observed newspaper photographs of Americans hurling their beverages and salves like basketballs. Some of them, I'm sure, shouting the cliché *"two points!"* to the polite laughter and applause of passers-by. There were countless newspaper, Internet and magazine photos of full-to-overflowing rubbish totes lined up within shrapnel distance of wall-to-wall travelers.

Remember when envelopes containing anthrax were being delivered to various news departments as well as Democratic Sen-

---

5   http://www.whitehouse.gov/news/releases/2006/08/20060812.html

ators Tom Daschle and Patrick Leahy (see the previous chapter)? During that series of terrorist attacks, when anything resembling white powder appeared inside of a very serious office building, the building was evacuated and very serious officials wearing those very serious containment suits from the movie *Outbreak* swept the building for any remote traces of the deadly toxin.

Compare that to the "Three Stooges Fix the Plumbing" routine taking place at our nation's airports during the liquid-explosives scare of 2006.

I had the opportunity to ask a former consultant from Homeland Security about this and he told me, "The TSA can't have people standing around in ordinance disposal suits and scaring the crap out of everyone. Not to mention sweating up a storm."

"Not even goggles? Hell, I wear goggles when I'm sawing wood," I replied.

The former DHS consultant responded by implying that such protective gear would be unnecessary because, "When was the last time there was an explosive-related incident at an airport security station? Never. Nor will there ever be. You could confiscate water, mouthwash, breast milk, eye drops and sodas for the next hundred years and never discover explosive material."

As for the "scaring the crap out of everyone," Americans and people around the world were plenty scared already. I don't think TSA officials sporting eye protection and ballistic tactical vests under their shirts would've incited any more fear than had already been injected into the national bloodstream by the red alerts and exploding cartoon airplanes. Furthermore, every time I go through a major airport security line, I can't help but notice that most of them have armed National Guard units flanking the chaos. I mean, literally, troops decked out in full combat regalia. So... why?

The answer to this question, of course, is that there wasn't really a serious threat in the first place, and, therefore, baseless fear-mongering is the only remaining motive. If the crisis had been truly urgent and truly deadly enough to raise the Homeland Security threat level to red and to instigate a nationwide panic, if the crisis was urgent enough for the news networks to create an animation of multiple airplanes exploding over the Atlantic Ocean, do you think that perhaps when the government ordered the confiscation of potentially explosive liquids, they would have ordered them to be disposed of just a *little* more carefully? They didn't even pretend to make it appear as if the dumped liquids were potentially harmful. If they intended to play out a charade they should've at least tried to make it appear legitimate. Instead, there they were. Government officials and average civilians throwing liquids around the security area like the food-fight scene in *Animal House*.

Meanwhile, as this was going on, we discovered that there were, in fact, security devices that had been specially designed to tell the difference between lemonade and evildoer explosives. On August 17, 2006 the *Boston Globe* reported:

> [Ahura Corp.] says its $30,000 handheld laser scanner, the First Defender, can answer the question. The device can "see" through glass or plastic bottles and identify any of 2,500 different chemical compounds in about fifteen seconds. The FBI and New York City police already use the Ahura system, which went on sale about a year ago.[6]

6   http://www.boston.com/business/technology/articles/2006/08/17/us_delays_security_for_liquid_bombs/

And why weren't these devices deployed long before these events? Naturally because the quiet deployment of such devices would've prevented the administration from scaring everyone. Why roll out a bit of technology when it's politically more advantageous to scare you into believing that the brown person in front of you is smuggling explosives inside a tube of spermicidal jelly? The official answer, of course, was:

> The TSA has not outfitted airports with the devices, in part, because officials have to prioritize where they spend limited dollars, according to Frank Cilluffo, former special assistant to President Bush for homeland security and now director of George Washington University's Homeland Security Policy Institute.

Too expensive. I would argue that if the goal was merely deterrence, as my DHS contact seemed to be implying, they could've used plastic $20 movie props instead of $30,000 handheld scanners. But money is no object when security *really* matters...

> "[The White House] purchased a unit from us [in 2005]," Kahn said of the TSA, adding that U.S. officials still aren't prepared to deploy the Ahura system.

That's right. A year earlier the White House and the Supreme Court had deployed the handheld units at their respective security checkpoints. But meanwhile it was okay for the rest of us to use garbage cans.

In 2007, the TSA purchased Fido Paxpoint handheld scanners from ICx Technologies and deployed them to seven major domestic airports. Each individual unit costs around $25,000—a lot of money considering, as the former DHS consultant I spoke with said, "You could confiscate water, mouthwash, breast milk, eye drops and sodas for the next hundred years and never discover explosive material."[7]

So which was it? A non-existent threat, allowing officials to go through the motions with garbage cans? Or a serious threat requiring a contract for a fleet of $25,000 scanners?

Could it be that our government actually lied to us about this and other threats? Could it be that, even though the use of liquid explosives was possible, it was, nevertheless, highly unlikely, and the Bush administration merely wanted to distract Americans from Ned Lamont's victory over White House tongue-kisser Joe Lieberman? Could it be that the Bush administration wanted to prove that their illegal and unconstitutional eavesdropping operation was somehow effective?

The prudent thing to do, as Olbermann so wisely recommends at the end of each of his Nexus reports, would have been to determine whether the threat was real in the first place, and then to behave with reason and rationality. Instead, the Bush administration cried wolf with a huge blaring Code Red alert, and in doing so, were so clumsy—so brazenly manipulative and amateurish—that it would otherwise be hilarious if it weren't so tragic.

Not only that, but the administration's stated policy has always been, at all costs and against all legalities, to withhold their terror-fighting tools and techniques so that "the enemy can't adjust." President Bush and his fear-mongering surrogates couldn't wait to question the integrity and patriotism of the *New York Times* when the newspaper published the details of the administration's illegal eavesdropping program. It was emboldening and

---

7   http://www.cbsnews.com/blogs/2007/05/23/primarysource/entry2843717.shtml

aiding the enemy, they cried. When asked about the administration's policy of waterboarding suspected terrorists, the president, after repeating "we don't torture" (we executed Japanese commanders for waterboarding our World War II fighting men, but okay), took up the position that he can't discuss our "enhanced interrogation" methods for fear that the terrorists will somehow adjust and adapt to the idea of drowning.

But it was full speed ahead with the mass panic incited by the liquids ban. It was all there on television. Dump the liquids into the garbage cans within explosive range of hundreds of Americans: this is how our government intended to thwart this so-called conspiracy to blow up airplanes, a conspiracy that had already been squelched by British intelligence officials. So we're left to believe nothing else except that the administration, yet again, perpetuated a fraud against Americans—a conspiracy to frighten and mislead the *We the People* as, perhaps, a means of distracting us from the dueling "bad news" of Ned Lamont's victory and the continued fallout from the illegal wiretapping investigation. Even if those specific bad news items weren't the inciting incidents for the distraction, and the fear-mongering of the Code Red and liquid ban were stand-alone events, we still have no other choice as thinking, reality-based people than to see this episode in Keith Olbermann's Nexus of Politics and Terror for what it really was: a poorly performed hoax by the administration.

And let's just suppose for a moment that the explosive liquid plot was real. Let's suppose for a moment that there were indeed many additional terrorists on the loose and making their way to airports in order to destroy airplanes using liquid explosives. Let's just suppose that the Bush administration was telling the truth about terrorism for a change and not using their go-to Argumentum in Terrorem. If it was all true, *this* was how our government in the midst of an all-encompassing war on terror officially and safely disposed of *potentially explosive liquids?* Sheesh. You may now join me in opening one or more bottled liquids and consuming them liberally.

5

THE FISA FEARGASM

When Congress was faced with the task of renewing the unconstitutional provisions in the euphemistically titled Protect America Act in the winter of 2008, the Bush administration erupted in what can only be described as a "feargasm." The Urban Dictionary defines the word "feargasm" like so:

> **feargasm:** *n.* when an [actress] in a movie makes a climactic orgasm face, but she is supposed to be playing the emotion of intense fear.

Okay, so it's not Merriam-Webster. But it works.

Whenever the Bush administration tries to legalize its illegal authoritarian programs, they go on the TV and have a feargasm. En masse. A feargasm is the usual Bush Republican fear-mongering routine, but turbo-boosted with a performance-enhancing cocktail of human growth hormone, Cialis, cocaine and intravenous injections of pure adrenaline. Adrenaline from a hyena. A hyena on Cialis. And much like the Urban Dictionary definition, the Bush Republican feargasms are: 1) fake, fake, fake, fake, 2) supposed to be about fear and seriousness, but shouldn't really be taken seriously, and 3) like an actual orgasm—intense, spastic and sometimes involving embarrassing outbursts.

And one of their most intense (and multiple) feargasms occurred during the battle over the Protect America Act, FISA and telecom immunity. Hence, the FISA Feargasm.

Some background. The Protect America Act (S.1927) was signed by the president in August of 2007.[1] The new law legalized the Bush administration's program of illegal wiretapping of phone conversations—without a warrant—essentially overruling the provisions of the Foreign Intelligence Surveillance Act (FISA). The administration believed that having to attain a FISA search warrant before eavesdropping on American citizens was somehow hindering their ability to smoke out the evildoers. This argument was, of course, ridiculous. If the administration desperately needed to listen to someone's phone call or retrieve someone's e-mail, they could have easily attained a warrant *after the fact*. More on that later. But the Bush administration insisted that it was above the law—certainly above the jurisdiction of the lowly FISA court.[2]

Despite clear Democratic majorities in both houses of Congress, the administration coerced and intimidated centrist Democrats into believing that the law was of the utmost urgency and that their unconstitutional and illegal searches had prevented numerous terrorist attacks.[3] Naturally, most of the terrorist attacks cited by the president were half-baked and didn't hold up to

---

1   http://thomas.loc.gov/cgi-bin/bdquery/z?d110:SN1927:

2   There's no verification of any politically motivated wiretapping. But don't forget that the Republicans used the Patriot Act's financial tracking provisions to take out Eliot Spitzer. In other words, there's no verification…yet.

3   The Fourth Amendment to the Constitution of the United States: "The right of the people to be secure in their persons, houses, papers, and effects, against unreasonable searches and seizures, shall not be violated, and no Warrants shall issue, but upon probable cause, supported by Oath or affirmation, and particularly describing the place to be searched, and the persons or things to be seized."

independent scrutiny—lies, basically. Sixteen centrist "blue-dog" Democrats voted for the bill and it easily passed. Sixteen Democrats and one Lieberman, that is. Senator Lieberman, by the way, justified his cowardly vote by saying, "We're at war. The enemy wants to attack us. This is not the time to strive for legislative perfection." Don't worry, Joe, no one is expecting perfection from you. By the way, that Lieberman quote was a McBush Republican triple play: 1) an appeal to patriotism, 2) an appeal to fear, and 3) an appeal to forgive incompetence.

Meanwhile, Senate Minority Leader and real-life *Land of the Lost* sleestak Mitch McConnell (R-KY) added a sunset clause, which meant that the law would automatically expire in February of 2008, and a new law would have to take its place. Great! It might go away. But not really. The sunset clause was kind of a dirty trick. A renewal vote meant another national debate about who wants to "protect America" and who doesn't, just in time for primary season when Republicans would be confusing fear-mongering with patriotism and looking for excuses to remind Americans that both Senators Clinton and Obama voted against the Protect America Act.

Yet a funny thing happened on the way to the trampling of the Constitution.

Within seconds of the passage of the Protect America Act, President Bush not only demanded that the law be made permanent, but he also demanded that it include retroactive legal amnesty for AT&T, Verizon and other telecommunication companies that had illegally handed over your private information to the government in the days after September 11. When the wiretapping story was first reported in January of 2006, we learned that AT&T and Verizon had illegally aided the National Security Agency (NSA) in mining data from phone calls and Internet communications.

Consequently, dozens of lawsuits were filed against the NSA and the phone companies, and rightfully so. They had clearly conspired, at the behest of an Executive Order signed by President Bush, to violate both FISA and the Fourth Amendment to the Constitution. And so by asking for and granting retroactive amnesty, the telecoms would be excused from any and all lawsuits. And what's worse is such a measure would establish precedent for corporations to do it again. To paraphrase the great Naomi Klein: in terms of the collusion of government and corporations, it's impossible to tell where AT&T ends and the NSA begins.[4]

So in the late autumn and early winter of 2007, the administration went to war with Congress. Inexplicably, Senator Majority Leader Harry Reid (D-NV) capitulated to the administration and allowed a new bill that would include telecom immunity in a new version of the law to be brought up for debate on the floor. Senator Chris Dodd used an obscure Senate procedure called a "hold" to try to stall the bill, but Senator Reid ignored the hold. So Senator Dodd threatened to filibuster the bill and Senator Reid backed off. Lots of Democratic in-fighting and a holiday break ensued.

Enter 2008 and the looming February 17 expiration of the Protect America Act.

Now bear in mind that Congress—members of both parties—was very much interested in at least renewing the law. Where many Democrats in particular parted ways with the president was, of course, on this issue of retroactive corporate amnesty. So the entirety of this feargasm had to do with the president wanting to protect Verizon over protecting America from terrorist attacks—or protecting your constitutional rights

---

4   Naomi Klein is the author of *The Shock Doctrine: The Rise of Disaster Capitalism*. Required reading.

from corporate violations of privacy. To put it another way, all of the quotes coming up from members of the administration are presented with the context that 1) Congress attempted on multiple occasions to extend or renew the law in order to "protect America" from terrorist attacks, 2) Some members of Congress, mostly in the House and under instructions from Speaker Nancy Pelosi, refused to pass any law or extension that granted immunity to the telecoms and 3) President Bush would rather have allowed the law to expire—leaving us, in his words, vulnerable to attack—than to allow the telecoms to be sued by *nonprofit* civil liberties groups like the Electronic Frontier Foundation[5] and the American Civil Liberties Union. (Contrary to what the president said throughout his various feargasms, the lawsuits were *not* being orchestrated by so-called trial lawyers. And as for that "liberal" organization the ACLU? This would be the same organization that helped Rush Limbaugh when he was arrested in Florida on drug charges.)

With these factors in mind, grab your protective goggles—it's time for the FISA Feargasm. Watch for repeated mentions of the following keywords and phrases: *September the 11th*, *9/11*, *protect, safe, weakened, harm, plotting, defend, terrorist, threats, critical, enemies, danger, dangerous, attacks, tragedy, security, al-Qaeda*. I've highlighted most of the fear-mongering passages in **bold**.

SEPTEMBER 19, 2007

The president calls for the Protect America Act to made permanent, while asking for corporate amnesty:

It's particularly important for Congress to provide mean-

---

5   http://www.eff.org

ingful liability protection to those companies now facing multi-billion-dollar lawsuits only because they are
believed to have assisted in efforts to defend our nation
following **the 9/11 attacks**. Additionally, without this
protection, state secrets could be revealed in connection
with those lawsuits—and **our ability to protect our
people would be weakened.**[6]

Holy crap on a stick! And in order to augment the insane fear-mongering ambience of his remarks, he delivered the feargasm at the NSA's
Threat Operations Center. I assume this was because the more terrifying We're All Going To Die Amphitheatre was booked that day.

"Believed to have assisted," by the way, was a lie. Director of
National Intelligence Mike McConnell admitted several weeks
earlier that the telecoms had, indeed, illegally assisted the NSA.
McConnell said in an interview with the *El Paso Times*, "Under
the president's program, the terrorist surveillance program, the
private sector had assisted us, because if you're going to get access, you've got to have a partner." The transcript was released to
the press on August 26, 2007, twenty-three days *before* President
Bush's "believed to have assisted" weasel words.

OCTOBER 10, 2007

President Bush has a feargasm all over the White House Lawn
when he warns that, unlike the Protect America Act, the terrorist threat will never expire. That conveniently means endless war,
endless emergency, endless orange alerts.

Unfortunately, when Congress passed the Protect Amer-

---

6   http://www.whitehouse.gov/news/releases/2007/09/20070919.
html

ica Act they set its provisions to expire in February. The problem is **the threat to America** is not going to expire in February. So Congress must make a choice: Will they keep the intelligence gap closed by making this law permanent? Or will they limit our ability to collect this intelligence and **keep us safe, staying a step ahead of the terrorists who want to attack us?**... The final bill ... must keep the intelligence gap firmly closed, and ensure that protections intended for the American people are not extended to **terrorists overseas who are plotting to harm us.** And it must grant liability protection to companies who are facing multi-billion-dollar lawsuits only because they are **believed to have assisted in the efforts to defend our nation following the 9/11 attacks.**[7]

Again with the "believed to have assisted" weasel words. Let's get this straight. He's feargasming all over that podium in an effort to seek retroactive immunity for corporations that have been confirmed to have participated in illegal eavesdropping on American citizens. But, then again, he's not so sure even though his top man confirmed it to the press.

Meantime, we're treated to scary phrases like "terrorists who want to attack us" and "terrorists overseas are plotting to harm us." No "believed to be" language there. No similar level of uncertainty. They're absolutely plotting to kill you and everyone you know. For this unforgivable feargasm, the president should've been forced to sleep in the wet spot.

NOVEMBER 15, 2007

Press secretary and distinguished resident of Whoville, Dana

---

7   http://www.whitehouse.gov/news/releases/2007/10/20071010.html

"Cindy Lou Who" Perino engaged in the first female FISA Feargasm. Notice that the president has had two feargasms already. That hardly seems fair. Selfish pig.

> A mere three months ago reasonable Democrats joined with their Republican colleagues to craft a bill that responsibly provides our intelligence professionals the tools they need **to protect our nation** and close a **dangerous gap** in our intelligence. We are disappointed that this kind of bipartisan cooperation was so quickly abandoned. Instead, the House Democrat's bill ... fails to protect companies facing massive lawsuits for allegedly stepping up and answering the nation's call for help after **the 9/11 terrorist attacks**. If this bill is presented to the president in its current form, the director of national intelligence and the president's other senior advisers will recommend that he veto it.[8]

This feargasm was the first veto threat for any FISA legislation over the corporate amnesty issue. Once again, the president would throw his own self-proclaimed security baby out with the amnesty bathwater. Protecting corporate criminals comes first, then that other stuff... the American people. Therein is the actual justification for the entire war on terrorism and the invasion of Iraq. Corporations first. Again, I highly recommend Naomi Klein's *Shock Doctrine* for more on this front.

DECEMBER 1, 2007

President Bush's Weekly Radio Address. The president, who's widely known as an unoriginal mope, used the same old routine

---

8   http://www.whitehouse.gov/news/releases/2007/11/20071115-15.html

here. Try not to roll over and fall asleep.

> Unfortunately, the law is **dangerously out of date.** In August, Congress passed legislation to help modernize FISA. That bill closed **critical intelligence gaps,** allowing us to collect important foreign intelligence. The problem is, this new law expires on February 1—**while the threat from our terrorist enemies does not.**
>
> Congress must take action now to keep the intelligence gaps closed—and make certain our national security professionals do not lose a **critical tool for keeping America safe.** As part of these efforts, Congress also needs to provide meaningful liability protection to those companies now facing multi-billion-dollar lawsuits only because they are **believed to have assisted in the efforts to defend our nation following the 9/11 attacks.**[9]

Yep. The same feargasm techniques. No wonder 70 percent of the American people reacted with a simultaneous, "Stop it. You're on my hair."

Nevertheless, we have a second instance of the ominous "the terrorists never expire" line. The reality is that as long as we're occupying Iraq, as long as we have bases in the Middle East, the terrorist threat won't expire. But with regard to the president's overall point, take away the Protect America Act, and the NSA could easily continue to eavesdrop using the existing FISA provisions. The only "downside" for the administration is that they'd have to get a warrant. And as we'll learn here shortly, getting a warrant is about as easy as getting the vice president to strangle a kitten for fun. Timothy B. Lee, an adjunct scholar with the Cato

---

9   http://www.whitehouse.gov/news/releases/2007/12/20071201. html

Institute, underscored both the timelessness of the original FISA provisions as well as the absurdity of the "expiration" lie:

> The Protect America Act allows the administration to "authorize" eavesdropping programs for a year at a time. That means that the government's various warrantless surveillance activities will continue to operate at least through August. And of course, if the need for new wiretaps arises after the act sunsets, the administration still has the opportunity to file for warrants under the Foreign Intelligence Surveillance Act (FISA).[10]

I think I figured out why August is a problem for the administration in terms of eavesdropping. Perhaps—and I'm just speculating here—perhaps after August, with several months to go before the presidential election, they wouldn't be able to eavesdrop on Democrats or unfriendly members of the press. Just speculating.

DECEMBER 7, 2007

Pearl Harbor Day. Vice President Cheney commemorated the day with a feargasm at the National World War I Museum in Kansas City.

> So we're asking Congress to take a look at the Foreign Intelligence Surveillance Act, or FISA. FISA sets out the legal framework to **monitor terrorist communications** while protecting the civil liberties of the American people. Unfortunately, the law is out of date. In August, Congress passed legislation to help modernize FISA. That bill closed critical gaps, allowing us to collect important foreign intelligence and to **help keep our coun-**

---

10   http://www.cato.org/pub_display.php?pub_id=9185

try safe. The only problem is the new law expires February 1. There's no point in putting a sunset provision on such vital legislation. **To protect the American people,** Congress needs to pass a new FISA law, and they need to make it permanent.[11]

The architect of one of the most oppressive authoritarian administrations in American history is talking about protecting civil liberties. Vice President Dick Cheney, who voted in favor of South African apartheid, is suggesting that he's going to protect civil liberties.

JANUARY 24, 2008

A written statement by the president. Sort of a Penthouse Letter version of a FISA Feargasm. But this time we're treated to the first of the countdown-style warnings. This technique will figure prominently later in February. But for now—

Dear Penthouse Forum,

I never thought this would actually happen to me, but...

> Unfortunately, Congress set this legislation to expire on February 1. That is just eight days from today—yet the **threat from al Qaeda will not expire in eight days.** If Congress does not act quickly, our national security professionals will not be able to count on **critical tools they need to protect our nation,** and our ability to respond quickly to **new threats and circumstances will be weakened.** That means it will become harder to figure out **what our enemies are doing to recruit terrorists and infiltrate them into our country.**[12]

---

11   http://www.whitehouse.gov/news/releases/2007/12/20071207-5.html

12   http://www.whitehouse.gov/news/releases/2008/01/20080124.html

It's important to underscore here that Congress passed updates to FISA as part of that cursed U.S.A. Patriot Act just after September 11. President Bush praised the updates to FISA at the time, suggesting that the modernized language "recognizes the realities and dangers posed by the modern terrorist." The administration still ignored the search warrant requirement, however, and, since having their illegal wiretapping and data mining program outed by the *New York Times* in late 2005, the administration claimed that the warrants would somehow slow down or hinder the process. That, of course, was a lie. Under FISA, it was possible to attain a warrant for up to seventy-two hours after the surveillance was underway. Out of 22,990 requests for warrants between 1979 and 2006, only six warrants were refused. *Six*. Out of 22,990. If the administration chose to seek warrants on grounds that were even remotely credible, they would never have been turned down and therefore wouldn't have had to circumvent the law.

JANUARY 26, 2008

President Bush's Weekly Radio Address. The Senate was on its way to passing a bill that would give the president everything he had been asking for. The feargasm appeared to be working. So much for the Democratic majority in the Senate.

> Congress is now considering a bipartisan bill that will allow our professionals to maintain the **vital flow of intelligence on terrorist threats.** It would protect the freedoms of Americans, while making sure we do not extend those same protections to terrorists overseas. It would provide liability protection to companies now facing billion-dollar lawsuits because they are **believed to**

have assisted in efforts to defend our nation following the 9/11 attacks. I call on Congress to pass this legislation quickly. We need to know who **our enemies** are and **what they are plotting.** And we cannot afford to wait until **after an attack to put the pieces together.**[13]

Here's a stupid question. Let's say the administration is telling the truth and the real purpose of the wiretapping really is to monitor terrorists and terrorist activity. Based on the administration's word, then, they're only eavesdropping on evildoers. Okay, so when they find a terrorist, why the hell aren't they just arresting them?

JANUARY 28, 2008

The president's last State of the Union address.

Unfortunately, Congress set the legislation to expire on February the 1st. That means if you don't act by Friday, **our ability to track terrorist threats would be weakened and our citizens will be in greater danger.** Congress must ensure the flow of **vital intelligence** is not disrupted. Congress must pass liability protection for companies **believed to have assisted in the efforts to defend America.** We've had ample time for debate. The time to act is now.[14]

In 2002, the president's State of the Union contained a sixteen-word lie: "The British government has learned that Saddam Hussein recently sought significant quantities of uranium from

---

13   http://www.whitehouse.gov/news/releases/2008/01/20080126.html

14   http://www.whitehouse.gov/news/releases/2008/01/20080128-13.html

75

Africa." This time, it was a seventeen-word feargasm: "Congress must pass liability protection for companies believed to have assisted in the efforts to defend America."

JANUARY 30, 2008

The day before the Protect America Act was due to expire. Vice President Cheney appeared on the "Rush Limbaugh Show" for a pre-expiration-date FISA Feargasm spiked with Limbaugh's very special Viagra-with-an-OxyContin-chaser feargasm recipe. Moments earlier, the House had passed a fifteen-day extension to the law.

> RUSH: I see here today an AP story that the House of Representatives has voted to delay the demise of the wiretap law by two weeks. So we've got a two-week extension on FISA. You know, we're in the middle of a presidential election year, and a lot of people's attention is focused on that, not on FISA and the **efforts that you and the people in the administration are doing to continue to detect potential attacks.** What's the status, what's the big deal about two weeks?

> CHENEY: Well, the legislation is absolutely essential, of course. They passed a six-month extension last August, which expires on Friday, with the idea that they would finish up the legislation by Friday. They've had six months to work on it. One of the main things we need in there, for example, is retroactive liability protection **for the companies that have worked with us and helped us prevent further attacks against the United States...** we do **badly need this legislation.** It's been essential in terms of **protecting the country against further at-**

tacks, vital, one of the most vital things the president's done **since 9/11, and it would be a tragedy if this authority weren't extended.**

RUSH: The opposition in the Senate is primarily from Democrats, correct?

CHENEY: Correct. People who don't want to—I guess want to leave open the possibility that the trial lawyers can go after a big company that may have helped. **Those companies helped specifically at our request, and they've done yeoman duty for the country, and this is the so-called terrorist surveillance program**, one of the things it was called earlier. **It's just absolutely essential to know who in the United States is talking to al-Qaeda.**[15]

Twice during this excerpt Vice President Cheney unequivocally confirmed that the telecoms had (illegally!) assisted with the administration's eavesdropping program. Also notice that the vice president confirmed that the program involves eavesdropping on people "in the United States." Without a warrant, this is both illegal and unconstitutional. As of this writing, the vice president is still at large.

The next day, President Bush signed the fifteen-day extension and the Protect America Act would live on for another two weeks.

FEBRUARY 13, 2008

The president addressed the nation from the Oval Office, flanked by Director of National Intelligence Mike McConnell. The day

---

15   http://thinkprogress.org/2008/01/31/cheney-rush-fisa/

before, Majority Leader Harry Reid, facing opposition from Republicans and centrist blue-dog Democrats, was forced to allow a floor vote on a bill that included retroactive corporate immunity. Senators Dodd and Feingold tried to attach an amendment to the bill that would slice away this cancerous corporate immunity provision, but a vote on the Dodd-Feingold Amendment failed: thirty-one yeas to sixty-seven nays.[16] It goes without saying that Senator Obama voted for the amendment. Senator McCain naturally voted with the Bush administration and against the amendment. You know. Because Senator McCain is a maverick. President Bush, meanwhile, grabbed the headboard, gnashed his teeth and feargasmed all over the Oval Office:

> **At this moment, somewhere in the world, terrorists are planning new attacks on our country. Their goal is to bring destruction to our shores that will make September the 11 pale by comparison...**

> In order to be able to discover enemy—the enemy's plans, we need the cooperation of telecommunication companies. If these companies are subjected to lawsuits that could cost them billions of dollars, they won't participate; they won't help us; **they won't help protect America.** Liability protection is critical to securing the private sector's cooperation with our intelligence efforts. The Senate has passed a good bill, and has shown that **protecting our nation is not a partisan issue.** And I congratulate the senators.

> The House's failure to pass the bipartisan Senate bill

---

16   http://www.senate.gov/legislative/LIS/roll_call_lists/roll_call_vote_cfm.cfm?congress=110&session=2&vote=00015

would **jeopardize the security of our citizens.** As Director McConnell has told me, without this law, **our ability to prevent new attacks will be weakened.** And it will become harder for us to **uncover terrorist plots.** We must not allow this to happen. It is time for Congress to ensure the flow of vital intelligence is not disrupted. It is time for Congress to pass a law that provides a long-term foundation to **protect our country.** And they must do so **immediately.**[17]

Now it was up to the House of Representatives and Nancy Pelosi. The clock was ticking and the feargasm was raging.

FEBRUARY 14, 2008

With time running out on the fifteen-day extension, the president had an enormous FISA Feargasm all over the White House lawn—again. This was a really long one, and probably represents the highest per-paragraph tally of fear-mongering phrases and sentences spoken by the president during his entire second term. No wonder he appears to be more squinty than usual these days.

This Saturday, at midnight, legislation authorizing intelligence professionals to **quickly and effectively monitor terrorist communications will expire.** If Congress does not act by that time, our ability to find out **who the terrorists are talking to**, what they are saying and **what they are planning** will be compromised. It would be a mistake if the Congress were to allow this to happen.

Members of Congress knew all along that this deadline was approaching. They said it themselves. They've had more

17   http://www.whitehouse.gov/news/releases/2008/02/20080213.html

than six months to discuss and deliberate. And now they must act and pass legislation that will ensure our intelligence professionals have **the tools they need to keep us safe.**

Earlier this week, the Senate did act, and passed a strong bill and did so with a bipartisan majority. The Senate bill will ensure that we can effectively monitor those seeking to harm our people. The Senate bill will provide fair and just liability protection for companies that **assisted in the efforts to protect America after the attacks of September the 11th.**

Without this protection, without this **liability shield,** we may not be able to secure the private sector's cooperation with our intelligence efforts, and that of course would **put the American people at risk...**

Failure to act would harm our ability to monitor new **terrorist activities** and could re-open **dangerous gaps** in our intelligence. Failure to act would also make the private sector less willing to help us **protect the country,** and this is unacceptable. The House should not leave Washington without passing the Senate bill...

The **lives of countless Americans** depend on our ability to monitor terrorist communications. Our intelligence professionals are working day and night to **keep us safe,** and they're waiting to see whether Congress will give them the tools they need to succeed or tie their hands by **failing to act.**[18]

There's no confirmation of the president joking to a staffer

---

18   http://www.whitehouse.gov/news/releases/2008/02/20080214-1.html

afterwards, *Did I get any feargasm on ya'? Eh-eh-eh!*

But Speaker Pelosi wouldn't blink. She refused to bring a House version of the law to a floor vote, effectively pushing back against the administration.

Shortly after the president's feargasm, House Republicans engaged in a ridiculous feargasm stunt: they literally walked out of the House chamber in protest against Speaker Pelosi's support of, you know, the Constitution. House Minority Leader John Boehner held his own mini-feargasm when he said during the walk-out, "Our number one objective as members of Congress is to protect the American people and if the Foreign Intelligence Surveillance Act were to expire, Americans would be at risk."[19]

You know, Americans in his home state of Ohio *are* at risk, but not from the terrorists. One of Boehner's biggest corporate contributors, AK Steel, is busy polluting the air and waterways of Ohio, and several others states for that matter (see the chapter "What's the Matter with Zanesville, Ohio?"). Who's putting whom at risk, Mr. Boehner?

FEBRUARY 15, 2008

President Bush, after a White House meeting with the bicameral Republican leadership, all but blamed the House Democrats for endangering the American people.

> House leaders blocked a good piece of legislation that would give our intelligence community the tools they need to **protect America from a terrorist attack...**
>
> [B]y blocking this piece of legislation our country is

---

19   http://thinkprogress.org/2008/02/14/republican-walkout/

more in danger of an attack...

[T]he House leaders must understand that the decision
they made to block good legislation has made it **harder
for us to protect you,** the American people, and we expect them to get a good bill to my desk—which is the
Senate bill—as soon as possible.[20]

In my best Beavis & Butthead voice... Huh-huh-huh. He
said "harder."

FEBRUARY 16, 2008

President Bush's Weekly Radio Address.

> **Because Congress failed to act, it will be harder for
> our government to keep you safe from terrorist at-
> tack.** At midnight, the attorney general and the director
> of national intelligence will be stripped of their power
> to authorize new surveillance against **terrorist threats
> abroad.** This means that as terrorists change their tactics
> to avoid our surveillance, we may not have the tools we
> need to continue tracking them—and we may lose a vital
> lead that could **prevent an attack on America.**[21]

He said, "The attorney general and the director of national
intelligence will be *stripped.*" He also said "harder" again, followed
by "tools." Are you detecting a pattern here? As the February 17
deadline approached, the FISA Feargasm appears to have taken
on a more obviously erotic tone. "Harder," "stripped," "tools"...
"Boehner." To further authenticate this surge in sexual meta-

---

20   http://www.whitehouse.gov/news/releases/2008/02/20080215.
html

21   http://thinkprogress.org/2008/02/16/bush-paa-deadline/

phors, I poured through the White House transcripts in search of more hilarious evidence of this theory. Sadly, I couldn't find anything along the lines of, *Unless the House, especially Congressman Sam "Dirty" Sanchez, reaches around and gives the private sector some protection for its tools, then the terrorists will be able to thrust themselves into America's delicate and vulnerable areas.*

On the same day, February 16, Mike McConnell, who again appeared desperate to tell the truth, confirmed the earlier observations made by Timothy Lee of the Cato Institute. The expiration of the Protect America Act, McConnell said, wouldn't necessarily hinder counter-terrorism efforts: "Some of the [surveillance] authorities would carry over to the period they were established for one year. That would put us into the August, September time frame. However, that's not the real issue. The issue is liability protection for the private sector."[22]

Did you see that? "The issue is liability protection for" corporations. None of this, according to the director of national intelligence, had anything to do with stopping the evildoers. "It's not the real issue," McConnell said.

With that, the clock ran out and the Protect America Act expired.

FEBRUARY 22, 2008

Desperate to convince someone—anyone—that their FISA Feargasm was for real, the Republican Party website, GOP.com, released a web-video spoof of the FOX series *24*. In it, the Republicans imply that House Democrats were putting us all at risk of a deadly terrorist attack, just like the ones on a fictional TV series.

---

22   http://thinkprogress.org/2008/02/16/bush-paa-deadline/

Shot of the earth

Text: "America is at risk"

Text blips onto the screen: "The Protect America Act allows our intelligence agents to intercept the plots of foreign terrorists. House Democrats have allowed the protect America act to expire."

Creepy "intensity" music rises.

Shot of the Capitol building with newscast audio: "Earlier this week, the Senate overwhelmingly passed a new bill extending those warrantless wiretap powers. But House Democratic leaders refused to bring up that bill because they know it will pass."

Text: "House Republicans demand immediate action to keep America safe."

Shot of the House floor with newscast audio: "Today, dramatic protest by House Republicans who walked off the House floor and out of the Capitol building."

Shot of the house Republicans walking out with more news audio: "The day when the president and these Republicans and a vast majority of the Senate feel as thought the law governing the electronic surveillance of terrorists in this country should be taken up. That bill right now in limbo, uh, because the Senate has passed a bill, uh, that House Democrats are vehemently against."

Text: "At midnight on February 16th, the Protect America Act expired."

FOX *News Sunday* clip of host Chris Wallace interviewing Mike McConnell. *Wallace:* "Would you say the country is in greater danger now for a terrorist attack because this law has expired?"

McConnell: "Increased danger, and it will increase more and more as time goes on."

Text: "Democrat [sic] intelligence chairman Sen. Jay Rockefeller."

Clip of Senator Rockefeller: "People have to understand around here that the quality of the intelligence that we're gonna be receiving is gonna be degraded. Is gonna be degraded. Is already gonna be degraded."

Text: "And what do House Democrats say?"

Music builds

Clip of House Majority Leader Steny Hoyer: "There is no urgency."

Graphic: Big red number 3 over black-and-white video of Middle Eastern men waving rifles in the air.

Clip of House Majority Leader Steny Hoyer: "There is no urgency."

Graphic: Big red number 2 over black-and-white video of Middle Eastern men waving rifles in the air.

Clip of House Majority Leader Steny Hoyer: "There is no urgency."

Graphic: Big red number *1* over black-and-white video of Middle Eastern men with rifles.

Music climaxes. Dramatic cut to black screen.

Text blips onto the screen: "Tell House Democrats to stop playing politics with our national security. Pass the bipartisan Senate bill to combat terrorism and keep America safe."

Text: "House Republican Conference. www.GOP.gov"

Now *that* is a huge steaming pile of feargasm. And I'm sure it worked on countless viewers who are generally susceptible to melodramatic claptrap like this. It probably also worked on people who know better but who tend to exhibit a cowardly and dangerous disregard for the Constitution. In Mike McConnell's own words (when he's not spreading administration propaganda on FOX News), terrorism "is not the real issue." But yet, there you go.

And in the immediate wake of this unabashed and epic feargasm, the White House had the audacity to wheel out Dana Perino to deny that the administration was using scare tactics…

FEBRUARY 25, 2008

The *Washington Post* published an op-ed written by Senator Rockefeller, Congressman Reyes, Senator Leahy and Congressman Conyers blasting the administration's unprecedented feargasm (they called it "sky is falling rhetoric" and "scare tactics").[23] And rightfully so.

But given the daily bombardment of fear, Perino had the audacity to issue the following feargasmic statement:

> [The Democratic authors of the op-ed] claim that the administration is using "scare tactics" and they claim that there is no cost to Congress' failure to pass long-term FISA modernization that will preserve the vital powers provided by the Protect America Act (PAA). ... **Stating that fact is not a scare tactic**—it reflects the considered judgment of the intelligence community, whose principal concern is not politics, but doing their jobs. [*Scare tactics ensue...*] That the failure to enact long-term FISA modernization legislation **is costly and dangerous is beyond any serious dispute.** ... The **grave concerns** raised by our private partners, combined with the House Democratic leadership's determination to block liability protection, **seriously jeopardizes** co-operation in the future. This is not **a risk** we should be taking. ... they have produced a **dangerously flawed** and unacceptable bill containing provisions that failed when debated as amendments in the Senate, and no retroactive **liability protection for companies alleged to have assisted in defending the nation after 9/11.** ... Pointing out the cost of Congress' failure to act is not

---

23   http://www.washingtonpost.com/wp-dyn/content/article/2008/02/24/AR2008022401668.html

a "scare tactic" and it is not a "wedge issue." Instead it is a sober, transparent assessment of **the terrorist threat our nation faces,** and the **critical importance** of the needs of our intelligence community **to combat that threat.** Unless this threat is taken more seriously in Congress, the ability to obtain the intelligence we need **will be at risk, and with it our national security.**[24]

Not a scare tactic? Did she *watch* that goddamn video? Later, in the press room, Perino further poo-pooed the accusation:

I think that fear-mongering and the use of the phrase "scare tactics" is something that the Democrats—it must be, like, one of their favorite words, or it must poll very well, because they use it almost every time.[25]

"Scare tactics" and "fear-mongering" are two words each. Not one word. Math notwithstanding, it's nearly impossible to find words suitable enough to counter this level of sheer ignorance. As we've documented here, it was literally months of this—climaxing with nearly an entire week of non-stop public statements of threats and danger from both the president himself and his hundreds of mouthpieces across the nation. Crazy, off-handed and irresponsible remarks like:

More than likely we would miss the very information we need to prevent some horrendous act from taking place in the United States.

–Mike McConnell

---

24   http://www.whitehouse.gov/news/releases/2008/02/20080225-1.html

25   http://www.whitehouse.gov/news/releases/2008/02/20080225-5.html

It's time for us to get serious and protect the companies and protect us.

–Senate Minority Leader Mitch McConnell

The people I hear about every morning, their fatwas do not have an expiration date.

–Attorney General Michael Mukasey

And did you notice the Senator Sleestak quote? We need to get serious in order to "protect the companies." That would stand to reason since Senator McConnell, during the 2006 election cycle alone, raked in $666,000 from corporate political action committees—62 percent of all of his contributions that year. In terms of telecommunications companies, Senator McConnell took money from Verizon, Comcast (who gave him $10,000), Clear Channel, AT&T, Vonage and Bell South. Now we wouldn't want these lawsuits to damage Senator McConnell's campaign finance operation, would we?

FEBRUARY 28, 2008

President Bush in another one of his snotty, petulant press conferences.

> And that is why a **dangerous intelligence gap** opened up last year, and that is why Congress passed legislation that reformed FISA—but they did so only temporarily. The law expired; the **threat to America has not expired.** Congress understood last year that FISA did not give our intelligence professionals the **tools they needed to keep us safe.** The Senate understands that the FISA—old FISA didn't give us the **tools needed to protect America.** The bipartisan bill it passed pro-

vides those **tools our intelligence professionals need.**
Yet the House's failure to pass this law raises the risk of
reopening a gap in our intelligence gathering, and **that
is dangerous.**[26]

You know what's really dangerous at this point? If there
were an actual threat, no one would take it seriously. Speaking
of which, I would be remiss if I didn't point out that he said
"tools" three times.

MARCH 13, 2008

The president headed back out onto the White House lawn.
One last go-around of the same tired feargasm remarks before
the ultimate climax:

> ...the House bill fails to provide liability protection to
> companies believed to have assisted in **protecting our
> nation after the 9/11** attacks. Instead, the House bill
> would make matters even worse by allowing litigation to
> continue for years. In fact, House leaders simply adopt-
> ed the position that class action trial lawyers are taking
> in the multi-billion-dollar lawsuits they have filed. This
> litigation would undermine the private sector's willing-
> ness to cooperate with the intelligence community, co-
> operation that is absolutely essential to **protecting our
> country from harm.** This litigation would require the
> disclosure of state secrets that could lead to the public
> release of highly **classified information that our en-
> emies could use against us.** And this litigation would
> be unfair, because any companies that assisted us after

---

26   http://www.whitehouse.gov/news/releases/2008/02/20080228-
2.html

9/11 were assured by our government that their cooperation was legal and necessary. Companies that may
have helped us save lives should be thanked for their
patriotic service...The American people understand
the stakes in this struggle. **They want their children to
be safe from terror.**[27]

For the first time, the president brought the children into
the feargasm. Which is just disgusting, both in terms of my silly
metaphor and in terms of the reality of it all.

And now, at long last, the climax.

MARCH 29, 2008

Attorney General Michael Mukasey spoke at a gathering of
the Commonwealth Club in San Francisco. During a question
and answer session, Mukasey choked up. Why? Because he
was claiming in his address that September 11 could have been
prevented if it wasn't for FISA. That's right. Mukasey tried to
blame the September 11 attacks on FISA. Not in a figurative
sense either. Literally. As was first reported in the *New York
Sun*, Mukasey said:

[Intelligence officials] shouldn't need a warrant when
somebody with a phone in **Iraq picks up a phone** and
calls somebody in the United States because that's the
call that we may really want to know about. **And before 9/11, that's the call that we didn't know about.**
We knew that there has been a call from someplace that
was known to be a safe house in Afghanistan and we
knew that it came to the United States. We didn't know

precisely where it went.

We'll come back to the content of Mukasey's remarks, but I'm interrupting to mention that Mukasey started to cry here. After a pause to compose himself, he continued:

> **We got three thousand...We've got three thousand people who went to work that day and didn't come home to show for that.**[28]

Apart from these quotes representing the obvious high-water mark of the Bush administration's extended FISA Feargasm, the attorney general of the United States just admitted in public that the administration knew about a phone call from Afghanistan to someone in the United States about the September 11 attacks before those attacks took place and did nothing to act upon that information. Furthermore, there is nothing in the 9/11 Commission Report indicating such a call took place. So, as Keith Olbermann pointed out on MSNBC shortly after this news hit the wires, either Mukasey was admitting that the United States government was complicit in the attacks by not using this information to prevent them, or Mukasey is lying. Based on the administration's record, the latter option is likely the answer.

The FISA law allowed more than enough latitude to eavesdrop on such a call if it, in fact, took place. The government can eavesdrop on whatever calls it wants—without a warrant—as long as the call originates from outside of the United States. But that's beside the point because there is no indication that there was any such call.

---

28   http://www.nysun.com/news/national/mukasey-makes-emotional-plea-surveillance-powers

Philip Zelikow, the executive director of the 9/11 Commission, was absolutely stymied, baffled and confused by the attorney general's ridiculous claim. In an e-mail reply to Salon.com blogger and author of *Great American Hypocrites*, Glenn Greenwald, Zelikow wrote that such a phone call never took place, to his knowledge. Vice Chairman of the 9/11 Commission Lee Hamilton told Greenwald, "I am unfamiliar with the telephone call that Attorney General Mukasey cited."[29]

Of course not, because it very likely didn't exist.

Later, the attorney general testified to the Senate Judiciary Committee that, in fact, the call didn't come from a safe house in Afghanistan. "One thing I got wrong," Mukasey told Senator Patrick Leahy, "I got the country wrong." Mukasey also referenced a letter that the Justice Department had sent to Congressman Reyes. In the letter, Mukasey and Mike McConnell explain that there had been a call between a "9/11 hijacker" while living inside the United States and "a known overseas terrorist facility." They go on to write that the intelligence community could have prevented the attack if they had only been able to tap into the domestic end of the call.[30]

The only problem with Mukasey's backpedaling is that, in the letter, they reference Executive Order 12333, which was signed by President Reagan in 1981, as the lone hurdle in tracking that call. Not FISA or anything of the like. And besides, 1) President Bush could've overturned such an order within seconds of needing to, and, in fact, President Bush did—twice,

---

29   http://www.salon.com/opinion/greenwald/2008/04/08/hamilton/index.html

30   http://www.talkingpointsmemo.com/docs/mukasey-mcconnell-reyes/?resultpage=3&

and 2) if such a call had occurred, whether originating here or there or inside Mukasey's crazy imagination, FISA could easily have been used to track it and identify the so-called hijacker.

Greenwald concluded on his blog that if the problem was this obscure Executive Order and not FISA, and that this Executive Order had long since been overturned by President Bush, why has there been such a feargasmic fuss over FISA?[31]

The answer, as far as I'm concerned, has to do with the telecoms and the lawsuits. After the administration's illegal eavesdropping operation was made public in final days of 2005, the reaction from the Republican Congress and the Bush White House was to change the law so as to make their program legal. Greenwald summarized the initial chaos like so:

> Congress passed a law in 1978 making it a *criminal offense* to eavesdrop on Americans without judicial oversight. Nobody of any significance ever claimed that that law was unconstitutional. The administration not only never claimed it was unconstitutional, but Bush expressly asked for changes to the law in the aftermath of 9/11, thereafter praised the law, and misled Congress and the American people into believing that they were complying with the law. In reality, the administration was secretly breaking the law, and then pleaded with the *New York Times* not to reveal this. Once caught, the administration claimed it has the right to break the law and will continue to do so.

But when the legal hammer fell onto the telecoms, it became evident that such court proceedings might shed way too much

---

31   http://www.salon.com/opinion/greenwald/2008/04/04/doj/index. html

light on whom or what the administration was truly targeting. The only way around that ugliness was to further alert the law, absolving the telecoms of their legal woes and therefore absolving the administration of any issues that might be revealed in the process.

If we eliminate the veracity of what they're telling us, the reality of what they're really doing becomes clearer. If their sole mission was to truly smoke out the evildoers, then, by expert consensus, they never really needed to amend FISA in the first place (and yet they successfully did so anyway with the Patriot Act and the overturning of whatever hurdles that Reagan Executive Order threw into their path). They never really needed to break the law by repeatedly and brazenly ignoring the search warrant provision and the FISA court. And they never really needed the Protect America Act to spy on terrorists.

The only explanation was that after September 11 the administration planned on doing some pretty heavy trampling on privacy, the Constitution and civil liberties. For what purpose, no one really knows. Yet. But once their conspiracy was outed—at least in terms of the "how" and not so much the "why"—they had no other choice but to uncork another Texas-sized bottle of Astroglide and go to town on the American public with a feargasm rivaled only by their pre-Iraq "mushroom cloud" campaign.

With their record of fear-mongering on everything from torture to re-election campaigns as the base-line standard, we really need to keep asking the question: why did this particular issue—creating an escape hatch for AT&T and Verizon, of all things—require such an intense and lengthy fear campaign? As with anything to do with the Bush White House, the rule is simple: the bigger the lie, the more elaborate the deception, the bigger and more elaborate the crime.

Now grab me a towel so I don't have to sleep in the wet spot.

THE CHICKENHAWK
AWARDS

Whether Senator Obama is elected the first black president or if Senator McCain is elected the first translucent-skinned president, a gloriously feathered sun will set upon the beaked faces of our nation's chickenhawk population. The chickenhawk era is coming to a close, at least in terms of chickenhawks occupying the White House. So too is an era in which chickenhawks are inexplicably regarded as more patriotic. That's not to say there won't be any more chickenhawks. On the contrary: as long as we're at war, there will be cowardly Republicans who mock our soldiers and veterans while questioning the patriotism of those who oppose war; even though, in their chickeny past, they themselves avoided military service.

And, of course, in a book about cowardice and fear-mongering, it only makes sense to include a few pages dedicated to this not-so-rare species of Republican. You know the ones. They question the military service and patriotism of veterans and war opponents, yet they themselves avoided military service when they had a chance. It's hypocrisy in one of its most deadly and ignorant forms.

This is a uniquely Republican character flaw. Sure, more than a few Democrats have been responsible for their fair share of military confrontations throughout recent history, but I can't scrounge a single example of any non-serving Democratic presidents or politicians—people like President Clinton, who famously received a college deferment—questioning the patriotism of military veterans or Republicans who opposed various Democratically favored military strikes. For instance, in 1999, when Sean Hannity vocally opposed the American and NATO military action in Kosovo (despite his more recent mandate that it's unpatriotic to oppose the president in a time of war), I can't find a single example of non-serving Democrats who painted Hannity as unpatriotic or emboldening-the-Yugoslavians-loyal-to-Slobodan-Milošević. As slogans go, that one doesn't especially glide off the tongue, but also to belch such an accusation doesn't make any sense unless of course you also happen to believe, as Hannity does, that scary real-life demons are living among us. This isn't a joke, by the way. Hannity dedicated an entire segment of his weird *Hannity's America* show on FOX News Channel to the imminent threat of demons living among people. So logical fallacies and outright fairy-tale reasoning isn't beyond the pale for this crew.

I personally never served in the military for several reasons, which I don't mind owning up to here: 1) At 6'4", 230 lbs., my nickname would be Private Bulletblocker, as in, *Private Bulletblocker! The platoon needs some cover, so run out in front and block some goddamn bullets with your freakishly oversized body!* 2) I don't take orders very well. Ask my publisher. 3) I'm afraid of, you know, being shot. I've also, however, never supported President Bush's wars, and would *never* presume to question the military service or patriotism of anyone who has served in those wars. I would never refer to any veteran as a "phony soldier," especially if my reason for avoiding the Vietnam draft was that I suffered a boil on my ass.[1] I also don't oppose war. In fact, I only tend to oppose, as Senator Obama aptly describes them, "dumb wars."

There's no rule—moral, constitutional or otherwise—that says our political leaders had to have served in the military. In fact, when President Washington resigned his commission prior to taking the presidential oath of office, he set the precedent that the commander-in-chief be a civilian post and that the military be subordinate to a civilian command structure. Imagine if every time a president had to order a military strike against an enemy, he or she had to resign in favor of someone who has served? Or worse, imagine, as an American, being hamstrung into only voting for politicians with military backgrounds. So the logic is flawed and, carried to its furthest extent, would essentially amount to a military junta. Military service should neither qualify nor disqualify an American from elected public service, as long as they're a civilian when they're sworn in. The key distinction is a rule of character—of decency, consistency and honor that mandates against being a chickenhawk. The distinction between an effectual commander-in-chief and a cowardly bastard chickenhawk is how a leader carries him- or herself.

It's immoral to avoid military service and then deploy the military for political and financial advantage, as chickenhawk

---

1   Everyone knows this story about Rush Limbaugh, but I really enjoy repeating that Limbaugh attained a military deferment and, thus, avoided the Vietnam draft because he was suffering from a condition known as a pilonidal cyst in his butt crack. This is caused by a simple skin infection or an—*ewww!*—ingrown butt hair. Rush Limbaugh, on his satirical radio show, also referred to veterans who oppose the Iraq occupation as "phony soldiers."

President Bush and chickenhawk Dick Cheney have. President Bush has repeatedly admitted to the political advantages of being a "war president." In terms of financial gain, a barrel of oil was $33 when George W. Bush used a team of lawyers (he claims to hate lawyers, by the way) to steal the presidency. Today, oil is well above $140 per barrel. So who's winning in Iraq? OPEC and the Bush-Cheney oil cronies (not to mention the scores of contractors and mercenaries whom the neocons are using as a means to rapidly privatize our military). And it's with no sense of satisfaction and a great sense of tragedy that I report that everyone else is losing.

It's also immoral to avoid military service and then question the patriotism and military record of those who have served simply because they don't happen to support your particular war.

And finally, it's immoral to deploy or to support the deployment of men and women to war if you have never served and subsequently exploit those men and women as an excuse when things don't go so well.

To that point, one of the most remarkable aspects of the Iraq invasion and occupation has been the president's predictably awful and irresponsible habit of placing the burden of the success or failure of this thing squarely on the shoulders of an already overburdened military. Specifically, President Bush and all of his apologists have scapegoated or are preemptively scapegoating the troops and the "commanders on the ground."

It's a strategy that could only come from a group of cowardly old bastards who, for the most part, deliberately avoided military service themselves. By way of a random sampling of mistakes and atrocities:

• When the Abu Ghraib torture photographs surfaced, the line from the administration wasn't about confronting the policies that fostered such atrocities. The line was, *Oh! That was just a group of bad apples. Destroy them now! Go!* In other words, don't blame the administration's medieval torture policy that everyone knows about. Blame the troops.

• When munitions were stolen from the formerly IAEA-sealed bunkers in al-Qa'qaa after the initial invasion took place, the White House and the Pentagon blamed the troops for not adequately securing the facility. No one in the administration was man enough to own up to the fact that the troops were, for the most part, ordered to secure the Iraqi Oil Ministry and not much else. Don't blame the goddamn policy. Blame the troops.

• The Mission Accomplished banner—clearly a product of the White House's obsessive need for sloganeering and plastering their message du jour on every smooth surface available—was ultimately blamed on the navy and the crew of the USS Abraham Lincoln. It didn't seem to matter to the cowards in the White House that the initial draft of the speech itself, in fact, contained the words "mission accomplished." Blame the troops, or at least make them partially to blame, and the White House's story turned into a roundelay of he-said, she-said. *We produced the banner, but the navy asked for it.* Or, *it was our idea, but the men aboard the Lincoln wanted to put something up.* And on and on and on.

• And in March of 2008, Vice President Cheney, who received five deferments from the draft during Vietnam, was asked by ABC News about the American military death toll in Iraq reaching the ignominious four thousand mark. The chickenhawk vice president noted the burden on military families, but then inexplicably replied: "The president carries the biggest burden, obviously. He's the one who has to make the decision to commit young Americans, but we are fortunate to have a group of men and women, the all-volunteer force, who voluntarily put on the uniform and go in harm's way for the rest of us."

The vice president's implication clearly being that four thousand soldiers had been killed... because they *volunteered* to be killed. These deaths, our vice president implied, were *their* fault. And it's the president who suffered the most from these four thousand losses.

Just a sampling. Naturally, no one is suggesting the military is absolutely blameless for random mistakes in the fog of war. But if the president is so comfy inside of his too-snug Chimpy Mc-Flightsuit commander-in-chief costume, then he ought to man-up and accept the blame for *all of it*. But he hasn't and he won't. And why should he? He's been bailed out his entire life. Why change now?

And then there's the preemptive scapegoating. When it all came down to the president's ridiculous plan for escalating the Iraq occupation last year, the president constructed yet another safeguard for himself. To paraphrase Willi Cicci from *The Godfather Part II*, "The president has lots of buffers." Rather than offering himself up as the spokesman for his cleverly marketed "surge," the president created a buffer, a lightning rod in the form of General David Petraeus who became the official whipping boy for the plan. The White House kicked their metaphorical Nerf football into the bloody prickers, and General Petraeus, as a man bound by duty, was the latest in a line of whipping boys who were shoved into the thorns after the ball. Even opponents of the war famously shifted focus onto General Petraus and so, in a way, the lightning rod worked.

All along, President Bush and his regime continued to repeat this familiar preemptive scapegoating refrain: *We listen to the commanders on the ground. We do what the commanders recommend. I'm a commander guy.*

> Troop levels will be decided by our commanders on the ground, not by political figures in Washington, D.C.
>
> –President Bush, July 11, 2007

> "I reminded our people that the best decisions are made when you listen to the commanders. And our commanders have got good, specific advice as to how to achieve our objectives, which I believe we'll achieve."
>
> –President Bush, May 17, 2007

> These elections are important, and we will respond… to requests of our commanders on the ground. And I have yet to hear from our commanders on the ground that they need more troops.
>
> –President Bush, November 4, 2004 *(the day after the 2004 election—arg!)*

> The question is, who ought to make that decision? The Congress or the commanders? I'm the commander guy.
>
> –President Bush, May 2, 2007 *(The president probably meant, "I'm a commander guy," as in he "supports the com-*

manders." Incidentally, the official White House transcript has been scrubbed and the "the" has been changed to an "a.")

Decisions about conditions for a drawdown of our forces in Iraq are best based on the recommendations of the commanders in the field and the recommendations of the gentleman sitting beside me.

−Donald Rumsfeld, August 3, 2006

And because things don't ever change, here's Rumsfeld's replacement two years later:

The question is about the pacing of the drawdown of troops. And that's where we will look for the recommendation of the commanders in the field and the president's other senior military advisers.

−Secretary of Defense Robert Gates, February 28, 2008

It's actually quite clever, albeit cowardly. When history is written, the president and his administration will be on record as saying that it was the military commanders who set the policies for the occupation. It was never the president's incompetence or intransigence; *it was those goddamn generals and troops who didn't come up with the good ideas. It was the troops who therefore undermined the process in Iraq.* And chickenhawk President Bush, as he has his entire life, is able to successfully avoid accountability and walks away, while other sons of bitches are forced to scoop up his giant mess.

So now, here at the end of the dark ride of the Bush years, it's appropriate to give out some chickenhawk awards. I've come up with three categories for this ceremony:

+ THE CHICKENHAWK BADGE OF AWFUL:
Chickenhawk agitprop that manages to simultaneously crap on every grave in Arlington.

+ THE MICHAEL SAVAGE WEINER MEMORIAL *"WTF DID HE JUST SAY?!"* LIFETIME ACHIEVEMENT AWARD: The craziest, most disrespectful thing said in reference to American soldiers.

+ THE CHICKENHAWK COMMANDER GUY: The crowning of a king and the ascension of a new regime.

CATEGORY 1:
THE CHICKENHAWK BADGE OF AWFUL

This was a tough call for the members of my elite panel of judges. A strong case was made for honoring those yellow-ribbon Support the Troops bumper magnets with the BADGE OF AWFUL. When those among us apply these magnets to the rear of their unnecessarily large SUVs, I don't believe they fully realize that by using more gasoline, they're creating a chain reaction that leads to the troops (whom they "support" by displaying a magnet) remaining continually deployed in the current McBush Republican wars for fossil fuels.

And the bumper magnets are made in China and sold for profit.

There was a time when war profiteering was frowned upon. But that was before America became, as the late George Carlin describes it, a gigantic shopping mall. So when people buy those magnets and adhere them to the ass-end of their SUVs and trucks, the only people they're supporting are fly-by-night profiteers. The troops, on the other hand, when they're done in Iraq fighting for SUV fuel, will probably be deployed in a war against China, where those magnets are made.

At the end of the day, my judges decided that the magnets weren't really agitprop, so they were disqualified.

Here now at the end of the Bush administration, THE CHICKENHAWK BADGE OF AWFUL for the last eight years has to be awarded to... those purple heart bandages worn by Republican delegates during the 2004 GOP convention as a shamefully disrespectful way to mock Senator Kerry who received three Purple Hearts for wounds sustained in the line of duty in Vietnam. (Senator Kerry also received the Bronze Star and the Silver Star.)

Accepting THE CHICKENHAWK BADGE OF AWFUL award on behalf of the purple heart bandages is the man responsible for distributing them during the 2004 Republican National Convention: Mr. Morton Blackwell.

Blackwell is a member of the Virginia Republican Party. He's also the founder of the Leadership Institute: a sort of Xavier Mutant School for wingnut X-men, with esteemed alumni including Grover Norquist and Jack Abramoff.[2] Blackwell is a noted member of the secret society known as the Council for National Policy (CNP), a group of radical far-right social conservatives including card-carrying members John Ashcroft, Brent Bozell, Phyllis Schlafly, James Dobson, Oliver North, Bob Jones, Tom DeLay, Trent Lott and cult leader Sun Myung Moon.[3] In his one-man show *A Patriot Act*, author Mark Crispin Miller described one of

---

2   http://www.leadershipinstitute.org/

3   http://www.policycounsel.org

CNP's organizing goals to be Christian Reconstructionism: to transform America into a fully theocratic state, with laws based on those described in the biblical book of Leviticus. Among other things, this would permit slavery and make homosexuality punishable by death. But until then, Blackwell is content with mocking decorated military veterans.

Oh, and no. According to CNN's Boston bureau chief Dan Lothian, Morton Blackwell never served in the military.[4] During the 2004 Democratic Convention, the late Peter Jennings asked Newt Gingrich, who also avoided military service, whether he "squirmed a little" when he saw the purple heart bandages. Newt Gingrich replied, "No. I think it's funny." Seriously. That's what he said.

And the Republicans are considered to be the patriotic, pro-military party? That's rich. In addition to around-the-clock mentions of September 11, the obvious wooden crucifix on the front of the convention podium, and Governor Schwarzenegger accusing Senator Kerry of being an "economic girly man,"[5] the purple heart bandages became *the* icon of the Republican Convention

---

4   From convention coverage transcribed by the conservative watchdog group, The Media Research Center. CNN's Dan Lothian filed the following report at around 11:30PM, August 30, 2004:

> This is the Band-Aid, it was put out by Morton Blackwell who is a member of the Virginia delegation. He is not a veteran but he said he distributed some three hundred Band-Aids with a purple heart in the middle to make a point against Senator Kerry. It was very controversial, denounced by the Democratic Party and also Republican officials. Ed Gillespie tonight, we are getting word now, has had a conversation with him, has told him that he should stop distributing these Band-Aids. He's agreed to stop distributing the Band-Aids and even has removed the one that he was wearing. http://www.mediaresearch.org/cyberalerts/2004/cyb20040831am.asp#1

5   Yeah, and President Bush's economic policy turned out to be peach, didn't it?

that year. That's right, one of the few visual centerpieces of the 2004 Republican Convention literally mocked the Vietnam War wounds of a decorated veteran.

During that convention, between August 30 and September 2, 2004, while all of those fat, white, unfunny George W. Bush Republican delegates waddled around the floor wearing those purple heart bandages, Sgt. Joseph C. Thibodeaux, age twenty-six, and Staff Sgt. Aaron N. Holleyman, age twenty-four, were killed in action in Iraq. Sgt. Thibodeaux was killed by hostile enemy fire, and Staff Sgt. Holleyman was killed by a roadside bomb.[6] Eight hundred and ninety-five wounded American soldiers became eligible for the Purple Heart during the month of August of that year, and 709 in September.[7]

If any of these soldiers should ever decide to run for office as a Democrat, I wonder if the race of cybernetic chickenhawk Republicans of the future will mock these veterans' Iraq wounds with the same disrespectful, tasteless zeal with which they mocked Senator Kerry's wounds. Incidentally, November 2004 was not only the month in which President Bush was elected to his second term, but also the bloodiest month in the five-year history of the Iraq occupation. A record 1,431 wounded American soldiers became eligible for the Purple Heart that month. The president, in his victory speech, thanked "the architect, Karl Rove" before getting around to mentioning the soldiers who gave everything so he could be a "war president."

And Newt Gingrich thought the purple heart bandages were funny. Yeah, they were hilarious—if you look at the world through douchebag-colored glasses.

---

6   http://edition.cnn.com/SPECIALS/2003/iraq/forces/casualties/

7   http://icasualties.org/oif/woundedchart.aspx

CATEGORY 2:

THE MICHAEL SAVAGE WEINER MEMORIAL "WTF DID HE JUST SAY?!" CHICKENHAWK LIFETIME ACHIEVEMENT AWARD

Without question, this award is going to be given to something that President Bush, the reigning king of all chickenhawks, has said. But which obnoxiously disrespectful-to-the-troops quote is deserving of such a high honor as THE MICHAEL SAVAGE WEINER MEMORIAL *"WTF DID HE JUST SAY?!"* CHICKEN-HAWK LIFETIME ACHIEVEMENT AWARD? After all, radio talk show host Michael Savage (real name: Michael Weiner), for whom this award is named, said one of the most disrespectful things about an American soldier ever. A statement so awful that he doesn't deserve to simply *win* an award... he deserves to have the award named after him. That's how awful this was. Let's rewind to November 2007.

CNN and YouTube hosted a Republican debate in which audience members and YouTube videographers asked questions of the full slate of GOP Reaganauts. One of the audience questions that night came from a decorated military veteran:

> My name is Keith Kerr, from Santa Rosa, California. I'm retired brigadier general with forty-three years of service, and I'm a graduate of the Special Forces Officer Course, the Command and General Staff Course, and the Army War College. And I'm an openly gay man. I want to know why you think that American men and women in uniform are not professional enough to serve with gays and lesbians?

A gay veteran—face to face with the entire Republican field. Steam began to shoot from Fred Thompson's ears like Uncle Fester and Mitt Romney's face-plate popped off revealing his positronic brain unit. And, predictably, the entire line-up dodged the question, which led General Kerr to remark, "With all due respect, I did not get an answer from the candidates." Of course he didn't. He's gay. I'm reasonably certain that when General Kerr was speaking, Tom Tancredo was thinking, *Can we erect a border fence around this gay so his gay won't spread to regular Americans? Wait. Did I just say "erect"? Oh no!*

As for the Republican audience… they booed General Kerr. They booed a retired general. Because he asked a tough question and, we can only gather, because he's gay.

It turned out that very few people remember *what* General Kerr asked that night. Shortly after the debate, he was "outed" as a member of the Lesbian, Gay, Bisexual, and Transgender Americans for Hillary Clinton steering committee, and, consequently, his question was removed from CNN's rebroadcasts of the debate.

Be that as it may, General Kerr is a decorated veteran. But his military service didn't stop Michael Savage from saying on his talk-radio program:

> I don't care about this old queen, frankly. He disgusts me to make—my flesh crawls from the old queen. That was a general? Now you wonder why we're still in Iraq five years later. General—with General Keith Kerr, you know why we're still in Iraq five years later.[8]

So not only did Savage, who never served in the military

---

himself, insult gay people, gay soldiers and, specifically, General Kerr, but he also insulted the troops serving in Iraq without realizing that General Kerr hadn't actually served in Iraq. Yeah, this is just about the most horribly disrespectful chickenhawk quote ever recorded and it's no surprise that it came from Savage, who boasts strong ratings in the coveted Males Aged 25-to-Asshole demographic.

This quote is in a category all its own, so it's really unfair to try to evaluate it with the rest of the field. It's a field of shame that includes more than a few disgraceful *"WTF did he just say?!"* statements from President Bush, who famously avoided Vietnam by enlisting in the Texas Air National Guard. And for his thoughtless chickenhawk remarks, President Bush deserves THE MICHAEL SAVAGE WEINER MEMORIAL *"WTF DID HE JUST SAY?!"* CHICKENHAWK LIFETIME ACHIEVEMENT AWARD.

This first of two significant quotes actually makes me physically and emotionally enraged when I think about it. It's from that wacky slide show, unveiled at the February 24, 2004 Radio and Television Correspondent's Dinner in which President Bush is shown hunting around the Oval Office for weapons of mass destruction.

"Those weapons of mass destruction have got to be around here somewhere," he said to laughs and applause from the very serious corporate press. "Nope. No weapons over there," he continued and the video projector displayed more hilarious photographs of the president looking under furniture and such.

Several hours later on February 25, Chief Warrant Officer Matthew C. Laskowski, age thirty-two, and Chief Warrant Officer Stephen M. Wells, age twenty-nine, were killed when their helicopter crashed into the Euphrates River near Haditha, Iraq. These men were killed in Iraq because the president thought Saddam Hussein was hiding weapons of mass destruction. This, as we all know, turned out to be untrue. And yet the president had the audacity to be publicly flippant about the nonexistent Iraqi weapons of mass destruction, and not just by way of another unfortunate gaffe. This was planned, scripted, vetted, photographed and presented to the world knowing that, as of the moment of his comedy routine, 150 American soldiers had already been wounded and seventeen American soldiers had already been killed that month alone in the name of finding weapons of mass destruction in Iraq. Hilarious.

But I really believe that the president deserves this award because of his most recent chickenhawk *"WTF did he just say?!"* remark.

On March 13, 2008, the president hosted a videoconference with the Provincial Reconstruction Team and various military commanders serving in Afghanistan: a nation rapidly descending into chaos and buried beneath a mountain of poppies. The White House website doesn't have a transcript of the discussion beyond the president's opening statement,[9] but we do know that, at one point in the discussion, the president said the following, as reported by Reuters:

> I must say, I'm a little envious... If I were slightly younger and not employed here, I think it would be a fantastic experience to be on the front lines of helping this young democracy succeed.
>
> It must be exciting for you ... in some ways romantic, in

---

9   http://www.whitehouse.gov/news/releases/2008/03/20080313-3.html

some ways, you know, confronting danger. You're really
making history, and thanks.[10]

While not directly insulting the soldiers serving in Afghanistan and Iraq, it was certainly a great big *fuck you* to anyone who
has ever served, especially to the boy who was sent to Vietnam
in President Bush's place back in 1969. From what we've been
told about the awfulness of the events in both nations, there's
very little happening that could be considered either "exciting,"
"romantic" or "fantastic." While some soldiers might enjoy the ca-
maraderie and adrenaline of the experience, the overall picture is
anything but "exciting," "romantic" or "fantastic." For the soldiers
returning home from Iraq with brain injuries, as few as 2,500[11]
to as many as 176,000[12] soldiers; for the tens of thousands of
amputees; for the estimated 83,000[13] soldiers rejoining society
with psychological injuries brought on by the war, among them
Post-Traumatic Stress Disorder; for those soldiers who arrived
at Dover, Delaware inside a flag-draped coffin: how are their ex-
periences "romantic" or "fantastic"?

What kind of human being orders men and women into
combat based on lies, then tells them that he is envious of their
front-line service, even though he himself deliberately avoided
combat? This kind of behavior could only come from President
Bush: a cynical, petulant, entitled chickenhawk elitist who has

10   http://www.reuters.com/article/politicsNews/idUSN1333111120080313

11   http://www.boston.com/news/nation/articles/2007/06/10/con-
cerns_grow_about_war_veterans_misdiagnoses/

12   In a sample of Iraq soldiers, 11 percent reported brain injuries, 1.6
million soldiers have served in Iraq, 11 percent of 1.6 million is 176,000.
http://www.usatoday.com/news/washington/2008-03-17-tbi_N.htm

13   http://www.boston.com/news/nation/articles/2007/06/10/con-
cerns_grow_about_war_veterans_misdiagnoses/

been handed everything in life, including the presidency, while sacrificing nothing except his golf game (and even that sacrifice is suspect). *Envious of the dangers of front line duty?* Is he kidding? The man who sat there in stunned silence while terrorists attacked the Pentagon and the World Trade Centers? He said that if he was "younger and not employed" he would do it. He would fight. Yeah, when he was younger and barely employed, he devoted his spare time to the noble pursuit of single malt and cocaine. And, credit where credit is due, Senator McCain once described anyone who romanticizes war as a "fool or a fraud." In the case of President Bush, Senator McCain got it exactly right.

If he was as genuine as his handlers describe him, he would, now at the end of his term, admit that these soldiers are better men than their commander-in-chief. Their character and convictions dwarf those of their president. A real man would own up to his shortcomings rather than, once again, using our fighting men and women as a prop, as a booster seat for his unprecedented smallness and his superficial patriotism.

Let's move on to the next category before I *really* go off.

CATEGORY 3:
THE CHICKENHAWK COMMANDER GUY

By rights, this award ought to be chucked in the direction of President Bush, especially considering the previous category. But the president already is THE CHICKENHAWK COMMANDER GUY, and besides, it's time to give this honor to a fresh chickenhawk from the coop.

So I scanned through my files from the last eight years and

tried to find that perfect fit. Someone with the full range of qualifications:

1) A backwards Bush-apologist Republican.

2) Didn't serve in the military but supports the continued occupation of Iraq.

3) Has said or done something to insult Americans who have served.

And then there are the all-important bonus corollaries required to be THE CHICKENHAWK COMMANDER GUY:

1) Has played dress-up in a military uniform (the Chimpy McFlightsuit Factor).

2) Has a punch-me face.

As I clicked through my digital archives of all things wingnut, no one really fulfilled all five qualifications, especially those last two bonus factors. For instance, Bill Kristol, while having a punch-me face, has never played dress-up, as far as I know. Same goes for Brit Hume. Rudy Giuliani played dress-up, but not in a military uniform. Now, Ted Nugent came really damn close. He plays dress-up a lot. He sure as hell has a punch-me face. And he never served in the military. But out of all of the crazy maxims and testostonaut remarks attributed to Nugent, I couldn't find anything that insults the troops. Rick Santorum: punch-me face but no dress-up that I'm aware of. Senator Saxby Chambliss compared a Vietnam veteran and triple amputee (Max Cleland) with Saddam Hussein and Osama bin Laden, but I can't find any instances in his dossier of playing dress-up.

Former Senator George Allen... oh so, so close. Punch-me face: check. Dressed up like a Confederate soldier in the movie *Gods & Generals*: check. But no troop insults on record to go with his racist Macaca epithets.

Congresswoman Jean Schmidt? I would love to give this award to her. On the floor of the House of Representatives, she said of former marine and combat veteran Congressman Jack Murtha, "...cowards cut and run, marines never do." That's off the charts awful, even for your typically thoughtless, cowardly chickenhawk. But even if I count the red, white and blue patriotic jumpsuit she was wearing that day as a military uniform, I can't, as a decent man, label a woman as having a punch-me face.

And then, buried deep in my 2005 file, I hit chickenhawk pay-dirt.

I re-discovered a man who satisfies all of the qualifications to be the next CHICKENHAWK COMMANDER GUY. I give you... Far-right talk radio host Mike Hussein Gallagher.[14]

---

14   "Hussein" isn't Gallagher's real middle name. As far as I know.

He's absolutely a Bush Republican propagandist. He never served in the military. He insulted someone whose son was killed in Iraq. And the bonus categories: he plays dress-up in military regalia as evidenced by the actual image on the proceeding page from his website; and he has "punch-me" written all over that doofus face.

So who is this peawit and why should we care? While not necessarily boasting the name recognition of Rush Limbaugh, Bill O'Reilly or even Bill Hussein Cunningham (see the chapter "The Ultimate Fear Bomb"), Gallagher has a national audience of around 2.25 million listeners.[15] He's also appeared on the FOX News Channel *Morning Zoo* (real name: *FOX & Friends*) and filled in for Sean Hannity on the unintentionally hilarious *Hannity & Colmes* television show. In fact, while doing so back in June of 2006, Gallagher suggested that Congressman Jack Murtha, a decorated veteran, might be "just plain crazy." And, according to Media Matters, "[Gallagher] is the eighth most recognized radio personality, according to Texas-based market-research firm the Benchmark Company."

But let's rewind to August of 2005, just prior to Hurricane Katrina.

President Bush was in the midst of a record setting five-week vacation in Crawford, Texas. Five goddamn weeks—you know, because he's just like regular folks. It's noteworthy that the president spent some time riding his mountain bike around his 1,600-acre estate with Tour de France champion Lance Armstrong. In fairness, Armstrong was there to lobby for increased government funding of stem cells and cancer research. Armstrong's not a Bush Republican, as far as I know. Nevertheless, it's worth not-

---

15   "Hussein" isn't Bill Cunningham's real middle name either. As far as I know.

ing that the president and Armstrong rode for seventeen miles without ever leaving the Bush property. Seventeen miles. Meanwhile, when the rest of us sneeze too loudly, our neighbors call the police to report a possible terrorist attack. I make it a policy not to praise Karl Rove, but the way he was able to package that spoiled, special-needs rich kid as a gritty man of the people is a modern day *My Fair Lady* story in reverse.

So while the president cleared brush and rode his bike (nickname: Bikey), the Iraq occupation continued to spiral out of control. Eighty-five American soldiers were killed that month. Five hundred and forty soldiers were wounded. And the man who sent them there for political and financial gain and without an exit strategy was enjoying an unprecedented five-week holiday.

Along the road leading to the president's estate, an ordinary American citizen and grieving mother named Cindy Sheehan waited with some fellow protesters for an opportunity to ask the president an important question. Cindy Sheehan's son, Casey, was killed in action in Iraq more than a year earlier—in April of 2004—and Mrs. Sheehan rightly wanted to know why. She wanted the truth about her son's death. After all, the reasons for which he was sent to war and eventually killed turned out to be horribly, horribly wrong. So what was the real reason? The president, Cindy Sheehan reasoned, owed her, at the very least, an honest answer. Mrs. Sheehan was and remains a mom and, I hasten to emphasize, a *patriot* whose boy was utterly sacrificed for the administration's unapologetically bogus invasion and occupation. At the very least, her constitutionally protected peaceful assembly in that sweltering gully along the road in Crawford was a valid and honest protest against the Iraq occupation and against the president who ordered it.

Regardless of all of it—regardless of her and her son's sacrifice—this squawking, disrespectful chickenhawk named Mike Gallagher thought it might be good for ratings to enlist some of his chickenhawk listeners and commission a bus to take them to Crawford in order to hen-peck and torment this grieving war mother.

Shockingly, the Mike Gallagher bus trip was called The Pro-America Bus Tour. As the Daily Kos blogger "Hunter" pointed out at the time, this begs the question: was Gallagher implying that Mrs. Sheehan's vigil was somehow un-American?[16] Well, of course, that's unequivocally what Gallagher was saying: if you oppose the Iraq occupation and protest against it, regardless of whether you have lost a son, you are hereby anointed as un-American and unpatriotic, according to a fringe talk-radio host who never served (and whose military-aged children aren't serving either).

In fairness, Gallagher claimed in the conservative online rag *Newsmax* that the bus trip was in support of the troops. That's odd because when Gallagher and his protesters set up shop in across the street from Mrs. Sheehan's Camp Casey, Gallagher's army shouted through bullhorns, "We don't care!"

I wish I was making that up, but that's what they shouted. THE CHICKENHAWK COMMANDER GUY even had a George W. Bush bullhorn with which to amplify his chickenhawkish behavior.

In terms of sheer ghoulishness, it came really damn close to the protests organized by the Westboro Baptist Church (WBC)—the God Hates Fags people who protest at military funerals, claiming that soldiers are suffering the wrath of God

16   http://www.dailykos.com/story/2005/8/12/182426/409

because of America's so-called support of homosexuality. Gallagher and his army clearly weren't *that* tasteless. But freakishly close. Decent human beings do not counter-protest the efforts of a gold-star mother, regardless of her politics. Yet there he was, our new CHICKENHAWK COMMANDER GUY, implying that Cindy Sheehan's sacrifice is irrelevant if she opposes the Iraq occupation.

Speaking of the Westboro Baptist Church, Gallagher gave this hate group an hour of airtime in exchange for a pledge to not protest at the funeral of the victims of the Amish school massacre. Later, he gave the Westboro Baptist Church the entire three hours of his show in exchange for a pledge to not protest at the funerals of the victims of the Virginia Tech massacre. Superficially, it sounds like it might be a good deal. But giving the Phelps family four hours of airtime and an audience of 2.25 million listeners is really a terrible, terrible idea.

Gallagher wrote a March 2008 column for Townhall.com in which he defiantly pledged to continue to use Senator Obama's middle name because it serves to underscore Gallagher's opinion that Senator Obama will meet with Iran.

> This, of course, is the same ridiculous tone that Obama himself tries to sound by suggesting that we should sit down and negotiate unconditionally with tyrants and terrorists, as if breaking bread with a lunatic who wants to break our neck would accomplish anything.[17]

So it's okay to negotiate with the God Hates Fags lunatics, but it's not okay to negotiate with Iranian lunatics? Admittedly,

---

17   http://mikegallagher.townhall.com/columnists/MikeGallagher/2008/03/07/barack_hussein_obama

Iranian President Mahmoud Ahmadinejad isn't the most centered guy in the world, but I don't think he'd win a *Who's Crazier?* contest against the Phelps family.

If Gallagher had kept his chickeny ass out of it, there are numerous other groups that voluntarily block or disrupt Westboro Baptist Church protests, including the Patriot Guard Riders and the Black Riders. Laws are being passed (of varying degrees of constitutionality), which are designed to keep funeral protests away from the direct view of the funeral participants. Despite this, Gallagher took it upon himself to swoop in and save the day—an earnest yet completely presumptuous, self-serving and self-important maneuver that only further enabled these wackaloons with more exposure and attention than they could ever possibly have gathered on their own. Four hours of syndicated time on *our* public airwaves. I hasten to note that, to date, Gallagher has yet to be fined by the FCC, even though Howard Stern was fined $27, 500 by the FCC for saying the word "blumpkin." Mike Hussein Gallagher? Gave four hours of airtime to a group who repeatedly used the homophobic epithet "fags." Not fined. Howard Stern said the word "blumpkin." Fined $27,500. American indecency standards in action.

It's ultimately difficult to make a clean distinction between protesting a military funeral, as the WBC family does, and shouting "we don't care" during a counter-protest against a mother whose son was killed in Iraq. There's no making sense of Mike Hussein Gallagher. Like most McBush Republicans, his reasoning is confined to the level of a bumper sticker. *If you protest against Bush's wars, you're unpatriotic*, even if, unlike Gallagher, the war has taken something dear away from you. This backwards reasoning mandates that only Gallagher, along with his fellow cowards, fear-mongers and chickenhawks, are the only truly patriotic Americans. Why? I can only gather that it's because *they say so*. They wave more flags and are therefore more patriotic, as if there's any direct correlation between the two. So they've injected this nonsensical association between mere symbolism and true patriotism into the mainstream. Okay, we get it. They love their country. And it's because they wear a lapel pin or a bumper magnet or, hell, a purple heart bandage. Tough gig, this brand of "patriotism." It's hard work.

But okay. If that's how they choose to define their love of America, who am I to argue? However, we all should be arguing against Americans like Gallagher who define themselves as such but then question or insult the integrity of men and women who have suffered physical or psychological trauma or have lost loved ones in the pursuit of patriotism.

Military service isn't a prerequisite for patriotism, just as military service isn't a prerequisite for being the commander-in-chief. But the Bush-era chickenhawks have truly tested the limits of patriotism by repeatedly overcompensating for their own cowardice and insulting the bravery and sacrifice—and even, remarkably, the patriotism—of those who *have* served.

7

WHAT'S THE MATTER
WITH ZANESVILLE, OHIO?

In the final days of the 2004 campaign, Vice President Dick Cheney delivered a stump speech in a small Ohio town fifty-two miles east of Columbus called Zanesville. Known for its unique Y-shaped bridge and active steel mill, Zanesville is a typical rust belt town of about 25,000 buckeyes: mostly white, mostly middle class. Despite a Democratic voting record that lasted until 1994, 57 percent of registered voters chose the Bush-Cheney ticket in 2004.

The voters of Ohio's Eighteenth Congressional District, which includes Zanesville, also re-elected chickenhawk Congressman Bob Ney that year.[1] You might remember Ney. Less than two years after Zanesville helped to send him back to Washington, he resigned in disgrace and was sentenced to thirty

---

1 Ney voted in favor of the Iraq war resolution; he voted to make Iraq part of the war against terror with no exit date; he voted for domestic surveillance without FISA oversight; and he voted to deploy the Star Wars missile defense system. Though he reached draft age in 1972, he didn't serve in Vietnam. And while I'm exposing Ney here for the chickenhawk he is, it's worth noting that Ney voted for a constitutional amendment banning gay marriage, ostensibly to "protect the sanctity of marriage." Ney divorced his first wife with whom he fathered two children, and is now re-married. Hooray for marriage!

months in prison after pleading guilty to federal charges of both conspiracy to commit fraud against the United States and lying on his financial disclosure documents. Regarding that last charge, he falsified his disclosure forms in order to hide the fact that he took tens of thousands of dollars in bribes from various business associates of indicted Republican lobbyist Jack Abramoff.

But how was Zanesville to know its congressman was a criminal? Like many Americans that year, they voted for Ney because they had the shit scared out of them by the Bush administration who told them that unless they voted for Republicans, the evildoers were going to attack. Right there in Zanesville. Yes, the McBush Republicans convinced Zanesville voters that al-Qaeda was plotting to attack their small town because, after all, the evildoers hated Zanesville for its freedom. And its three Dairy Queen locations.

Back to the vice president's last-minute stump speech at the Hallowed Hills Conference Center in Zanesville. Bob Ney was there, by the way, and the vice president led off his remarks by telling his Zanesville supporters, "[Bob Ney] does a superb job for everybody here." By "does a superb job for everybody here," Cheney probably should've said: *Bob Ney will totally disgrace and embarrass everybody here,* but that sort of honesty can get a guy like the vice president booted out of the Legion of Doom.

During Cheney's remarks that day, he attacked Senator Kerry by saying, "John Kerry will say and do anything to get elected," and then he proceeded to show off his mighty political integrity by using *not-just-saying-things-just-to-get-elected* words like "terror," "terrorism" and "terrorists" a total of sixteen times during his brief remarks. He also invoked September 11 three times. He mentioned the Pan Am Flight 103 disaster; he mentioned the

USS Cole bombing; he mentioned the attack on the U.S. Marines barracks in Beirut; he mentioned the embassy bombings in Africa; and he mentioned the first World Trade Center bombing. The usual Bush administration feargasm.

Further attacking Senator Kerry, the vice president told his Zanesville audience, "Our goal is not to reduce terror to some acceptable level. Our goal is to defeat terror, and with George Bush as president, that's exactly what we will do." For the record, the Bush administration hasn't *exactly* defeated "terror." He probably meant "terror*ism*," which he also didn't defeat and, in fact, made worse. Whenever the Republicans use the broad, imprecise word "terror," I half expect them to also promise to defeat other emotional conditions like "the heebie-jeebies" or "the willies." If they could have figured out a way to involve Blackwater's mercenary army in fighting "the skeevies," I'm sure they would have tried.

One year before Cheney's fear-mongering stump speech, *USA Today* published a story that rapidly evolved into a very serious cable-news scandal. The story revealed how Department of Homeland Security (DHS) anti-terrorism funding was going to municipalities that, you know, weren't in any danger of a terrorist attack… *whatsoever*. The article spotlighted Zanesville's $87,500 anti-terrorism bounty from 2002, which included:

> …a $13,500 thermal imager to help find victims in heavy smoke. An $800 thermal heat gun to test the temperature of gases that might ignite. A $1,250 test kit for deadly nerve agents such as VX and mustard gas. A $1,300 monitor to gauge oxygen and carbon monoxide levels in the air. Four air packs at $3,800 each, with masks and extra bottles. Four chemical suits at $875 apiece. And much more.

The following year, 2003, Zanesville received $312,000 in DHS grants. The USA Today exposé noted, "[The county hazardous-materials] office plans to buy two $5,000 search cameras, a $15,500 communications trailer, emergency sirens—maybe even a radiation detector." If only they had invested in a crapola detector, they could've smoked out the truth about Bob Ney and the Bush administration before it was too late.

The article quoted the Zanesville assistant fire chief who cautioned, "If you do all the preparation in the big cities, the terrorists will come here." This of course would entirely change the dynamic of the war on terrorism. Zanesville, the chief implied, was kind of like that last unwanted donut in the office lunch room. The stale hideous-looking one with remnants of the other more popular donuts stuck to its side. When all of the delicious powdered donuts and cream donuts and chocolate donuts are eaten, all that's left is *that one*. Such a shift in evildoer strategy from targeting big cities to attacking tiny, lonely burgs would also require Zanesville's finest to adapt to being evildoer hunters. After all, the article noted, the most critical emergencies in the town had previously included, "a farmer pinned in a grain silo, a city worker trapped in a trench and a vacant building that collapsed."

Zanesville wasn't the only stale donut in the nation. USA Today reported that Outagamie County, Wisconsin received $500,000 in federal grants for, "chemical suits, generators, rescue saws, disaster-response trailers, emergency lighting, escape hoods and more. Coming soon: a bomb disposal vehicle."

"Anything can happen any time, anywhere, and we have to be prepared," the Outagamie County emergency management chief is quoted in the article. What else was this guy supposed to think? During that particular era, DHS was raising the threat level every time the president's approval numbers dipped below 1,000 percent. To this day, President Bush and Senator McCain are continuing to lie to the people of Wisconsin and Ohio and all points in between, telling them that they'll be killed by terrorists unless the executive branch is given unprecedented authority to police the world. Anything can happen at any time, they say.

People believed and, naturally, repeated whatever their president told them, and, during that period of time, few in the very serious corporate media possessed the sense of professional integrity to debunk the tsunami of unmitigated hyperbole. Americans, for better or worse, will trust their president—especially during a war, and especially those 30 percent of Americans (60 percent in 2003 and 2004) who have somehow been blinded to the president's utter incompetence.

Meanwhile, America's larger, already-have-been-attacked cities—you know, like New York and Washington, D.C.—were only receiving around a third of the funds they needed to protect their skyscrapers and monuments and centralized populations. The *USA Today* article reported that as much as 40 percent of the DHS terrorism preparedness funds were dispersed irrespective of population, which meant that Wyoming of all places received the largest sum of government cash per capita. By the way, isn't Wyoming the vice president's home state? Yeah, I thought so.

So the DHS funding process was tweaked and reconfigured to make sure more heavily populated areas received more of the cash.

But it still wasn't enough for cities like New York. Last year, Senator Clinton blasted New York's relatively piddling $134 million share of the preparedness cake. DHS Secretary Michael

"Shirt-off" Chertoff[2] replied with typical Bush administration petulance, "If those who criticize have a better way, they should come forward and propose that better way and see if they carry the day in the debate."[3]

Well, it turns out that Shirt-off Chertoff's boss, President Shirt-off, proposed a better way. There's very little bureaucratic gray area in this lede from December 2007:

> The Bush administration intends to slash counter terrorism funding for police, firefighters and rescue departments nation-wide by more than half next year, according to budget documents obtained by the Associated Press.[4]

The president's "better way" included the complete elimination of programs and funding for ports, emergency management and transportation. Ostensibly because terrorists have never tried to use transportation—say, airplanes for instance—as a means to attack.

The president, the AP story reported, "does not believe previous homeland security grants have been well spent and does not believe the nation's highest-risk cities have satisfied security needs." To translate, the president believed that rather than continuing to tweak the system until it actually makes sense, he ought to instead just starve it do death while focusing on initiatives that serve to consolidate his power. Or at least it seems that way.

So even though we're told ad nauseam that the terrorists could strike at any moment, requiring us to vote Republican,

---

2   Not his actual nickname. But he loves to run around shirtless, constantly flexing for people.

3   http://www.cnn.com/2007/US/07/18/homeland.security.grants/index.html

4   http://www.wnbc.com/news/14742469/detail.html?rss=ny&psp=news

we don't need to spend as much money on first responders like police and firefighters. We don't need to secure the ports or the bridges and tunnels. Just as long as the McBush Republicans can scare you and coerce you into supporting their military-industrial welfare programs, they're satisfied to ignore actual measures that could save lives in the event of an attack. After all, it's easier to ignore, you know, the Constitution, than it is to actually direct some cash to where it's needed. And the destruction of checks and balances has the added bonus of consolidating unprecedented and, I hasten to add, largely *unchallenged* executive powers.

But what about Zanesville?

Like so many other Americans in small towns across the face of this continent, the buckeyes living in that small Ohio town with the Y-shaped bridge were deceived into voting for criminals like Bob Ney and President Bush and Vice President Cheney after being subjected to ceaseless fear-mongering—a macro-brainwashing effort that began the moment American Airlines Flight 11 blasted through the North Tower. Zanesville was told by its local authorities that all sorts of expensive gadgets were required to protect them from the evildoers. The very acquisition of such items sent a clear message to the people of Zanesville, Muskingum County and the Eighteenth District: *If we need these Homeland Security grants, there must be a good reason. Maybe it can happen here.*

Zanesville, in a way, was a microcosmic reflection of what has happened in America for the better part of this decade.

The significantly understated irony is that terrorism—especially as it pertains to towns like Zanesville—is nowhere near the most significant threat we ought to be confronting.

That active steel mill in the heart of Zanesville? It turns out that it's been pumping thousands of pounds of toxins into the air and water. It turns out that AK Steel Holding, the corporation that owns and operates the Zanesville steel works along the Muskingum River, is one of the nation's biggest polluters.

Some history.

In 2000, the Environmental Protection Agency ordered AK Steel to distribute bottled water to the people of Zelienople Borough and Butler, Pennsylvania (about an hour north of Pittsburgh) after the EPA discovered that the corporation had been dumping 29,000 pounds of pickling chemicals (used to remove impurities from stainless steel) into the Connoquenessing Creek... every day.[5] The Connoquenessing Creek had been the secondary and the primary source of the borough's drinking water. Not any more.

The EPA allows up to ten parts per million of nitrates in drinking water and anything above that level is considered to be hazardous. The pickling liquors that AK Steel had been dumping into the drinking water caused nitrate levels in the creek to spike to as high as 175 parts per million. Nitrate levels of this magnitude cause "blue baby syndrome," a birth defect that results in both heart defects and prevents the blood from carrying normal levels of oxygen to the rest of the body. From 1998 to 2000, the EPA ordered AK Steel to provide bottled water for pregnant mothers in the area, but as of June 2000 when this potentially deadly spike occurred, they were ordered to provide safe bottled water for *everyone*. The creek, meanwhile, is still contaminated— so much so that swimming is prohibited.

Four years later, the EPA and AK Steel settled a government lawsuit in which AK Steel was forced to pay a ridiculously in-

---

5   http://www.epa.gov/region03/r3press/pr00-01.htm

significant $300,000 penalty and $900,000 in "programs" (corporate community service) for the following crimes against the environment and the people of the United States:

> Violated federal and state hazardous waste regulations through improper storage and disposal of baghouse dust generated at the plant. The baghouse dust, containing high concentrations of the known human carcinogen hexavalent chromium, was stored on the ground at the facility. AK Steel was also cited for failing to conduct inspections of hazardous waste storage tanks, and failing to train employees on hazardous waste management.

> Violated the Clean Water Act with an unpermitted discharge of process waters and storm water to the Sawmill Run Reservoir, a tributary of the Connoquenessing River. In September 2000, EPA ordered AK Steel to cease this unpermitted discharge. The company subsequently obtained a Clean Water Act permit for this discharge.

> Violated Clean Air Act safeguards designed to prevent equipment leaks of ozone-depleting refrigerants containing chlorofluorocarbons (CFCs) on 145 separate occasions from mid-1998 through the fall of 2002. CFCs deplete the ozone layer which protects the earth from ultraviolet radiation. Ultraviolet radiation exposure results in increased incidence of skin cancers and cataracts, suppression of the immune system, and damage to plants including crops and aquatic organisms.[6]

---

6   Verbatim from the EPA press release: "AK Steel Settles Lawsuit Over Environmental Violations at Butler Mill—Steelmaker to Pay $300,000 Penalty and $900,000 in Pollution Reduction Projects to Settle Hazardous Waste, Air and Water Pollution Violations"

Next door, in Ohio, the AK Steel works in Zanesville dumped at least 2,122,813 pounds of nitrates into the Muskingum River in 2002, according to the watchdog group Scorecard.org. From 1998 to 2002, the amount of nitrates dumped into the river increased by an alarming 849,080 percent. Muskingum County is ranked twenty-fifth in the nation for nitrate water pollution and it's entirely due to AK Steel's Zanesville works.[7] To paint a

America's TOP 25 Water Polluters

1. **AK Steel Corp. (Rockport, IN)**
2. BASF Corp. (Freeport, TX)
3. IBP Inc. (Lexington, NE)
4. Smithfield Packing Co. (Tar Heel, NC)
5. Excel Corp. (Fort Morgan, CO)
6. DSM Chemicals N.A. Inc. (Augusta, GA)
7. **AK Steel Corp. (Coshocton, OH)**
8. Tyson Foods Inc. (Sedalia, MO)
9. IBP Inc. (Hillsdale, IL)
10. USS Gary Works (Gary, IN)
11. Anheuser-Busch Inc. (*Baldwinsville*, NY)
12. US Army (Radford, VA)
13. Du Pont (Belle, WV)
14. Excel Corp. (Schuyler, NE)
15. Du Pont (Deepwater, NJ)
16. McCain Foods USA Inc. (Easton, ME)
17. J.R. Simplot Co. (Heyburn, IN)
18. John Morrell & Co. (Sioux Falls, SD)
19. Motiva Enterprises LLC (Port Arthur, TX)
20. McCain Foods USA (Burley, ID)
21. IBP Inc. (Dakota City, NE)
22. **AK Steel Corp. (Zanesville, OH)**
23. Samoa Pacific Cellulose (Samoa, CA)
24. Choctaw Maid Farms (Carthage, MS)
25. Taylor Packing Co. Inc. (Wyalusing, PA)

Source: Scorecard.org

---

7   http://www.scorecard.org/chemical-profiles/rank-counties.tcl?edf_
chem_name=NITRATE+COMPOUNDS&edf_substance_id=EDF-
038&how_many=100&drop_down_name=Water+releases&fips_state_code
=Entire+United+States

picture of how terrifically awful that ranking is, there are 3,141 counties in the United States and Muskingum is number twenty-five. Comparatively, Butler County, Pennsylvania, where AK Steel was ordered to give bottled water to the people of Zelienople in order to prevent blue baby syndrome, is ranked sixty-fourth.

Let's be clear about this. According to Scorecard.org, Zanes-ville's river water is more polluted with nitrates than the poten-tially deadly Connoquenessing Creek. And all of that nitrate pollution comes from the Zanesville works. Three of the top twenty-five most nitrate-polluting facilities in the United States are owned by AK Steel, and one of those three mills, in Rock-port, Indiana—also known as The Rock—is number one on the list, making AK Steel the biggest water polluter in the nation. In other words, among all corporations everywhere in America, AK Steel's Rockport plant dumps more toxins into the water than any other corporation.

Twenty-eight miles north of Zanesville, up Rt. 60 then north-west on Rt. 16, the Coshocton AK Steel works is ranked seventh on the list of America's top twenty-five water polluters. The Co-shocton factory, coincidentally enough, is *also* actively polluting the Muskingum River, miles and miles before those waters travel southward to flow beneath the Y-shaped bridge in Zanesville.

The Zanesville AK Steel mill is ranked second in the na-tion for nitric-acid air pollution.[8] The Zanesville mill is ranked twenty-second in the nation for overall water pollution. Again, line up every corporate facility in the United States of America in numerical order of which pollutes the water more, and the

---

8   http://www.scorecard.org/chemical-profiles/rank-facilities.tcl?edf_chem_name=NITRIC+ACID&edf_substance_id=7697-37-2&how_many=100&drop_down_name=Air+releases&fips_state_code=Entire+United+States&sic_2=All+reporting+sectors

Zanesville steel mill is number twenty-two.

All of these factors combined have led Scorecard.org to rank Zanesville in the 80-90 percentile for cancer-causing air and water pollution. Zanesville also scored in the 90-100 percentile for total environmental pollution.

A recent poll indicates that the people of Muskingum County support tougher restrictions on corporate pollution. The non-profit environmental watchdog group called Earth Justice polled voters in the Ohio Eighteenth District and determined that they are overwhelmingly concerned about pollution in their waterways by a margin of nearly nine to one.[9] Earth Justice reported that 87 percent say they are concerned about clean drinking water and 55 percent say that the government hasn't gone far enough to protect the environment. But here's the rub: 67 percent of these voters *aren't* "worried" about drinking their tap water. Considering what AK Steel has been responsible for in other areas, Muskingum voters should probably be *a lot* more worried about the safety of their drinking water.

But I wonder whom our fear-mongering politicians tend to side with: the people or the polluters. Over the last eight years, the AK Steel Political Action Committee has donated hundreds of thousands of dollars to mostly Republican politicians from Ohio, Pennsylvania, Indiana, Kentucky and other states.

So who has taken the most money from the biggest water polluter in the nation?

---

9   http://www.earthjustice.org/library/references/oh18marginals.pdf

AK Steel PAC – 2008 Election Cycle All Stars

Rep. John Boehner (R-OH)	$2,000
Senator Sherrod Brown (D-OH)	$2,000
Rep. Steve Chabot (R-OH)	$1,000
Rep. Philip English (R-PA)	$1,000
Rep. Zachary Space (D-OH)	$1,000

Total disbursements as of March 2008: $50,050

AK Steel PAC – 2006 Election Cycle All Stars

Senator Evan Bayh (D-IN)	$6,000
Rep. John Boehner (R-OH)	$10,000
Rep. Steve Chabot (R-OH)	$5,000
Former Senator Mike Dewine (R-OH)	$5,000
Rep. Philip English (R-PA)	$6,500
Senator Orrin Hatch (R-UT)	$1,000
Senator Mitch McConnell (R-KY)	$7,000
Former Rep. Bob Ney (R-OH)	$1,000
Former Senator Rick Santorum (R-PA)	$2,500
Rep. Jean Schmidt (R-OH)	$3,000

Total disbursements: $109,051
Paid to 28 Republicans, 4 Democrats

AK Steel PAC – 2004 Election Cycle All Stars

Senator Evan Bayh (D-IN)	$7,000
Rep. John Boehner (R-OH)	$10,000
Senator Jim Bunning (R-KY)	$5,000
President George W. Bush	$5,000
Rep. Philip English (R-PA)	$2,500
Former Rep. Dennis Hastert (R-IL)	$1,000
Rep. Bob Ney (R-OH)	$1,000
Senator George Voinovich (R-OH)	$5,000
Former Senator Rick Santorum (R-OH)	$2,000

Total disbursements: $169,601
Paid to 27 Republicans and 3 Democrats

AK Steel PAC – 2002 Election Cycle All Stars

Senator Evan Bayh (D-IN)	$1,000
Rep. John Boehner (R-OH)	$9,000
Senator Mitch McConnell (R-KY)	$2,500
Former Rep. Bob Ney (R-OH)	$1,000
Former Senator Rick Santorum (R-PA)	$2,500

Total disbursements: $166,972
Paid to 21 Republicans, 1 Democrat

AK Steel PAC – 2000 Election Cycle All Stars

Rep. John Boehner (R-OH)	$7,500
Former Senator Mike Dewine (R-OH)	$3,000
Rep. Philip English (R-PA)	$1,500
Senator Dick Lugar (R-IN)	$2,000
Rep. Anne Northup (R-KY)	$2,000

Total disbursements: $127,975
Paid to 18 Republicans, 4 Democrats

Total Political Contributions 2000-2008: $623,649
Source: http://www.campaignmoney.com

Scanning this list, you'll notice that Bob Ney received $3,000 from AK Steel. Sadly, his Democratic successor, Congressman Zach Space (real name) is carrying on the polluter tradition by accepting $1,000 from these corporate criminals.

Congressman Phil English, meanwhile, of Pennsylvania's Third District has received $11,500 from AK Steel over the last eight years. Congressman English's district happens to include the town of Butler, Pennsylvania, which is of course the home of the AK Steel works that totally destroyed the Connoquenessing Creek and polluted the drinking water of Zelienople Borough with toxic chemicals. So it's with significant levels of snark that I congratulate Congressman English for winning the 2008 Distinguished Community Health Defender Award from the National Association of Community Health Centers (seriously—it's on his website).[10] It's awesome that he can take so much cash from one of America's worst polluters while also receiving an award for being a defender of health.

House Minority Leader John Boehner is clearly the winner, though, raking in $38,500 over the last eight years. Leader Boehner represents Ohio's Eighth District, which is the home of AK Steel's Middletown works. The Sierra Club lists Middletown as a Community at Risk due to this corporation's criminal activity. The AK Steel plant is reported to be coating nearby homes with layers of black soot. One resident died recently from a rare form of cancer that typically attacks steel workers called renal cell carcinoma. The Sierra Club reported:

> [Throughout the past twenty-five years] the Ohio EPA failed to take effective action to protect Middletown resi-

---

10   http://www.house.gov/english/biography.shtml

dents' health. Finally, in June 2001, the U.S. EPA took legal action against AK Steel's more than two hundred violations of the Clean Water Act, numerous spills of up to one million gallons into the Great Miami River and Dick's Creek, and violations of the Clean Air Act and the Resource Conservation and Recovery Act for improper disposal of hazardous waste... Signs are now posted along Dick's Creek, a six-mile waterway running through Middletown, that read, "Unsafe Water, Do Not Swim, Bathe, Drink or Fish." ... AK Steel has committed more than 200 Clean Water Act violations and dozens of Clean Air Act violations since 1995. A benzene leak in January 1996 resulted in the demolition of half a block of houses... AK Steel responds to questions regarding its environmental record by threatening to leave town, taking local workers' jobs with them. [11]

AK Steel hasn't moved the works from Middletown. It remains right there, polluting Ohio's natural resources and allegedly killing its citizens. However, they've evacuated their corporate headquarters, formerly based in Middletown, and relocated to West Chester, north of Cincinnati. I suppose their chairman and CEO James L. Wainscott grew tired of sucking in all of that soot and benzene.

It's no shocker that over the last eight years, Republicans like Leader Boehner and Congressman English and Bob Ney and George W. Bush have taken the vast majority of AK Steel contributions: ninety-seven Republican contributions compared with fourteen contributions to Democratic candidates. Obviously (and primarily) it's the fear-mongering Republicans who would rather

---

11   http://www.sierraclub.org/communities/2002report/ohio/

their constituents remain horrified at the prospect of a terrorist attack, while one of their best contributors, AK Steel, is actively polluting the air and water with carcinogenic toxins—toxins that also cause deadly birth defects. Speaking of which, it's a fine thing for the "pro-life" party to be taking money from a company that's risking the health of the unborn, isn't it? How staggering is it that a Republican politician can tell a woman what to do with the fetus growing inside of her, all the while taking cash from a corporation that could be killing that fetus with corporate pollution?

All across the nation, the threat of terrorism (and other scary distractions) routinely overshadows the very real dangers we face from white men in tailored suits and very serious haircuts who rationalize the destruction of our environment. Their attacks breach the walls of our home every day in our air and drinking water. Who are the real evildoers confronting small towns like Zanesville? Are they insurgents in Iraq or militants in Afghanistan or are they the American corporatists who seem to have no problem whatsoever with dumping carcinogens of all varieties in our water and air and, consequently, into our bodies?

What's the matter with Zanesville and the rest of the country? Priorities. What should we really be afraid of? The relatively remote odds of a terrorist attack in our small towns, or the very real and verifiable toxic contamination of our most basic life sustaining resources: our air and water? Clearly, it's the latter. And in a broader sense, attention to the climate crisis suffers at the hands of the same inconsistent priorities. At the heart of this problem are the Republicans who deny that humans are causing the climate crisis—if not outright defining it as a myth—while, on the other hand, trying to convince us of this fairy tale about how the terrorists in Iraq will follow us home and turn Zanesville into Basra. They're trying to tell us that our patriotism is defined by the degree to which we blindly support this ill-defined and poorly executed war on terrorism, rather than defining it in terms of guarding our people, our land, our water and our air. Did Vice President Cheney, during his last-minute stump speech, mention one damn thing about the nitric-acid vapors that were being pumped into the air while he spoke? Or the chemicals being injected into the river just a few clicks north of where he was stumping for votes?

If the administration was half as tenacious about protecting you and me and our natural resources from deadly polluters as they are about this futile misadventure in the Middle East, corporations like AK Steel would have no choice but to sit down and come up with a way to do business that doesn't involve flagrantly dumping toxins into the air and water. If we redirected just a small fraction of our half-a-trillion-dollar defense budget (that we, the public, know about) into tax incentives, as well as into actually enforcing—I mean, really dogging—corporate criminals and polluters until they take advantage of existing technology and future innovation to safely and cleanly dispose of industrial waste and emissions, we might one day be able to reclaim for ourselves and our posterity these commonly held resources.

But the McBush Republicans have allowed the EPA to be gutted. Hundreds of enforcement staffers have been dropped. Billions of dollars have been sliced from the EPA's relatively modest budget. And 20 percent of the EPA's research facilities are scheduled to be closed by 2011. All the while, the Republican-controlled EPA has, in turn, attempted to nullify the Clean Air Act, prompting then-New York Attorney General Eliot Spitzer to sue the administration.[12] In 2003, the administration also attacked the Clean Water Act by attempting to erase certain waterways and wetlands from being protected,[13] while inexplicably declaring 2002 and 2003 to be the Year of Clean Water. Meanwhile, more than 40 percent of our lakes, streams and rivers aren't safe for swimming or fishing.[14] The Clean Water Act, signed by President Nixon, was supposed to eliminate water pollution by 1985. But polluters like AK Steel have bought their way out of compliance with the law.

Zanesville might have been temporarily bought off with carbon-monoxide gauges and chemical suits and test kits for nerve gas to protect its people against the terrorists. But I really wonder if they'd be better served by protecting themselves against the enemy within their city limits—the enemy that's slowly poisoning them.

---

12   http://www.oag.state.ny.us/press/2002/nov/nov22b_02.html

13   http://www.commondreams.org/news2003/0609-04.htm

14   http://www.ens-newswire.com/ens/mar2006/2006-03-24-05.asp

8

THE ULTIMATE FEAR BOMB

They threw in the obvious, ultimate fear bomb.
"When all else fails, be afraid of his name, and
what that could stand for, because it's different."

–Michelle Obama
February 28, 2008

Too many far-right politicians and very serious corporate media pundits can't bring themselves to use the word "Democratic" when referring to the Democratic Party and instead use the grammatically incorrect epithet *Democrat* Party, partly because "crat" rhymes with "rat."[1] Get it? *Har-har!* Imagine if Senator Obama began to retaliate by pronouncing Republican with a long *u* sound, as in \ri-pyüb-li-kən\, so the middle syllable sounds like the word "pube." This way, the Republicans will become subliminally regarded as a party of pubic hair. *ZING!*

---

1   The *Democrat* Party epithet was originally used by President Hoover and later popularized by Newt Gingrich and Frank Luntz during the 1990s as a way to not just draw the subliminal "rat" comparison, but also to diminish the association between "Democratic" (the party) and "democratic" (the system of government). In addition to pundits and bloggers, it's often used by President Bush and other Republicans. Because they're so dignified.

Even though it's funnier than *Democrat* Party, Senator Obama would never do any such thing because it's ridiculous and totally beneath the dignity of a presidential candidate, much less anyone who's older than a third-grader.

Silly name-calling, however, has always been part of the American political dynamic: from cutesy titles like His Accidency for vice presidents who rose to the presidency due to a tragedy, to ad hominem epithets designed to smear a candidate or president.

During the election of 1800, President John Adams was hammered by a Richmond, Virginia propagandist named James Callender with one of the most colorful rants in all of American politics. Historian David McCullough documented the attacks in his legendary biography *John Adams*:

> Not satisfied that the old charges of monarchist and warmonger were sufficient, Callender called Adams a "repulsive pedant," a "gross hypocrite," and "in his private life, one of the most egregious fools upon the continent." Adams was "that strange compound of ignorance and ferocity, of deceit and weakness," a "hideous hermaphroditical character which has neither the force and firmness of a man, nor the gentleness and sensibility of a woman."[2]

During the election of 1836, the William Henry Harrison campaign and his Whig Party supporters wrote a song in which they called President Martin Van Buren a "squirt-wirt-wirt." Later that year, they began to refer to the president as Martin Van Ruin. That same year, liberal Democrats known as Equal Righters (politically not unlike today's liberals and progressives) were

---

2   David McCullough, *John Adams*. pg. 537

called a wide variety of old-timey epithets like Rowdies, Sweepings and Remnants, Noisy Brawlers, Disorganizers, Unclean Birds and Pledge Spouters.[3] Four years later, New York Whig party boss Thurlow Weed coined the name Sweet Sandy Whiskers for the foppish Van Buren.

And of course there were the famously nasty things said and written about President Lincoln. The *Charleston Mercury* wrote in 1860:

> A horrid looking wretch he is. Sooty and scoundrelly in aspect, a cross between the nutmeg dealer, the horse swapper, and the night man, a creature "fit evidently for petty treason, small stratagems and all sorts of spoils." He is a lank-sided Yankee of the uncomliest visage, and of the dirtiest complexion. Faugh! after him what decent white man would be president?[4]

In 1864, supporters of Democratic candidate George McClellan were quoted in *Harper's Weekly* as using the following epithets for President Lincoln: Filthy Story-Teller, Ignoramus Abe and Old Scoundrel. And I'm sure these were just the epithets that were suitable enough for publication.

Admittedly, name-calling is a fun and creative endeavor in politics. The subtitle of this book contains two epithetical terms. Really good name-calling is a comedic art form all its own and we liberals have all the (good) comedians, so our nicknames are more than a little worthy of historical note. The names we've coined for President Bush, for instance, have been part and parcel of the liberal blogosphere. The really funny names involve the

---

3   From *Presidential Campaigns* by Paul F. Boller. Oxford University Press.

4   Ibid.

combination of a general epithet or simian word like Chimpy or Monkey for the first name and, for the last name, any negative word combined with the prefix Mc.

The George W. Bush Derogatory Nickname Theorem:

[(simian word ending in 'y') or (random obscenity with or without a 'y')] + [(Mc) + (epithet, which can end in 'y' but isn't mandatory)] = Hilarious Bush Epithet

You can fill in the blanks with just about any word combination. One of my personal favorites is Chimpy McSmirky. I also dig Chimpy McTwitchy, due to his unexplained jaw twitch circa 2004-2005.[5] The Daily Kos version of Wikipedia, known as dKospedia, compiled the following list of derogatory names for President Bush:

Arbusto, aWol, Baby Bush, Beelzebush, Blotchy, Boy President, Boy Emperor, Bubble Boy, Bush Leaguer, Bush Lite, Bush, Inc., BushCo, Bushit, Bushwa, C-Plus Augustus, Caligula, Chimp, Chimp-in-chief, Chimpy, Chimpy McCokespoon, Chimpy McFlightsuit, Chimpy McHalliburton, Chimperor, Commander Codpiece, Deserter-in-Chief, Dim Son, Disaster Monkey, Dubya, Dubyanocchio, Dumbya, Flight Suit-In-Chief, Furious George, Idiot Prince, Idiot Son of an Asshole, Incurious George, Jesus W. Bush, Junior, King George, Liar-

---

5   During the second Fall 2004 presidential debate between Senator Kerry and President Bush, I noticed that the president's jaw would inexplicably spasm—shifting left and right briefly—following a remark. This twitching continued throughout the following year and reached its high-water mark during the Hurricane Katrina disaster, when Harry Shearer compiled for the *Huffington Post* a video of the spasms. By the beginning of 2006, it had almost entirely vanished. No one from the administration has remarked on this bizarre presidential twitch.

in-Chief, Moronarch, Miserable Failure, Post Turtle, Preznit, President Monkey, Pretzel Boy, Shrub, Shrubya, Smirk, Squatter-in-Chief, Toxic Texan, Twig, Whistle Ass, Wimp, Jr. [6]

Chimpy McFlightsuit is probably the funniest thing associated with George W. Bush. And that's a long and storied list, which includes the president dropping his foo-foo dog Barney onto the hard pavement of an airport tarmac in front of a group of little-league softball players. Chimpy McFlightsuit and all of the rest of the Bush epithets are worthy of historical, museum-quality names like "squirt-wirt-wirt" or "unclean birds" any damn day.

This past year, variations of Governor Mike Huckabee's name became a short-lived yet popular pastime for those of us in the blogosphere. During the height of the primary season, I coined the nickname Huckaboner to describe Governor Huckabee's penchant for gaffes, bloopers and various creepy evangelical pledges to rewrite the Constitution based on God's law (boner used here as a synonym for a mistake). Meanwhile, Cliff Schecter, author of *The Real McCain*, coined the nickname Huckacrazy on Sam Seder's radio show. Other variations included Huckleberry, Huckabounce, Huckabomb, Huckaburst, Huckabye-bye, Huckaboondoggle, Huckabandwagon, Huckanutter Sandwich and Huckmaster General.[7]

All of the above nicknames illustrate the difference between liberal name-calling and authoritarian conservative name-calling.

---

6   http://dkosopedia.com/wiki/George_W._Bush#Derogatory_Nicknames

7   Microsoft Word spell checker suggestions for the name Huckabee: Chickadee, Huskies and Hoecake.

It's a phenomenon indicative of a well-known difference between the two political schools of thought: liberals are generally funny or clever while conservatives are generally neither. Therefore, one could say that liberal name-calling is creative and funny and in line with a history of innocuous, albeit muddy, American discourse. Conservative name-calling, on the other hand, is predictably unfunny and, more often than not, racist or sexist or both. Name-calling in American politics can only be funny and creative only when, beyond any satirical content, it's ultimately harmless.

Until recently, the McBush Republicans have historically only *compared* the Democrats to terrorists. But now the far-right has expanded its "bin Laden is rooting for the Democrats" gimmickry into the realms of literally and dangerously implying that Senator Obama *is* a terrorist, or helping to spread the false notion that Senator Obama is a Muslim with terrorist sympathies. The strategy includes everything from whisper campaigns to not-so-accidental mispronunciations of the senator's last name to self-satirical stunts like the time FOX News Channel conducted a poll in which they asked voters:

Who is Usama Rooting For?

Who does Usama bin Laden want to be the next president? More people think the terrorist leader wants Obama to win (30 percent) than think he wants Clinton (22 percent) or McCain (10 percent). Another 18 percent says it doesn't matter to bin Laden and 20 percent are unsure.[8]

I wish I had been called to participate in this poll because

---

8   FOX News Poll, February 28, 2008. http://www.foxnews.com/story/0,2933,331691,00.html

when the pollster got to this question, I would've replied: "bin Laden? Who's he rooting for? I'm so glad you asked because I think bin Laden is rooting for the munchkin who lives in my shoe! I call him Senator Fiddlesticks and he's a bionic rat bastard just like my replicant brother Linda. Tomorrow, Senator Fiddlesticks the Shoe Munchkin is receiving the endorsement of the FOX News Is Full Of Shit PAC. And then onward to Washington, D.C. to take back the White House! *YAARRRR!* I hope my answer was adequately ridiculous to match the ridiculousness of the question. Bye!"

But at some point beginning around 2005 and spreading like a cancer into this year's presidential campaign, we've been witness to a form of name-calling-meets-whisper-campaign-meets-racial-smear-meets-fear-mongering the likes of which we really haven't before seen in American politics.

Soon after Senator Obama entered the Senate, Rush Limbaugh, being the Rosetta Stone of all that is comedy, began to deliberately confuse the names Osama bin Laden and Senator Barack Obama as a recurring bit on his drug-tainted, flaccid-weinered radio program. For instance, according to Media Matters, during a single July 2005 broadcast, Limbaugh said "Obama-Osama" seven times in one segment.[9] Hilarious! Limbaugh noticed a similarity in the names and then, like the kindergartener he is, deliberately confused the names. Genius. However, the subtext is more sinister. He succeeded in conflating Senator Obama with the al-Qaeda leader in order to incite fear and, secondarily, as a pathetic attempt to be funny. Limbaugh's idea of comedy is also illustrated by, for instance, the time he thought it would be hysterical to imitate and mock Michael J. Fox's Parkinson's Syn-

---

9   http://mediamatters.org/items/200507120008

drome tremors.

Then, in December of 2006, CNN's *Situation Room* exploded in a full-blown cuckoo's nest of mispronunciations and evildoer comparisons thanks to Jeanne Moos and Jeff Greenfield. First, the Jeanne Moos statement, as described by Media Matters:

> "[O]nly one little consonant differentiates" Obama and Osama. She then added, "[A]s if that similarity weren't enough. How about sharing the name of a former dictator? You know his middle name, Hussein."[10]

Very good, Moos! Observant! I wonder if Jeanne Moos is presently working on a special investigation into the mysterious nexus of *Kim* Jong Il and Disney Channel's cartoon heroine *Kim* Possible; Ted *Bundy* and Al *Bundy*; OJ *Simpson* and Jessica *Simpson*. But of course it was inexplicably considered to be newsworthy by CNN to mention Senator Obama's middle name with pejorative intent. And Moos was in good moronic company that day in the form of Jeff Greenfield. The Media Matters summary:

> Jeff Greenfield compared the similarity of Obama's "business casual" clothing to Iranian President Mahmoud Ahmadinejad's "jacket-and-no-tie look." Greenfield concluded the segment by saying: "Now, it is one thing to have a last name that sounds like Osama and a middle name, Hussein, that is probably less than helpful. But an outfit that reminds people of a charter member of the axis of evil, why, this could leave his presidential hopes hanging by a thread."

What kind of life-changing kick to the groin transformed

---

10   http://mediamatters.org/items/200802120007

Jeff Greenfield from a brilliant speechwriter for Robert F. Kennedy into an insufferable, fear-mongering douchebag? Strike that. Apologies to Mr. Greenfield. He's not *literally* a douchebag, he just *reminds* people of one. That's probably less than helpful for him. See what I did there?

The following month, in January of 2007, *Insight* magazine, a subsidiary of the conservative *Washington Times*, published a story claiming that "researchers connected with the Clinton campaign" had incorrectly discovered that Senator Obama was schooled in a madrassa—a Muslim seminary—during his childhood in Jakarta, Indonesia. The Clinton campaign later denied it; however, considering a remark by Clinton supporter and former-Senator Bob Kerrey in December of 2007, and a statement by Senator Clinton before the Texas and Ohio primaries, I'm not so sure about the veracity of that denial. Be that as it may, the article falsely claimed that Senator Obama was hiding his past:

> "He was a Muslim, but he concealed it," the source said. "His opponents within the Democrats hope this will become a major issue in the campaign"...
>
> "The background investigation will provide major ammunition to his opponents," the source said. "The idea is to show Obama as deceptive."[11]

Legitimate media sources, including CNN and the Associated Press, promptly debunked the lies and set the record straight, thankfully.

On the flip side, CNN, that month, aired videotape of

---

11   *Insight Magazine*, January 16-22, 2007. "Hillary's team has questions about Obama's Muslim background" http://www.insightmag.com/Media/MediaManager/Obama_2.htm

Osama bin Laden with text that read: "Where is Obama?" Yeah. Good job, CNN. Though, to their credit, Wolf Blitzer offered to apologize to Senator Obama in person even though Blitzer had nothing to do with the on-screen graphic blunder. So that's something. The truth is that, while living in Jakarta, Senator Obama attended Catholic school for several years, and then spent two years in a secular public school. The public school happened to be the one that *Insight* claimed (and Republicans subsequently repeated) was a madrassa. It wasn't. Nedra Pickler of the Associated Press reported within several days of the fear-mongering (and false) *Insight* story:

> "The allegations are completely baseless," said Akmad Solichin, the vice principal at SDN Menteng 1, who added, "Yes, most of our students are Muslim, but there are Christians as well. Everyone's welcome here... it's a public school."

> A spokesman for Indonesia's Ministry of Religious Affairs said claims that Obama studied at an Islamic school are groundless.

> "SDN Menteng 1 is a public primary school that is open to people of all faiths," said the spokesman, Sutopo, who goes by only one name. "Moreover, he studied earlier at Fransiskus Assisi, which is clearly a Catholic school."

But we live in a nation where a war hero can be swift-boated and, even though the lies are thoroughly debunked, the egg can never entirely go back into the shell. We live in a nation where *John Kerry looks French* can be perceived as *John Kerry is French*, which becomes *John Kerry is effete*, which is eventually misinterpreted as *John Kerry is gay*. So it's no surprise that an ambitious operative decided to morph "public school with Muslim students" into "Muslim school" into "madrassa that teaches Wahhabism."

And it's no surprise that people bought it. The strategy behind this conspiracy is indicative of the ugly, cynical side of American Bush-Rove Republican politics. The idea was to manipulate as many less-educated, less-informed Americans as possible; Americans who inaccurately believe—probably because they were told by fear-mongering authority figures—that all or most Muslims are terrorists. These easily manipulated simpletons, so the conspirators believe, will make the same inference about Senator Obama if they're told that he's a Muslim who's concealing his true religion from the American people. These exploitative tactics are neither funny nor clever within the bounds of the historical name-calling tradition. This non-reality based fusion of the senator, a lie about his past and the so-called terrorist threat continues to be nothing if not baseless, disgraceful fear-mongering at its very worst and rather than being reserved for the commentariat and snark-master generals occupying the blogosphere and late-night comedy shows, has perpetuated at the highest levels of authoritarian Republican leadership.

Nevertheless, the whisper campaign had begun. Far-right blogs and talk-show hosts throughout the so-called liberal media ran with the story. And even though the rumor wasn't true, it was enough to fuel the whispering. And when combined with both the deliberate name mispronunciations and the pejorative use of the senator's middle name (Hussein), the far-right had a smear-and-fear campaign that could freely permeate across the semi-osmotic membrane, which divides legitimate and subversive far-right discourse.

And it gets worse. The viral e-mail called "Who is Barack Obama?" continues to be circulated by gullible people to this day. Among other things, it claims that Senator Obama, who is a Christian, is actually a Muslim. Furthermore, even though there exist dozens of photographs and videotape showing the senator's distant cousin, Vice President Cheney, swearing-in Senator Obama on a Bible, the e-mail falsely claims he was sworn in on the Koran. Why is this? Probably because Congressman Keith Ellison, who really is a Muslim, was sworn in on the Koran and the sick bastard who created this e-mail probably figured no one would be able to tell the difference. The e-mail also falsely claims that Senator Obama refuses to say the pledge of allegiance, even though he's on video leading the United States Senate in the recitation of the pledge. This claim is based on a silly photograph taken in Iowa during a performance of the Star Spangled Banner. Senator Obama is shown standing respectfully with his hands cupped, while Senator Clinton and Governor Bill Richardson opted to hold their hands to their heart, which isn't mandatory for National Anthem etiquette. The upshot of the e-mail reads as follows (bad punctuation included):

> Let us all remain alert concerning Obama's expected Presidential candidacy. The Muslims have said they plan on destroying the US from the inside out, what better way to start but at the highest level - through the President of the United States , one of their own!!!!

As ridiculous and dangerous as that appears, it's worth underscoring that too many Americans believe every word of it. Sure, these are likely the same Americans who give their PIN numbers to various dying Nigerian princes who just won the international lottery and need a place to stash their billions of dollars in nonexistent winnings but, nevertheless, they believe.

Recently, Dr. Danielle Allen of the Institute for Advanced Study investigated the origins of the e-mail and determined that the information probably came from a disgruntled former political opponent of Senator Obama named Andy Martin who began to compile these Muslim lies about the senator soon after the 2004 Democratic convention.[12] Dr. Allen discovered further that the whisper e-mail contains information provided by anonymous far-right commenters—also known as "freepers"—from the conservative website FreeRepublic.com. It goes without saying that these self-proclaimed patriotic Americans, who have no evidence with which to back up their claims, refused to go on the record with their actual names and instead continue to hide behind their protective Internet handles.

In late September of last year, Rush Limbaugh reached well beyond his unfunny Obama-Osama gag by combining the deliberate name mispronunciation with a direct comparison between Senator Obama and bin Laden:

> Well, we've got another tape from—I get these guys confused—Usama bin Laden. Another tape says he's going to invade Pakistan and declare war on Pakistan and Musharraf, which, ladies and gentlemen, puts him on the same page with a Democrat presidential candidate—that would be Barack "Uss-Obama."[13]

---

12   "An Attack that Came Out of the Ether" *Washington Post*, June 28, 2008. By Matthew Mosk. http://www.washingtonpost.com/wp-dyn/content/article/2008/06/27/AR2008062703781.html?sid=ST2008062703939&pos
=

13   http://mediamatters.org/items/200709210002

Before I get into this one, and for the record: Sorry, Limbaugh, you impotent McDonaldland Grimace character,[14] Senator Obama didn't say he would randomly invade and occupy Pakistan. The senator said, quite clearly, that if Pakistan were to fail to act upon specific intelligence about a terrorist target, that he would take the initiative himself: "If we have actionable intelligence about high-value terrorist targets and President Musharraf won't act, we will." The Bush administration bombed al-Qaeda strongholds inside Pakistan in February of this year, based on similar reasoning, Limbaugh, you fatheaded puzzle-wit.

So the evolution of the "accidental" mispronunciation of Senator Obama's last name from a name-calling joke into a fully actualized excuse for comparing the senator to a terrorist grew in prevalence as the autumn turned to winter last year. Republican presidential candidate Mitt Romney, who has the most cartoonish-sounding political name since Boss Hogg, elevated the name mispronunciation to the presidential candidate level. According to the *New York Times* blog, the Caucus, Mitt Romney said on October 23, 2007:

> I think that is a position which is not consistent with the fact… Actually, just look at what Osam — uh — Barack Obama, said just yesterday. Barack Obama calling on radicals, jihadists of all different types, to come together in Iraq. That is the battlefield. That is the central place, he said. Come join us under one banner.[15]

Presidential candidate Mitt Romney said that Barack Obama, a United States senator and presidential candidate, was

---

14   With apologies to Grimace.

15   http://thecaucus.blogs.nytimes.com/2007/10/23/romney-makes-obama-osama-gaffe/

"calling on radicals, jihadists of all different types, to come together in Iraq." A Romney spokesman told the *New York Times* that Romney "misspoke," which is always the best excuse for saying awful things.

Republican fear-mongers absolutely understand that when they say things like this, the tooth-impaired demographic of the American electorate will believe it and perhaps use it as an excuse for their racist, refusal to support a black presidential candidate. As Senator Obama secured the Democratic nomination, multiple YouTube videos began to surface in which residents of various small, mostly white rural towns were asked about who they would vote for. When Senator Obama was mentioned, the interviewees would invariably cite either the senator's race or the senator's misperceived religion as their reason for not voting for him. The trend being the conflation of "black," "weird name" and "Muslim" (or "Arab").

For racist white people, the Muslim excuse is a convenient one. If they perceive the black candidate as being a Muslim and possibly a terrorist sympathizer, they conveniently have a legitimate excuse for their bigotry and don't have to necessarily admit to their racism. Two years ago, Tennessee Republicans gave bigots a similar excuse to vote against Harold Ford in his unsuccessful Senate campaign. The smear commercial that probably tipped the scales against Ford featured a semi-naked white woman imploring Ford to "call her." The conceit of the commercial was that if Harold Ford were elected to the Senate, his next move would be to come for the white women. In the simplest of terms, the Republican leadership, by endorsing such a message, legitimized bigotry because if the TV says it's okay... then it's okay.

This leads us to the ratings-impaired, far-right CNN *Headline News* personality, Glenn Beck, who was somehow able to weasel his way onto the December 17, 2007 edition of ABC's *Good Morning America*, on which he said this:

> They just want someone they think they can trust. I think Osama—unfortunate name. Obama!

Here's the weird thing. Sometimes when I want to say the name Glen Beck, I accidentally blurt out Glass Cock. The words are so similar that when I say Gleek Duck—whoops! See? I'm always doing that. Wow. Glenn Beck has such an unfortunate name.

And no, Mr. Beck (yes!), Barack Obama is a noble and unique name. Gonads Van Rapist—now *that's* an unfortunate name. Barack Obama is most certainly *not*, Mr. Beck, you twit. You're a professional broadcaster, for Pete's sake, and you can't properly say the last name of a major presidential candidate? Or is this mispronunciation not so accidental, sir?

Later, in a statement, Beck excused his inability to properly pronounce a simple three-syllable name by recycling Jeanne Moos's excuse from a year earlier: *silly me—the names are only different by one consonant.* Of course one consonant (and one vowel) is the difference between "Beck" and "cock," but no one with a complete set of chromosomes would seriously believe that confusing those two words was merely accidental due to their "unfortunate" similarities.

And then there's the middle name. Even though the far right, as a matter of policy, disgraces the Constitution and America's reputation in the world, they also crack me up. Not a lot, but sometimes. It's okay for the Bush family to do business with the bin Laden family and the Saudis, but it's not okay for Senator Obama to have a middle name that happens to be a common name in the rest of the world, outside of our white, sheltered, Puritanical excuse for culture. I mean, I presently live near Reading, Pennsylvania, which is mostly Pennsylvania Dutch and German and very, very white and—I just checked—there's a guy in the phone book with the last name Hussein.

And so, because they apparently have no other plan of attack, screeching racists like Ann Coulter have taken to referring to Senator Obama as "Barack Hussein Obama" or "B. Hussein Obama." The excuse? Well, shit, it's really his middle name.

This naturally goes well beyond a mispronunciation and turns a man's given middle name—the name of his father—into something foul and obscene, what Michelle Obama called "the ultimate fear bomb."

In June 2007, Ann Coulter took Senator Obama's middle name one step further by making a hilarious terrorist-hijacking joke on FOX News Channel's *Hannity & Colmes*:

> COULTER: No, but I do think anyone named B. Hussein Obama should avoid using "hijack" and "religion" in the same sentence.

> COLMES: I see. So, in other words, you want to paint him as a terrorist by continuing to use—to highlight that his middle name is Hussein?

> COULTER: Just avoid those two together.

> COLMES: So, in other words, he—only you can talk like that. Only conservatives. Someone whose middle name is Hussein should not talk like that.

COULTER: Avoid "hijack" and "religion."

Okay, so if having the middle name Hussein automatically makes someone a terrorist who hijacks airplanes, then it's fair to say that because Coulter has the same hairstyle as Saruman from *The Lord of the Rings*, she ought to be considered similarly evil. Of course that's a ridiculous means of comparison, but I'm proving a satirical point. What's Coulter's excuse, given her reputation, other than to pass of as humor the deliberate perpetuation of the fear-bomb campaign against Senator Obama?

Months later, on a very special Valentine's-and-Fear-Monger's-Day-2008 episode of *Hannity & Colmes*, Coulter the White Wizard lapsed into an unhinged Hussein Tourette's Syndrome outbreak when Alan Colmes challenged her on the comedic value of her sinister Hussein bit. Coulter's Hussein fest began with this exchange:

COLMES: What does his middle name have anything to do with—

COULTER: You know, it's really irrelevant because our gal—

COLMES: But why do you do that?

COULTER: Hillary is doing a fine job now.

COLMES: Yeah, but why do you do that? Why do you keep emphasizing his middle name as if you're trying to associate him with Saddam Hussein?

COULTER: Because I think it's funny. Okay, back to Hillary. She won in New Mexico—

COLMES: I hear the gales of laughter. [16]

I love the sarcasm from Colmes, who got it exactly right. It's not funny. What we have here is a Republican who doesn't know how to be funny, and who is also lying about trying to be funny. Merely repeating something that's true isn't comedy. It's repeating something that's true and, in this case, implying something that isn't true. Chimpy McFlightsuit is funny and harmless, but still biting and creative enough to augment a satirical point about the president's insubstantial nature. B. Hussein Obama (in a pejorative context) is unfunny, simplistic, too easy and, worst of all, incites racist anti-Muslim hatred against someone who isn't a Muslim in the first place. Coulter might fancy herself a comedian, but B. Hussein Obama isn't comedy. It's dangerous and simplistic. Cut ahead a few seconds when Coulter said:

Get ready for President Hussein, and let's start planning for the next president.

In other words: get ready for the first terrorist president. I wonder what an unstable wingnut in a pair of too-tight rubber pants—polishing his constitutionally protected assault weapon while watching from his "compound"—took away from that statement.

This could be why, remarkably, some Republicans have opted to stop using both Hussein and the Obama-Osama mispronunciation. In a shocking development, two of the most prominent Republicans to walk away from this game have been race-bait-

---

16   http://mediamatters.org/items/200802150002

ing blogger Michelle Malkin and ratfucker Karl Rove.[17] Apparently they're even chastising other Republicans to cut the crap as well, like talk-radio chickenhawk Mike Gallagher who wrote in his March 7, 2008 column that Rove told him that using Senator Obama's middle name as a pejorative "isn't helping John McCain."[18] And Michelle Malkin told Gallagher that to misuse Senator Obama's name to make a point isn't necessary. Naturally, Gallagher protested with the predictable *Duh-huh? But it's really his middle name!* excuse, figuring this would confuse and fluster everyone into ignoring *why* Gallagher was mentioning Senator Obama's middle name in the first place: to incite fear and hatred.

But, make no mistake, I'm not praising either Malkin or Rove for their discretion and inexplicable embracing of, you know, taste. Rove has been responsible for one of the most terrible and destructive presidencies in American history; and Malkin has been a loyal cheerleader and water-carrier for Rove's shish kebob of horrors. One rational decision in a world of shit doesn't mean a whole hell of a lot, especially when the thing is already out there.

The Rove-Malkin memo apparently didn't make it to the hairy ears of cranky old man and talk radio host Bill Cunningham, who erupted in a Barack Hussein Obama feargasm at a February 26, 2008 John McCain rally in Cincinnati. When I first saw the footage, I seriously thought the codger on stage was Dana Carvey's Cranky Old Man character. But I was wrong. I was so, so wrong.

---

17   Actual political term for someone who engages in dirty tricks.

18   Townhall.com, "Barack Hussein Obama" http://www.townhall.com/columnists/MikeGallagher/2008/03/07/barack_hussein_obama

Senator McCain later publicly apologized for Cunningham's remarks,[19] and that's pretty much how the Republican fear bomb has functioned: stoke the fires using surrogates and pawns to keep the rumors fresh and up-to-date; then publicly distance Senator McCain from the remarks; and repeat. Josh Marshall, the founding editor of the website Talking Points Memo described this dynamic like so:

> Don't insult your intelligence or mine by pretending that John McCain's plan for this race doesn't rely on hundreds of Cunninghams—large and small—across the country, and the RNC and all the GOP third party groups, to

---

19   The conservative blog Hot Air reported on Senator McCain's apology in a post titled "McCain Disavows Cunningham's Barack Hussein Obama Shtick." Unlike Bill O'Reilly, I don't think it's fair to quote commenters as representatives of the sites on which they post, but the following Hot Air comment about Senator Obama's middle name grabbed my attention:

> I like the fact that it bothers the libs and PC police on HA to say ones middle name or any variation thinkable. I enjoy saying Hillary Rotten, BJ Clinton, Hussein Obama, McShamnesty, Flip Romney, etc… If saying Hussein shows disrespect then that is a perfectly fine goal. I have no respect for Hussein and if saying his middle name draws attention to his darker side, then so be it. Even if it doesn't have any effect other than disrespecting a pandering Marxist, I am fine with that also. Hussein needs to disassociate himself from any hint of potential to have sympathetic policies (or turn a blind eye) to sharia creep and such. The U.S. needs a leader who will be practically forcing the so-called "moderate" Muslims to come out of the closet and denounce what is going on with their religion and the disgusting sharia in the U.S. and abroad. It is up to Hussein and his sympathizers to fix the button that's being pushed or how they think about it. It's not up to the commenters. If you don't like it, you might as well get used to it.

As awful as this is, the intention isn't to indict Hot Air based on this comment. But it's indicative of the views way, way too many Republican voters. http://hotair.com/archives/2008/02/26/video-mccain-disavows-cunninghams-barack-hussein-obama-shtick/

be peddling this stuff nonstop for the next eight months
because it's the only way John McCain have a real shot at
contesting this race.[20]

Previously on his syndicated radio show, Cunningham is
quoted as having taken the Senator Obama fear-bomb concept
to a new and crazier level. On a January 6 episode of his show,
Bill Cunningham referred to Senator Obama as "Barack Hussein Mohammed Obama." He added a Mohammed in there.
Which—oh my—I just snarfed beverage out of my nose because it's so funny. But actually it's just dirty, sinister and, hence,
typically Republican. It really is a window into what passes as
the Republican creative soul. It simply and falsely implies that a
decent, patriotic American public official is, in fact, a terrorist,
without any sense of irony. It's illustrative of the entire modern
conservative movement. Tasteless, unsubstantial, cynical, destructive, racist.

The day after Cunningham went publicly batshit, the fully
legitimate Tennessee Republican Party issued a press release
titled "Anti-Semites for Obama." Seriously. The release has been
removed from the Tennessee GOP's website, but fortunately the
Internet tubes allow us to save incriminating evidence for posterity. The memorandum began with:

> The Tennessee Republican Party today joins a grow-
> ing chorus of Americans concerned about the future of
> Israel, the only stable democracy in the Middle East, if
> Senator Barack Hussein Obama is elected president of
> the United States.[21]

---

20   http://talkingpointsmemo.com/archives/180471.php
21   http://www.talkingpointsmemo.com/images/2008-02-27-tn_
gop_obama.jpg

The memo goes on to mention Louis Farrakhan's unsolicited and famously "rejected and denounced" endorsement of Senator Obama, and then ends with:

> Obama has pledged to hold a Muslim Summit to deter-
> mine Middle East policy with the very leaders that have
> as their to goal to remove Israel from the map, referenced
> Jews to be "dogs" and "pigs," among other vile references.

This is the Republican Party, not some fringe conspiracy group or cowardly far-right talk-show host.

Then came the photograph. On February 25, the day be-fore Bill Cunningham exploded at that McCain rally and at the outset of the Clinton campaign's famous "kitchen sink" assault on the Obama campaign, Matt Drudge posted on his Drudge Report website a photograph of what appeared to be Senator Obama wearing a white turban of some sort. Uh-oh.

As I poured through the Drudge story and other reports about the photograph, I learned that this was an actual Asso-ciated Press photograph showing the senator wearing non-reli-gious Kenyan (at the time, the outfit was incorrectly described as Somalian) garb during an official congressional visit to Africa in 2006, and I knew that this would fit perfectly into the far-right's fear-bomb narrative. And then I read that the photograph had apparently been sent to Drudge—as a way of saying *look what we found in the AP archives*—not by a random Republican operative but instead by a staffer inside the Hillary Clinton campaign.

At least, that's what Drudge wrote. To date, no other news organization has confirmed that a Clinton campaign staffer sent to photograph to Drudge. Given his record of, frankly, stirring up shit, I tend to believe that he was doing just that.

Around that same time, however, several Clinton campaign volunteers were fired after they were caught circulating the "Who is Barack Obama?" whisper-campaign e-mail. And after Drudge's turban photograph story hit the fan, Senator Clinton's campaign manager Maggie Williams issued a rather bizarre and defensive statement. The *New York Times*:

> Enough... If Barack Obama's campaign wants to suggest that a photo of him wearing traditional Somali clothing is divisive, they should be ashamed. Hillary Clinton has worn the traditional clothing of countries she has visited and had those photos published widely.[22]

Regardless of the source of the photograph, for Williams to not understand the true implications of the photograph and the misperceptions it would help to feed indicated that the Clinton campaign, in the throes of the "kitchen sink," weren't interested in helping to defuse—or to even sympathize with—the fear bomb. After all, it didn't matter how many foreign outfits Senator Clinton had sported over the years, there has never been a whisper campaign circulating about Senator Clinton being a Muslim and, subsequently, a terrorist Manchurian Candidate. That's why the photograph was regarded as "divisive." Sheesh. It wasn't about the clothing and the turban. It was entirely about the larger fear-bomb narrative.

And remember the Tennessee Republican Party memo that falsely accused Senator Obama of conspiring with the Iranians to destroy Israel? This Kenyan-turban photograph of Senator Obama was part of it. The memo described the photograph: "Obama, (pictured dressed in Muslim attire in a 2006 visit to

---

[22]   http://www.nytimes.com/2008/02/26/us/politics/26clinton.html

Africa)..." *Muslim attire*, the Tennessee Republican Party said. If they had described the garb as a replica Boba Fett costume, it would've been equally as inaccurate.

All of these events—the photograph, the Clinton campaign's cheap response, the Cunningham tirade, the Tennessee Republican Party memorandum—all occurred within one week of what ought to be more appropriately described as a *shock-and-awe* fear-bombing of a presidential candidate, and not because of some kind of gaffe or indiscretion, but simply because of an ignorant misinterpretation of his name and his humble Kansas-meets-Kenya heritage.

The only reason this is an issue is because a nest of fear-mongers somewhere decided that the only way they could take down Senator Obama was to create this whisper campaign around his name and background. This is an entirely invented series of lies and among smart, normal people, there is no disputing any of it. Humans breathe air, water is wet, dogs lick their own balls, and Senator Obama is a Christian man as well as a patriotic American.

Nearly one week after the release of the Drudge Kenyan photograph, *60 Minutes* interviewed Senator Clinton.[23] Steve Kroft asked the senator if she thought her opponent was a Muslim. Senator Clinton replied:

> Of course not. I mean, that, you know, there is no basis
> for that. I take him on the basis of what he says. And, you
> know, there isn't any reason to doubt that.

With the words "of course not," this seemed like a reasonably

---

23   http://www.cbsnews.com/stories/2008/02/29/60minutes/main3894659_page4.shtml

strong refutation by Senator Clinton. But then came the less certain, "I take him on the basis of what he says." As if there's some gray area. As if he might not be telling the truth. "There isn't any reason to doubt that," she continued. But, see, it was never a question of doubt versus belief. It has nothing to do with anything Senator Obama said or didn't say. It's about the lies perpetuated by the far-right. Kroft continued:

> "You said you'd take Senator Obama at his word that he's not…a Muslim. You don't believe that he's…," Kroft said.
> "No. No, there is nothing to base that on. As far as I know," she said.

"As far as I know"? That was an awfully big opening at the end there, wasn't it? As far as *I* know, these responses, if they were calculated, indicated that, much like Maggie Gallagher's statement, Senator Clinton wasn't inclined to outright dismiss these rumors, and instead placed the burden of truth on Senator Obama who had nothing to do with any of it, other than to run for public office in a world that's partially occupied by fear-mongering McBush Republicans. And if she didn't want to dismiss the rumors, it can be concluded that she was fine with letting them fester—a festering which, at that point in the game, could only have served to help her chances in the primaries. After all, it wasn't her problem and therefore it's not her responsibility. Technically, that would be true. It wasn't up to her to debunk the rumors. But, whether her equivocation was deliberate or innocent, the hesitant phrases in her remarks succeeded in keeping the fear bomb fully activated. It's no wonder that later in the report, Kroft spoke with a Democratic voter in Ohio who said he wasn't sure whether he could vote for someone who was sworn in on Koran. It's the gray area. The uncertainty. For a whisper campaign to work, uncertainty is all the oxygen it requires for survival. And Senator Clinton blew plenty of air into its lungs.

Author Eric Boehlert, writing for Media Matters on March 11, 2008, defended Senator Clinton against the corporate media (and some of us in the blogs) who had, in his opinion, purposely exaggerated the "as far as I know" and "I take him on the basis of what he says" quotes as a means of perpetuating the calculating Clinton narrative. Boehlert wrote:

> The fact is, if you look at Clinton's exchange with Kroft in its entirety, which lasted less than one minute, I count eight separate times in which she either plainly denied the false claim that Obama was Muslim, labeled that suggestion to be a smear, or expressed sympathy for Obama having to deal with the Muslim innuendo. *Eight times.*
>
> But to set aside Clinton's denials and suggest that "as far as I know" captured her entire response is patently dishonest. Yet that's exactly when many media players did.[24]

And, in the mayhem of the Democratic primary race, I did, too. With the clarity afforded by some objective distance, perhaps her responses were magnified by the context of both the "kitchen sink" strategy and the other fear-bomb incidents of that two-week span. That said, if someone asks me if so-and-so is a Muslim, and he isn't, then my answer is, "No. Next question." If someone asks me if, I don't know, Senator Fiddlesticks the Shoe Munchkin is real, my honest answer would be, "No." Yet what if I answered, "No. But, come to think of it, I haven't checked

24   http://mediamatters.org/columns/200803110002

recently," people will rightly begin to talk. Yes, it's true that Senator Clinton said, "Of course not," and, "No. No." But then she interjected two of what even Boehlert described as "qualifiers." Qualifiers—even though this is a question that didn't require any escape pods.

Menacing voices don't have to say that so-and-so is a terrorist in cahoots with al-Qaeda. In fact, all they have to do is to mention that he could be a Muslim, or mention that his middle name is evildoer-ish. And that's it. The whole conspiracy is an insinuation rather than a black-and-white statement. Again, the unhinged and racist elements in our society believe that most, if not all, Muslims are terrorists. *So this guy is a Muslim, but he doesn't admit to it. What's he hiding? Hmm. Well, shit, we better not risk voting for a terrorist.* Everyone can deny, deny, deny. But words matter and people hear the qualifiers and they draw their own conclusions. Sadly, many of those conclusions are terribly, terribly wrong.

Consequently, this isn't a topic on which someone in an authority position ought to be hedging. Right or wrong. You don't hedge about something this deadly serious. Politicians of all shapes and sizes use language to say things without saying things. Politics is all about hedging and poking and prodding for effect and reaction. Probing the line. Words matter. And in presidential politics, words are everything.

On the same day the "as far as I know" *60 Minutes* interview aired, in a nation that boasts a Constitution that explicitly forbids religious test, Senator Obama had to underscore to the media the next day that he, in no uncertain terms, is a Christian and a member of the United Church of Christ.

"I am a devout Christian. I pray to Jesus every night and try to go to church as much as I can," he told reporters in Toledo, Ohio just one week after the release of the Drudge photograph.

But after all of it, the shock-and-awe bombing quieted, but the surgical airstrikes continued.

TIME magazine's Marc Halperin is a former ABC News producer and professional corporate media stooge who fancies himself the purveyor of very serious conventional wisdom in Washington. On March 8, 2008, Halperin published a series of tips for how Senator McCain could defeat Senator Obama in the general election titled: "HALPERIN'S TAKE (updated): Things McCain Can Do To Try To Beat Obama That Clinton Cannot (some already on display)." The tips included a lot of heinous things such as a recommendation that Senator McCain, "Allow some supporters to risk being accused of using the race card when criticizing Obama." Or, simply put, tell your support-ers to be bigots. Again, I hasten to underscore that this isn't some radical far-right splinter group. This is *TIME* frickin' magazine. And it gets so much crazier. Here's Halperin's contribution to the fear bomb:

> 11. Emphasize Barack Hussein Obama's unusual name and exotic background through a Manchurian Candi-date prism.

In other words, *TIME* magazine just recommended to Senator McCain that he proceed with his campaign using the same racist, fear-mongering lies popularized within that insidious "Who is Barack Obama?" viral e-mail. Take a giant crap on what remains of your dignity, Halperin recommended to Senator McCain, and tell everyone that Senator Obama is a terrorist.

The Bush administration and Senator McCain, aided by

very serious traditional media, have been screwing things up since September 11. We know for a fact that their endless fear- and war-mongering has actually served to strengthen terrorism. Al-Qaeda is better positioned to strike the West than at any time since 9/11. How do we know this? It says so in the July 2007 National Intelligence Estimate (NIE) titled "Al-Qaeda Better Positioned to Strike the West." The NIE summarizes that al-Qaeda has been entirely reconstructed during the Bush administration, and is now training new recruits in the tribal areas of western Pakistan while its leadership is exploiting the invasion and occupation of Iraq as a means of spawning new generations of anti-American terrorist recruits (see also the chapter "Endless War").

Yet we're to believe from Glenn Beck, Ann Coulter, Rush Limbaugh and the rest of the far-right fear-mongers that Senator Obama's middle name might actually be more dangerous than Senator McCain's continuation of the Bush administration's bloody and destructive policies? That's rich.

McBush Republicans view the world chiefly in terms of symbolism. In simplifications. Mainly because their wiring doesn't allow for complex or multiplexed thought. Flag lapel pins *are* patriotism. Having a Support the Troops bumper magnet on the ass-end of your Hummer means you *are* supporting the troops, even though the troops are dying for the oil used to fuel the Hummer. Airing a fancy logo that says "fair and balanced" means FOX News Channel really *is* fair and balanced. Symbols. President Bush purchased an estate in Crawford immediately prior to running for president because it would symbolize a well-fabricated cowboy persona, regardless of the president's wealthy, Yale-cheerleading-squad, New-England-elite heritage. So it stands to reason that they'd look at a guy's name and use it to define—to symbolize—the man. It's this brand of simplistic, destructive, fear-mongering politics that Senator Obama, in every aspect of his very being, seeks to derail.

There will always be silly nicknames circulating on the fringes of American politics. It's part and parcel of system in which free speech is permitted, encouraged and necessary. And for those of us who are political junkies, the name-calling is part of the fun. But when it's used by menacing operatives as a means of inciting fear and intolerance, it ceases to be a fun aspect of our political fabric. And, most alarmingly, it potentially cultivates violence against its target.

To be precise, if we're at war against terrorists, and frightened Americans are manipulated into believing that a public official *is* a covert terrorist conspirator who's part of a fatwa aimed at destroying America, the symbolism of such a smear campaign triggers a reflex in the most reptilian, knee-jerk cortex of our notoriously paranoid, semi-evolved brains… to do harm to that so-called Manchurian Candidate.[25]

So this isn't about some trivial issue of political correctness, nor is it a joke. This whisper campaign is an ill-conceived, cowardly, unfunny psy-op, carrying with it the unintended consequence of potentially precipitating violence against a charismatic American leader, simply because he has a unique name and a multicultural heritage.

---

25   In June 2008, the Obama campaign opened a website, fightthesmears.com, which is aimed at debunking these and other rumors. If you're still not sure about the senator's background after reading this chapter, please go to the fightthesmears.com website. You'll be glad you did.

IT'S 3 A.M.

*One of Clinton's laws of politics is: if one candidate is trying to scare you,
and the other one is trying to make you think; if one candidate is appealing
to your fears, and the other one, appealing to your hopes.
You better vote for the person who wants you to think and hope.*

–President Bill Clinton
October 2004

It was February 24, 2008. Just ten days before the crucial Texas, Ohio, Rhode Island and Vermont primaries. William Kristol, who had repeatedly and very publicly recommended to Senator McCain that he use fear-mongering tactics against Senator Obama in the general election (see also chapter two, "Endless War"), passed along the following words of wisdom—free of charge—to Senator Clinton on the weekend comedy show *FOX News Sunday*:

> [Obama's] riding a wave of euphoria. She [Clinton] needs to puncture it. **The way you puncture euphoria is reality, or to be more blunt, fear. I recommend to Senator Clinton the politics of fear.**[1]

---

1   *FOX News Sunday*, February 24, 2008. http://thinkprogress.org/2008/02/24/kristol-politics-of-fear/

Just five days later, Senator Clinton premiered her now-legendary "3 a.m." television commercial, written by her campaign's chief strategist (pollster) Mark Penn. The commercial cleverly featured stock footage of sleeping Caucasian children inside an idyllic suburban household, backed with the sound of a phone ringing (six times). A deep-voiced narrator intoned the following:

> It's 3 a.m. and your children are safe and asleep. But there's a phone in the White House and it is ringing [*six times*]. Something is happening in the world your vote will decide who answers that call [*after six rings*]. Whether it is someone who already knows the world's leaders, knows the military—someone tested and ready to lead in a dangerous world. It's 3 a.m. and your children are safe and asleep. Who do you want answering that phone?

Dissolve to videotaped footage of Senator Clinton on a telephone in the middle of the night while diligently writing thank-you notes to Mark Penn and the editors of the commercial for helping her to successfully carry out Bill Kristol's most-excellent fear-mongering stratagem.

You're aware of Bill Kristol's past advisory hits: the Iraq invasion and occupation, the "surge," and his cheerleading for an attack against Iran. His chronic wrongness has, naturally, landed him a position at the *New York Times*. If you're a student of journalism, the ultimate advice Kristol can offer by his own example is that, in the very serious corporate media, you can be wrong all the time and, even though your roadmap for a short and triumphant war turned out to be a disaster, you can still fail your way to the top. Be that as it may, there's no way of knowing whether the idea to use this commercial against a fellow Democrat actually came from Bill Kristol. It probably didn't. But the very fact that Mark Penn's and Senator Clinton's decision to produce and release the commercial coincided with the chronically wrong advice of Bill Kristol on *FOX News Sunday* cuts to the painful and disappointing heart of the thing: The Clinton campaign and neocon wunderkind Bill Kristol actually agreed on how to attack Senator Obama. By using fear.

Regarding the "idea" for the commercial...

One week earlier, the Clinton campaign charged Senator Obama with "plagiarizing" a line of his stump speech from Governor Deval Patrick of Massachusetts, Senator Obama's national campaign co-chairman. The charge was thin and ultimately a non-starter, but it was enough ammunition to coerce everyone everywhere into saying the words "Obama" and "plagiarism" in the same sentence for a few days. Senator Clinton, during a debate in Austin, went so far as to use the line, "It's not change you can believe in; it's change you can Xerox." *Hoo-hoo!* Ironically enough, the line was written for Senator Clinton by the Democratic Leadership Council (DLC) president, Bruce Reed.

Compounding the irony of the plagiarism charge was the hilarious truth that the ringing phone commercial wasn't a Clinton invention either. The concept was almost identical to a commercial that was used to scare up votes by Walter Mondale during the 1984 Democratic primary battle between Mondale and Gary Hart. It featured a ringing phone and an ominous deep-voice narration warning Americans about the scary consequences of voting for the younger, "less experienced" Democrat. And what happened? Mondale won the nomination but was crushed by President Reagan in the general election. And yet he could have just as easily won the nomination and been crushed by President Reagan *without* having lowering himself to fear-mongering against a fellow Democrat.

Ultimately, the goal of the 3 a.m. commercial was to suggest that Senator Clinton, and Senator Clinton alone, was strong and experienced enough to respond to a terrorist attack. The subtext implied that if her opponent, the young, skinny black man was in the Oval Office and answered that ringing phone, your children would be in considerably more danger. So if you're interested in protecting your children, you had better goddamn vote for Senator Clinton. However, if you don't pay attention to the scary deep-voice guy and vote for Senator Obama anyway, well, crap, you're an irresponsible parent who's tempting a horrible death upon your over-medicated, quiescent children.

The commercial also implied, quite by accident, that Senator Clinton and her staff might allow the emergency evildoer bat-phone to ring *six times* before anyone picked up to find out what the heck was going on at three in the morning. I can only assume that there exist other phones tied to the same line in the Oval Office: the chief of staff's office and the Situation Room, for two. And of those three West Wing locations, no one's answering within six rings? My cell-phone voice mail picks up after four rings, and, even then, I'm at least holding the phone after one or two rings to check the caller-ID to determine whether I'd like to speak with Scarlett Johansson—again!—or to go back to sleep with my lovely wife whom I love (stop calling me at home, Scarlett!). The NSA, meanwhile, taps into my phone *before* the first ring, which really is amazing. And yet, in this commercial, the emergency phone at the White House kept ringing and ringing and ringing. The first thing I look for in a president is the ability to actually grasp a telephone receiver and speak clearly into the mouthpiece. If a politician is simply unable to master this task, it's maybe time to resign, Mr. Bush.

Naturally, Senator Clinton's 3 a.m. commercial made a difference in her narrow popular vote victory in Texas (she lost the Texas caucuses and lost the pledged-delegate totals). Texas was the only state that was specifically targeted with the commercial, ostensibly to win back some of the voters who had previously begun to swing over to Senator Obama. However, it's entirely possible that it boosted Senator Clinton's margin of victory in Ohio and Rhode Island due to the reality that the commercial was aired around the clock during the very serious prime-time pundit shows on all of the cable-news networks. So one could argue that it was, essentially, a national TV ad-buy based on the wall-to-wall coverage it received.

The commercial, as Harvard sociology professor Orlando Patterson observed in the *New York Times* several weeks later, was obviously targeted at white, suburban, middle-class Texans.[2] Of course it was—the people in the commercial, after all, were white, suburban, middle-class citizens. That is, except for the white, *upper-class fear-monger* at the end. Patterson observed that, during the previous week, Senator Obama had surpassed Senator Clinton's narrow lead among white Texans. Senator Obama was leading with 47 percent to Senator Clinton's 44 percent. Yet by the following Tuesday, primary day in Texas, Senator Clinton ended up winning 56 percent of the white vote—a swing, Patterson observed, of 12 percentage points in just a few days.

No one ever said fear-mongering didn't work. Knocking over banks and mugging old ladies sometimes nets a few bucks, too.

---

2   "The Red Phone in Black and White," by Orlando Patterson. March 11, 2008. http://www.nytimes.com/2008/03/11/opinion/11patterson.html

The head-scratchingly inexplicable side to the 3 a.m. commercial was that if Senator Clinton had actually won the nomination, Senator McCain (who has set off on his own fear-mongering crusade against the Democrats) could have used this exact same commercial—the whole damn thing—against Senator Clinton and just tagged it with footage of himself writing at a desk in the middle of the night. It's an unfair fact of life in politics that the Republicans, despite the reality of their gross incompetence on the issue, are considered the "national security" party. The fact that the Clinton campaign threw caution to the wind and allowed this massive blunder to slide was indicative of the campaign's insane level of desperation. They had lost eleven primaries and caucuses in a row and they simply *had* to win a primary—and soon. So I'm sure the campaign pegged any blowback as something they'd deal with…later. Senator Obama and the Democratic Party, on the other hand, weren't consulted for their input regarding the wisdom of airing such a poisonous commercial and its potentially negative effect on Democratic candidates at large, so it would be Senator Obama and the Democrats who would have to deal with the blowback…later.

This could be said for the entire Clinton fear-mongering stratagem. All of it. She essentially handed the Republicans some ass-kicking material. Free of charge. It was very Kristol-ish of her.

Soon after the debut of the ad, my friend Marc Evan Jackson and his improv troupe, the Public Service Administration, produced one of the most brilliant and memorable spoofs of the commercial, which perfectly underscored the "be afraid" message of the spot.[3] In their YouTube video, Jackson plays an ominous

---

3   www.publicserviceadministration.com or http://www.youtube.com/
Election08

voiceover narrator who's literally standing in the child's bedroom with his headphones and professional microphone. The child's dad rushes in and boots the narrator out of the room. The child asks, "Dad? Why do narrator people keep coming into by bedroom and scaring the crap out of me?"

DAD: It's election season, son. There's a lot of people who just want to scare you.

CHILD: Are they bad people?

DAD: They're not bad people, son. *Horrible* people.

[Shows photos of Mark Penn, Bill Kristol and the logo for FreedomWatch.org]

DAD: People who want nothing more between now and November than to spend every day scaring you craptastic.

CHILD: Well, what do we do?

DAD: You don't let 'em. You look 'em in the eye and say, "The world's a tough and dangerous place—it always has been. No reason to reupholster the inside of your trousers and vote like a moron every time they say BOO!

CHILD: Is that why I'm thirty years old and still wearing a diaper?

[Freeze frame. TEXT: America, It's Time To Grow Up! Don't let them scare you. Don't be afraid of their narrators anymore.]

CHILD: Are you gonna make the ominous narrators go away?

DAD: Be brave, son. You're tougher than they are.

That pretty much summarizes the thesis of this entire book. Sadly, I was unable to coerce Jackson and his fellow cast members to ghostwrite for me.

And despite an extraordinarily vocal backlash against the commercial, Senator Clinton didn't let up on her attempt to paint Senator Obama as the weaker candidate, with the fear of not being able to hack a 3 a.m. phone call during a terrorist attack (or you name it) as the subtext of every statement. She continued onward with an equally desperate and inexplicable attack. During a single March 1 media blitz in which Senator Clinton appeared via satellite across the nation, she praised Senator McCain's national security credentials over Senator Obama's:

> Now I think you will be able to imagine many things Senator McCain will be able to say. He has never been the president. He will put forth his experience. I will put forth my experience. Senator Obama will put forth a speech he made in 2002.

Wrong, wrong, wrong. There's more:

> I have a lifetime of experience that I will bring to the White House. I know Senator McCain has a lifetime of experience that he will bring to the White House. And Senator Obama has a speech he gave in 2002.[4]

---

4   A YouTube user compiled multiple clips of Senator Clinton endorsing Senator McCain here: http://www.youtube.com/watch?v=zMVOT-IH8sg

And:

> Of course, well, you know, I've got a lifetime of experi-
> ence. Senator McCain has a lifetime of experience. And
> you know, Senator Obama's whole campaign is about
> one speech he made in 2002.

So now that the general election has come down to Senator
McCain versus Senator Obama in, what Bill Kristol calls, "a national security election," Senator Clinton, who otherwise would
be regarded as a statesperson and party leader, chose to bally-
hoo the qualifications of Senator McCain—the crotchety, fear-
mongering Republican—over Senator Obama, the Democratic
frontrunner at that time.

But this was a campaign that didn't plan for any of the primaries after Super Tuesday, thanks to its former chief strategist,
Mark Penn. They felt as though they were entitled to the nomination and would have it secured by that stage, and when Senator
Obama defied the odds, the Clinton campaign appeared to have
diverged into a thousand different and contradictory directions.
Senator Clinton was, on one day, conciliatory toward Senator
Obama, and then, on the next day, she was sucker punching him
and the entire Democratic Party with fear-mongering attack ads.
It's no wonder the Clinton campaign was so desperate to verbally
and figuratively stroke Senator McCain. For a bunch of weeks
there, the Clintons were behaving like McMurphy in *One Flew
Over the Cuckoo's Nest*, scrambling for votes in order to convince
Nurse Ratched to let the patients watch the World Series on
television. Only McMurphy wasn't nearly as spasmodic as the
senator and her surrogates. Let's try *this* and *this* and *this*, and
the general in his wheelchair and the weird chronics in the back

of the ward. The desperation, at times, was embarrassing to observe. It was like watching Albert Brooks's weekend-news scene
in *Broadcast News* when he suffered an over-the-top case of the
flop-sweats and no remedy could adequately sandbag the shirt-
drenching tsunami of failure.

However disorganized and unhinged the campaign was at
that point in time, nothing excuses or forgives the Clinton campaign's disgraceful use of fear-mongering.

Not only that, but she was potentially sabotaging herself.
Had she won the nomination, she was playing into Kristol's recommendation for a "national security election," which would be a
difficult contest to win against a former U.S. Navy fighter pilot,
Vietnam veteran and POW survivor. It would be like Senator
McCain framing the campaign against Senator Obama in terms
of youth and change. In other words, you absolutely do not frame
a campaign on your opponent's terms. It's a huge mistake. And
the Clinton campaign screwed up on this one. It inadvertently
agreed with Kristol's assessment and helped to set up the general election on Republican terms. Without a doubt, Senator
Obama can win on national security, given his Iraq record and
the Republicans unprecedented bungling of everything from
anti-terrorism to the 9/11 Commission to the reconstituting of
al-Qaeda's pre-9/11 strength, but in American presidential politics in a Bush-Rove-Cheney world, you *do not* give ammunition
to the Republicans under any circumstances. Still, the Clinton
campaign needed to win at any cost and were willing to engage
in slash, burn and fear-mongering politics. Everything Senator
Obama is running against.

In the movie adaptation of *Primary Colors*, Libby, Kathy
Bates's character, refuses to use smear-mongering politics against

a fellow Democrat, played by Larry Hagman. And if the (quasi-Clinton-ish) Stanton campaign leaks information about Hagman's cocaine and bisexual past, Bates threatens to reveal to the press all of the women Jack Stanton had fucked. When the Stantons try to call her bluff, she paraphrases an American soldier after the battle of Ben Tre, suggesting, "Yes, I will destroy this village in order to save it." Or as Internet satirist Lee Stranahan wrote in his "3:02" YouTube spoof of the commercial: "Hillary Clinton: she wouldn't punch a baby in the face unless it would help her win this fucking election."

So what exactly was Senator Clinton suggesting by her commander-in-chief rhetoric? Simply put, the senator was using terrorism to, as Senator Obama says, "scare up votes." Military preparedness, in a post-September 11 world, implies an ability to face down a terrorist attack, to act swiftly and powerfully against a threat or to retaliate against an attack. Digging into the rabbit hole even further, a strong commander-in-chief implies a fierce gravitas that will actually serve to deter a terrorist attack. Conversely, a weak commander-in-chief might actually *invite* a terror attack. Therefore, our natural lizard-brain instinct to experience fear instructs us to make decisions in favor of strength.

This is game they played.

But the implications of Senator Clinton's rhetoric notwithstanding, the very fact that she preyed upon the fears of the American people made her, in these specific instances, no better than the Republicans. Here's a Supervillain Cheney classic:

> If we make the wrong choice, then the danger is that we'll
> get hit again—that we'll be hit in a way that will be dev-

astating from the standpoint of the United States. [5]

–Vice President Dick Cheney, 9/07/04

And the Supervillain henchman...

Whoever is elected in November faces the prospect of another terrorist attack. The question is whether or not we have the right policies in place to best protect our country. That's what the vice president said.

–Cheney's Spokeswoman Anne Womack clarifying the vice president's above statement

Compare that with Senator Clinton's remarks the day before the New Hampshire primary—a contest she needed to win in order to stay in the race.

I don't think it was by accident that al-Qaeda decided to test the new prime minister. They watch our elections as closely as we do, maybe more closely than some of our fellows citizens do. Let's not forget you're hiring a president not just to do what a candidate says during the election, you want a president to be there when the chips are down. [6]

Prior to this statement, I didn't really dislike the Clinton campaign. I simply favored the Obama campaign and worried that maybe Senator Clinton had it in her arsenal the ability to get really ugly. When I wrote my endorsement of Senator Obama for the *Huffington Post*, I wondered out loud if Senator Clinton

---

5   CNN, "Cheney: Kerry Win Risks Terror Attack" http://edition. cnn.com/2004/ALLPOLITICS/09/07/cheney.terror/

6   January 7, 2008. Marcella Bombardieri for the *Boston Herald*, "Clinton heightens terrorism rhetoric." http://www.boston.com/news/politics/politicalintelligence/2008/01/clinton_heighte.html

was a little too Cheney-ish to take over when—especially on humid Washington afternoons—the slippery stench of the actual Dick Cheney still oozes from the wood trim of the West Wing. But when the senator resorted to this obviously Cheney-ish fearmongering statement in New Hampshire, it was one of the most disturbing and disillusioning moments in the early primary race and the portend of much worse.

Go back and compare Anne Womack's remarks to Senator Clinton's. Senator Clinton even threw in the "it's no accident" line made famous by the Republican No Attacks Mythology (see chapter three, "The No Attacks Mythology"). As in, "It's no accident that we haven't been attacked."

Senator Clinton wasn't mincing words. The terrorists, she implicitly stated, will surely test the next president by attacking the United States (on the scale of September 11... or worse), and if the people of New Hampshire choose Senator Obama— a lesser, weaker candidate in her estimation—then we'll all be killed and the nation will be thrown into chaos while Senator Obama, so she implied, hides. Only President Hillary Clinton, Awesome Commander-in-Chief, will be able to handle such an attack, ostensibly by personally answering the phone at 3 a.m. and not letting voice mail pick up.

In an MSNBC exit poll, New Hampshire voters were asked the usual terrorism question: "How worried are you that there will be another major terrorist attack in the United States?"[7]

The results indicated that 73 percent of New Hampshire voters responded "very/somewhat worried." If the Clinton campaign didn't have similar polling information in hand leading up to Senator Clinton's *ooga-booga!* remarks on that Monday in Jan-

---

7   http://www.msnbc.msn.com/id/21225995/

uary, Mark Penn wasn't doing his job (what a shocker!). I would be surprised if the most poll-driven political campaign in the race didn't have New Hampshire data on terrorism. Nothing is said that isn't polled for effect. That's modern politics, especially within the Clinton Loop. Without the proper intel, she never would have stood up at that Dover rally in front of live television cameras and leaned on the jolly, candy-like panic button: *a vote for Senator Obama is a vote for another terrorist attack—because the evildoers are watching!*

My very first presidential vote was absentee for then-Governor Bill Clinton in 1992. I remember unfolding the Virginia ballot on my desk in college and carefully studying the options after having worked diligently on campus for the campaign (after having previously supported Paul Tsongas in the primaries). It was a great day. A day when I could chose hope over fear: the "Clinton law of politics." Hope.

And throughout the 1990s, I supported the Clintons even in their darkest days. On my various middle-to-late-1990s radio shows, I did what I could to defend the Clintons at a time when progressive talk radio was unheard of.

So it was with great pain that I observed and documented Senator Clinton's slow descent into Republican-style fear-mongering during the latter days of her campaign; and it's with greater pain that I've had to type the words "Clinton" and "fear-monger" in the same sentence. In a book about fear-mongering, ignoring this episode in recent political history would be nothing if not conspicuous in its omission. Fear-mongering is fear-mongering regardless of a politicians ideology or party affiliation. But I think it's because I had previously admired Senator Clinton and, naturally, President Clinton, that their campaign's "kitchen sink" tactics had become so unseemly to me. Or maybe it was because I, like so many others, was infected with the idealism of a better way forward.

Having studied and observed and documented politics for most of my adult life, it's always too easy to be cynical about it. But there's an Aaron Sorkin/Frank Capra idealism that keeps me from sliding off the rails and into the shadow realms of talkers like Chris Matthews, who appears to only see politics as a contest, as a horserace. In the vernacular of Senator Obama's campaign, my interest in politics grows out of *hope* for a better nation. Hope is an intangible thing that we only really know about when we're feeling it. Frank Darabont, screenwriter of the modern classic *The Shawshank Redemption*, carried hope as a theme throughout the film. The following line, delivered by Morgan Freeman's Red, perfectly describes the quality of hope:

> I find I'm so excited, I can barely sit still or hold a thought in my head. I think it's the excitement only a free man can feel, a free man at the start of a long journey whose conclusion is uncertain. I hope I can make it across the border. I hope to see my friend, and shake his hand. I hope the Pacific is as blue as it has been in my dreams. I hope.

The power of this sequence is the ultimate transformation of Red from an institutionalized, ambivalent character—a cynical, beaten-down inmate trapped on a long, dark ride—a character who earlier had earlier in the story cautioned, "Hope is a dangerous thing. Hope can drive a man insane," into a character who was inspired to feel that beautiful energy again. Through the example of his friend, Andy, played by Tim Robbins, Red was transformed by hope, rather than succumbing to the fear of a larger world, a fear that drove the Brooks character to hang himself from the rafter of that lonely halfway house. Only Darabont and Stephen King, who wrote the book on which the movie is based, might know what became of Red and Andy in Zihua-tanejo, Mexico. But the hope—the experience of that bus ride towards the blue waters of the Pacific was enough to satisfy even the most acerbic soul. Likewise, if the Obama presidency turns out to be a letdown, we have to believe that this present blue tide of hope for a better future—if perchance only fleeting—is enough. And if it means pushing back a tide of fear, then yeah. It's absolutely enough.

THE GREAT FEAR OF 2008

*There's an old saying about those who forget history.
I don't remember it, but it's good.*

–Stephen Colbert

My original idea for this chapter was to write a hilarious chronology of fear-mongering throughout American history. I was planning to write about these historical events as if I was live-blogging them in real time from the cockpit of a time machine.

And then Pat Buchanan ruined it. Like always.

I was planning to begin at the logical fear-mongering starting line: the Salem witch trials. Guest blogger: Cotton Mather.

Then I planned to fast-forward a hundred years to the John Adams administration and the Alien and Sedition Acts of 1798. The French, at that time, were the evildoers, and so the conservatives in Congress passed a pair of laws designed to smoke out French extremists and to restrict seditious speech, be it in public or in private. War-mongering, fear-mongering, anti-French Federalists (not unlike modern day McBush Republicans) used the

Sedition Act as a means to imprison congressmen, newspaper publishers and even the Newark, New Jersey town drunk who joked to a bartender that President Adams ought to be shot in the ass with a cannon. True story. Luther Baldwin, the drunk who joked about the presidential ass, was held in prison indefinitely until he could pay the fine, while a Richmond newspaper editor named James Callender was sentenced to nine months in jail and fined $200 for publishing, at the covert request of Thomas Jefferson, editorials critical of President Adams. Shortly after the election of 1800, in which both Jefferson and Aaron Burr narrowly defeated Adams, the Sedition Act expired without ever being challenged in the Supreme Court. It failed to give the Federalists the lasting military power they craved and became an historical albatross for President Adams who, as a patriot and champion of liberty, should have known better.

Nevertheless, a similar law would emerge more than 120 years later, in 1918, at the urgent request of President Woodrow Wilson, just after America entered World War I. The Sedition Act of 1918 gets mostly ignored in the shadow of its more famous ancestor, even though the sheer audacity of its unconstitutionality confounds reason:

> ...whoever, when the United States is at war, shall willfully utter, print, write or publish any disloyal, profane, scurrilous, or abusive language about the form of government of the United States or the Constitution of the United States, or the military or naval forces of the United States, or the flag of the United States, or the uniform of the Army or Navy of the United States into contempt, scorn, contumely, or disrepute, or shall willfully utter, print, write, or publish any language intended to incite,

provoke, or encourage resistance to the United States, or to promote the cause of its enemies, or shall willfully display the flag of any foreign enemy, or shall willfully by utterance, writing, printing, publication, or language spoken, urge, incite, or advocate any curtailment of production in this country of any thing or things, product or products, necessary or essential to the prosecution of the war in which the United States may be engaged, with intent by such curtailment to cripple or hinder the United States in the prosecution of war, and whoever shall willfully advocate, teach, defend, or suggest the doing of any of the acts or things in this section enumerated, and whoever shall by word or act support or favor the cause of any country with which the United States is at war or by word or act oppose the cause of the United States therein, shall be punished by a fine of not more than $10,000 or the imprisonment for not more than twenty years, or both.

Whenever they say "it can't happen here," they're misinformed. It can and it has, and in the form of the world's most unconstitutional run-on sentence.

The Alien and Sedition Acts of both 1798 and 1918 were obviously the precursor to the U.S.A. Patriot Act and the Military Commissions Act—neither of which, I'm sorry to report, have been repealed by the Democratic Congress.

I was going to write about President Andrew Jackson's genocide against the Cherokee Nation, an effort driven by greed and fueled by fear of the "savages." Whenever you glance at a twenty dollar bill, always remember that you're gazing at an engraving of an American president who used overreaching executive power to ignore a decision by the United States Supreme Court.

In *Worcester v. Georgia* (1832), the Supreme Court ruled that the Cherokee Nation could retain its sovereignty and thus retain the right to live where they pleased in Georgia. President Jackson ignored the ruling and used military force to eject the Cherokee from their ancestral territory, sending them on a forced march to Oklahoma, during which approximately four thousand Cherokees "died from hunger, exposure and disease," according the Cherokee Nation Record of the Trail of Tears.[1]

Modern anti-immigration fear-mongers who seek to deport twelve million Latinos living in America—many of who work for slave wages in corporate factories and on corporate farms—can boast a grand tradition here in America. The penalty, meanwhile, for using an obscenity on the radio is more than twenty times greater than the penalty against a corporation that hires an illegal immigrant (maximum of $16,000 per illegal immigrant; $325,000 per use of the slang word "blumpkin" on the radio).

I was planning to write about the Japanese internment camps during World War II. Like Adams and Wilson before him, this is a blight on the historical greatness of the Franklin Roosevelt administration, and justifiably so.

I was planning to write about the second Red Scare (the first occurred during the Bolshevik Revolution) and the House Committee on Un-American Activities, when communists were the enemy and Senator Joseph McCarthy set about on his self-ordained patriotic duty to protect America from the influence of alleged Soviet evildoers in America who were seeking to overthrow the government. I was going to dovetail this into some clever comparisons between Bill O'Reilly and Joe McCarthy, beginning with their striking physical resemblance. (To be fair

---

1   http://www.cherokee.org/Culture/CulInfo/TOT/58/Default.aspx

to McCarthy, as crazy as he was, never sent his interns to stalk people at their homes. And unless I'm terribly wrong, McCarthy never sexually harassed a member of his staff with discussions of soapy loofas and falafels.)

I was planning to summarize all of it with an historical kicker from Civil War historian and author Robert Krick about a myth that circulated during the various battlefield victories by Confederate General Thomas "Stonewall" Jackson:

> Nannies in the north would try to shush crying children by saying, "Stonewall will come get you!" Part of being larger than life is that you were a bit of a bogeyman to the enemy.[2]

Sounds exactly like the nannies in the McBush Republican Party. *If you don't support our authoritarian policies, the evildoer bogeymen will come and get you!* So naturally everyone who believes the fear-mongering and this overly exaggerated terrorist threat is successfully shushed.

But then, shortly after Senator Obama delivered his legendary Philadelphia Address ("A More Perfect Union") at height of the Reverend Jeremiah Wright controversy last spring, I read the following disgruntled rant written by the notoriously disgruntled white man Pat Buchanan. I've included more than the usual pull-quote in order to give Buchanan some context.

> How would he justify not walking out as Wright spewed his venom about "the U.S. of K.K.K. America," and howled, "God damn America!"...Barack then listed black grievances and informed us what white America must do to close the racial divide and heal the country.

---

2   From the History Channel documentary: *Civil War Journal: Stonewall Jackson.* Greystone Communications.

It is the same old con, the same old shakedown that black hustlers have been running since the Kerner Commission blamed the riots in Harlem, Watts, Newark, Detroit and a hundred other cities on, as Nixon put it, "everybody but the rioters themselves"... White America needs to be heard from, not just lectured to. This time, the Silent Majority needs to have its convictions, grievances and demands heard. And among them are these:

First, America has been the best country on earth for black folks. It was here that six hundred thousand black people, brought from Africa in slave ships, grew into a community of forty million, were introduced to Christian salvation, and reached the greatest levels of freedom and prosperity blacks have ever known... Second, no people anywhere has done more to lift up blacks than white Americans. Untold trillions have been spent since the '60s on welfare, food stamps, rent supplements, Section 8 housing, Pell grants, student loans, legal services, Medicaid, Earned Income Tax Credits and poverty programs designed to bring the African-American community into the mainstream... Is Barack aware that black-on-white rapes are one hundred times more common than the reverse, that black-on-white robberies were 139 times as common in the first three years of this decade as the reverse?[3]

Yeah, white people have been awesome to black people. Slavery and Jim Crow aside, for every Pell grant or Section 8 housing project, there are untold hundreds of terrible things black Americans have been subjected to at the hands of white Americans. Everything from segregation to mandatory-minimum sentences

---

3   http://buchanan.org/blog/?p=969

and three-strikes laws that have disproportionately imprisoned black people, while white corporate criminals are excused with small fines and leisurely vacations in minimum-security country clubs. What about the Tuskegee Syphilis experiments? What about, as Douglas Blackmon covers in depth in his groundbreaking book *Slavery By Another Name*, the practice of neoslavery in the South, when black citizens were arrested on bogus charges like "vagrancy" or simply abducted off the street and sold to wealthy, white farming and mining cartels—a practice that endured until the beginning of World War II?[4]

Pat?

If Native Americans were the topic, I'm sure Buchanan would have written, *What about the casinos and the whiskey?*

The very fact that Buchanan is lording, of all things, food stamps and Section 8 housing over the heads of black people is a major part of the problem here. Buchanan believes that offering up, in his estimation, forty trillion dollars worth of relief for African-Americans ought to have earned him some gratitude. "We hear the grievances. Where is the gratitude?" he wrote. How does he expect anyone to be grateful for items that he just listed as "grievances"? What he's really saying is, *Hey, I hate all this welfare shit we've given you, and I opposed it every step of the way. Now come on, where's my "thank you"?*

At the end of the day, penance ceases to be penance when it's regurgitated in the form of ruling-class braggadocio.

I would write up a full parsing of Buchanan's white-power rant, but I think his nearsightedness is self-evident. Also, I can't

---

4   This is one of the most horrible and yet unspoken chapters in recent American history. For more information, see www.slaverybyanother-name.com

help but to wonder why Buchanan wasn't suspended or fired by MSNBC given that the cable-news network fired serial racist Don Imus for calling the Rutgers' women's basketball team "a bunch of nappy-headed hos"; and given the fact that MSNBC suspended the otherwise competent reporter David Shuster for suggesting that the Clinton campaign was "pimping" Chelsea Clinton. Not that I'm hoping for Pat Buchanan to be fired, mind you. I'm crazy into the First Amendment like that. I think it's better that far-right racist fear-mongers remain out in the open where we can see them and where we can shame them, rather than flushing them underground to be hidden away in the slag like the cowards they truly are. For instance, I'd rather see Limbaugh on the air where he can humiliate himself and self-destruct in front of the *entire nation*. That's a much more satisfying way for him to flame out, isn't it? An impotent gasbag mentally disintegrating *in private* is no fun. Besides, I want to know about it when he suggests that Philadelphia Eagles quarterback Donovan McNabb was only celebrated in the media because he's black. Or when he told a black caller to "Take the bone out of your nose and call me back." Or when Limbaugh referred to New Orleans Mayor Ray Nagin as "Ray Nager." And how can we forget Limbaugh's hilarious "Barack the Magic Negro" song parody?

Buchanan's column, titled "Whitey is Awesome (Food Stamps, For Example)!" (kidding—it was titled "A Brief for Whitey") reminded me of several eras in our nation's history in which racial fear-mongering reached grotesquely new and wicked heights. And to Buchanan's point that America has been the greatest country for black folks (and Native Americans—don't forget the casinos!), these historical markers serve to underscore why, perhaps, certain segments of the African-American community—Reverend Wright's generation, for instance—might be disgruntled and might not be able to appreciate all of those awesome programs Pat Buchanan so proudly hailed.

The election of 1860 was known as The Great Fear, borrowing from the 1789 *grande peur* that swept through France just prior to the French Revolution.

Author and historian Stephen B. Oates in his landmark biography *With Malice Toward None: A Life Of Abraham Lincoln* discussed how, when Lincoln received the nomination of the newly formed Republican Party,[5] southerners were absolutely convinced that Lincoln and the "Black Republican, free love, free nigger" party were organizing and mustering slaves to take up arms against their masters. These rumors were invented by the southern "fire-eaters" (pro-slavery extremists) who exploited John Brown's poorly executed and limited skirmish in Harper's Ferry as their "Pearl Harbor event"[6]—their September 11—as a means to scare up votes and incite secession. The rumors of a slave rebellion have never been verified, of course. Nevertheless, the fire-eaters also propagandized the Bleeding Kansas affair and the brutal Senate-floor bludgeoning of Massachusetts Senator Charles Sumner (whose seat would eventually be held by President John F. Kennedy and his brother Senator Edward Kennedy) by the cane-wielding Congressman Preston Brooks of South Carolina, who, the fire-eaters said, was simply defending

---

5   The Republican Party of Lincoln was ideologically closer to the modern Democratic Party. For example, the Republicans supported a strong central government and, of course, civil rights. Each are modern staples of the Democratic Party. Political party ideologies have shifted and swapped between the parties over time.

6   Another reference to the Project for a New American Century (PNAC) memo titled, "Rebuilding America's Defenses." http://www.newamericancentury.org/RebuildingAmericasDefenses.pdf

the honor of the South against a radical northern abolitionist.

Smear- and fear-mongers such as the fire-eater Robert Barnwell Rhett spread lies about other menacing black conspiracies including one in which Lincoln, when elected, would urge slaves "to copulate and marry with white women." Not that there's anything wrong with that, but the specter of blacks and whites marrying in those days—and even well into post-World War II America, by the way—was perhaps more terrifying to racist white voters than emancipation. To back up these horror stories, there were rumors that Hannibal Hamlin, Lincoln's running mate, was half black (Rush Limbaugh would've called Hamlin a Halfrican-American).

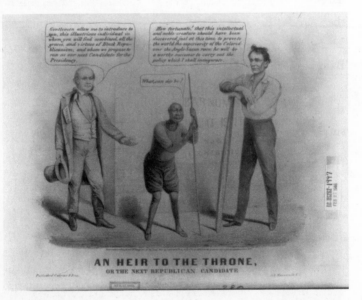

AN HEIR TO THE THRONE,
OR THE NEXT REPUBLICAN CANDIDATE

Along those same lines, fire-eaters in Tennessee organized a propaganda campaign implying that, when elected, the candidate for Senate there was planning to "miscegenate" with Tennessee's white women. Oh wait. Sorry, that happened in the 2006 mid-term election with the Tennessee Republican Party's "call me" ad.

When the *Charleston Mercury* published an article describing President Lincoln as being "of the dirtiest complexion," (see also chapter eight, "The Ultimate Fear Bomb") the *Mercury* editor probably meant to imply that Lincoln looked "black." Shockingly, the southern press never once referred to Lincoln, Hamlin or his supporters as Macaca, former Senator George Allen's favorite racist epithet.

And long before television or YouTube, there were plenty of awful cartoons and pamphlets used to stir up white fears. An artist named Louis Maurer published a cartoon titled "Heir to the Throne" in which Horace Greeley, the famously liberal editor of the *New York Tribune*, is shown introducing both Lincoln and Lincoln's "presidential successor," who turns out to be a black P.T. Barnum sideshow performer from that era named "What is it?"

The same artist, Maurer, published another cartoon that shows Lincoln elevated to national prominence via his "secret" support for the abolitionist movement.

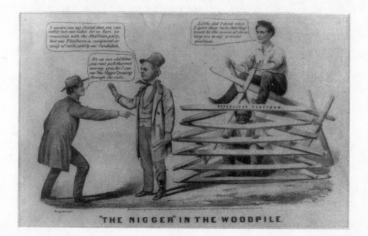

"THE NIGGER" IN THE WOODPILE.

"'The Nigger' in the Woodpile" cartoon shows candidate Lincoln sitting atop a cage made of split rails inside which hides a slave, representing Lincoln's "hidden agenda" for emancipation. In the middle is a caricature of Horace Greeley, once again serving as the spokesman for Lincoln and "lying" to the southerner on the left by explaining that the Republican platform is about split-rails and not abolition. The incredulous southerner is shown pointing and exclaiming, "It's no use old fellow! You can't pull that wool over my eyes for I can see 'the Nigger' peeping through the rails!"

Fast-forward to Lincoln's reelection campaign of 1864. At the outset of the campaign, the term "miscegenation" was first coined by a political dirty-trickster. In 1863, a pamphlet was published that called for the mixing of the races until everyone looked the same. It was published anonymously but attributed to the liberal Republicans aligned with President Lincoln, only, it was actually written by a race-baiting pro-slavery operative as a way to scare white voters: a classic double-cross not unlike the dirty tricks employed by Karl Rove and other Republicans.[7] A broadside cartoon was published at the time in order to fully illustrate this impending white doom (notice Lincoln and Senator Charles Sumner on the far left).

I can't make out all of the details or read all of the speech balloons, so there's no way of telling if one of the white women is making a telephone-hand gesture and whispering, "Harold! Call me!"

The majority of the anti-Lincoln, anti-emancipation fearmongering campaigns, while insulting and degrading to African-Americans, were mainly targeted at white voters as a way to discredit white politicians. The slave revolt conspiracies were, by in large, attributed to white abolitionists and the warnings of "miscegenation" were attributed to the policies of white northern officials. It wasn't until after the fall of the Confederacy when African-Americans became the direct target of racist fear-mongering efforts.

With the invention of the moving picture, fear-mongering took on a seriously unforgivable degree of ugliness.

The rise of silent movies and "flicker shows" at the beginning of the twentieth century happened to coincide with a nationwide movement to repair the damage caused by the Reconstruction era. Historians, public figures, poets and authors of the late nineteenth century began to formulate the Lost Cause mythology, which, in what would be one of America's most insidious misinformation campaigns, rewrote history and defined the Confed-

---

7   During his ascension into Texas politics, Rove allegedly bugged his own office, then blamed his political enemies. A classic Rove double-cross.

eracy and the South as victims, rather than the instigators of the war and the subjugators of an entire race of people. In order to reunify the nation, southern whites would have to be reevaluated and redefined as the ones who had been subjugated. It's the sort of Orwellian opposite-day chicanery we've become all too familiar with during the Bush presidency. See "the surge worked" or the Healthy Forests Initiative. But put into perspective, this reunification strategy was far more damaging.

The intention of reunification, I suppose, was noble, but the way it was handled and the glorification of racism and slavery is still, to this day, one of the most notorious episodes in the history of American propaganda and fear-mongering. Author and film historian Bruce Chadwick describes this misguided effort nicely, "All of these writers, politicians and civic leaders probably did a very wrong thing to bring about a very right thing."[8]

Right. But the phrase "wrong thing" tends to understate the depths of awfulness to which this effort plunged. It's one thing to write poems about grand southern plantations and frail southern belles. But it's another thing entirely for early filmmakers like D.W. Griffith to echo the bigotry of white Americans who continued to think of African-Americans as devilish proto-humans.

So unlike the Great Fear of 1860 and the Mini-Great Fear of 1864 (my title), which mostly involved pro-slavery southern whites attacking abolitionist northern whites, the reunification effort sought to repair the divide between the two groups and, in order to do so, the propagandists turned their focus to the most common link between northern whites and southern whites: their mutual bigotry against African-Americans. Nowhere is this

---

8   Bruce Chadwick, *The Reel Civil War: Mythmaking in American Film.* pg. 10

more evident that in the silent films of that era.

By the first decade of the twentieth century there were ten thousand movie theaters in America, and many of the very short, very awful silent movies exhibited in those theaters make D.W. Griffith's *Birth of a Nation* seem tame, especially by today's standards. There were of course the relatively "harmless" shorts by the Pathé brothers, who created bastardized versions of minstrel shows. The shorts featured stereotyped black characters like Rastus, Mammy and Little Black Sambo. The Rastus films, in particular, sported offensive titles like *How Rastus Got His Chicken; another, Rastus in Zululand*, is described as being about "a darky who needs warmth."

Filmmakers who carried on the reunification effort presumed that African-Americans didn't possess a cultural identity and therefore identities could be entirely invented for them, without their consent. What emerged was wholesale cultural subjugation for the purposes of fueling preexisting white bigotry and fear: the manufacturing of the stereotype of the black man as an unpredictable, sex-crazed thief. The mid-nineteenth century legend of the aforementioned Sambo, for example, was that of a slow-witted, subservient "darky," who could at any moment transform, Incredible Hulk-style, into a frothing rapist.

In *The Reel Civil War: Mythmaking in American Film*, film historian Bruce Chadwick describes *Minstrels Battling in a Room* (1896) as "black minstrels beating up a white man with bottles." There was *Prize Fight in Coon Town*, described in the distribution catalogue as featuring "two bad coons." There was *The Interrupted Crap Game*: a movie about two black men who interrupt a round of craps in order to capture a chicken. Uh-huh. In his book, Chadwick quotes a line from a film catalogue description of the blacks who appear in one of the shorts: "These darkies are of the 'Old Virginny' type." Another movie's catalogue describes the movie as, "the catching, tarring and feathering and burning of a Negro for the assault of a white woman." Again, the Sambo-rapist stereotype is carried on from one film to the next. Chad-wick laments that, "...existing racial attitudes were exacerbated by these movies." When Pat Buchanan, in his "Whitey" rant, made sure to highlight present-day rape and burglary statistics in his indictment of African-Americans, he—perhaps deliber-ately—played to these thieving, rapist stereotypes.

And then there was the movie that's more responsible for modern stereotypes and racism than just about anything else from twentieth-century American culture: D.W. Griffith's *Birth of a Nation*. Based on a play by Thomas Dixon called *The Clans-man*, *Birth of a Nation* is a watershed document of racial intol-erance and demonization, of sociological projection and white rage, a move that set the table for another one hundred years of American racial division.

Birth of a Nation is largely the story of a southern family, the Camerons, who endure the horrors of the American Civil War and Reconstruction and eventually find a way to reclaim their southern way of life. Through terrorism and fear-mongering. But the Cameron story is really just a conveyance for the overt racist and revisionist goals of the film.

The main character, Ben Cameron, forms the Ku Klux Klan terrorist organization with his fellow Confederate veterans as a way to take back his white southern heritage. Even the formation of the white ghost-like regalia is shown in the movie from a fear-mongering perspective. In the "idea for the costumes" scene, Ben sits near a cliff, contemplating his "unfair" southern white hard-

ships, when he observes a group of white children hiding under
a white sheet. Several black children come along and the white
children frighten them away by acting like ghosts. *A-ha! Black
people are afraid of ghosts!* Clever.

Cameron's Ku Klux Klan is portrayed as an avenging army
of swashbuckling heroes who flock to the rescue of a white woman being surrounded in her cabin by a platoon of lascivious black
soldiers. Naturally, the black soldiers are played by white actors
in blackface who behave in offensively stereotypical ways.

Black Union soldiers are shown suppressing and intimidat-
ing *white* voters: several bayonet-wielding black soldiers are seen
yanking a pair of white voters away from a ballot box. As we all
know, the exact opposite occurred in the South during Reconstruction, not to mention the decades that followed. (See also the
disenfranchisement of black voters in Florida…eight years ago.)

Black politicians, including the Silas Lynch character, are
unanimously elected to the state legislature via the intimidation
of white citizens at the hands of black soldiers. The all-black legislature goes on to pass laws that strip white people of their right
to vote. The politicians, meanwhile, ogle and harass white women
in the street, but only when they aren't getting drunk and eating
chicken legs. The through-line of the entire movie is as follows:
Black men, who really can only really be controlled under the
banner of slavery, seek to overthrow the government so they can
freely dominate white men and freely rape white women. The
solution? Only the KKK can save the day.

In other words, without white vigilance, blacks will destroy
America.

So when the videotaped clips of Reverend Wright were
broadcast over and over, the subtext from the far-right fell into

line with their most effective and reliable scare tactic: clearly this angry black preacher and his America-hating cohort, Senator Obama, would use their newly discovered presidential power to undermine American (white) values.

The preceding historical samples of racial fear-mongering have served as the catalyst for all of the stereotypes and misperceptions that modern Republican operatives have exploited and continue to exploit right now, as I write this.

Civil War and Reconstruction-era racial politics exist in our time as the infamous modern-day Republican Southern Strategy. The strategy, in a nutshell, began during the Nixon administration as a way to paint the Democrats as the party of race and the party of "black radicals"—exactly the same goal of the fire-eaters from 1860. By doing so, racist white southern voters would be forced to switch from the Democratic Party to the Republican Party in order to avoid being associated with black voters and civil rights causes. It was so successful for Nixon that it helped to generate one of the largest scale party identification shifts in modern political history: southern whites moving in droves to the Republican Party.

Speaking of which, I looked up the term Southern Strategy on Conservapedia.com, the conservative answer to Wikipedia (which is, contrary to far-right opinion, a non-partisan resource). The entry for Southern Strategy was predictably weak and incomplete. Here's the entry in its entirety:

> The Southern strategy was the method Richard Nixon
> used to win support for the Republican Party from the
> south.

Wow. Thorough and insightful, as we've come to expect from

McBush-era conservatives. Then again, to include the history of race-baiting, ugliness and fear-mongering would've been too honest for the Conservapedia readers.

After all, the Southern Strategy of the modern era requires *implicit* racism, rather than the more obvious tactics of the past. In a 1988 *New York Times* interview, George H.W. Bush's late campaign strategist Lee Atwater explained the transformation of conservative race-baiting from *the obvious* to *the implicit*:

> You start out in 1954 by saying, "Nigger, nigger, nigger." By 1968 you can't say "nigger"—that hurts you. Back-fires. So you say stuff like forced busing, states' rights and all that stuff. You're getting so abstract now [that] you're talking about cutting taxes, and all these things you're talking about are totally economic things and a byprod-uct of them is [that] blacks get hurt worse than whites.
>
> And subconsciously maybe that is part of it. I'm not say-ing that. But I'm saying that if it is getting that abstract, and that coded, that we are doing away with the racial problem one way or the other. You follow me—because obviously sitting around saying, "We want to cut this," is much more abstract than even the busing thing, and a hell of a lot more abstract than "Nigger, nigger."[9]

It's certainly more abstract than letting fly with the n-word all over the place. But notwithstanding what Atwater had suggested, abstractions and implicit racism are clearly the exception for the Republicans. Overt racism is as ubiquitous and obvious as it's ever been. To overlook or ignore it is to endorse that fuckwitted Conservapedia definition of Southern Strategy.

---

9   Alexander P. Lamis, *Southern Politics in the 1990s.*

Rewind to 1988—just twenty years ago—and the grotesquely racist Willie Horton commercial. Horton was a black
prison inmate in Massachusetts who had been released on a
weekend furlough; he never returned to prison and was eventually arrested in Maryland for robbery, assault and rape. Make
no mistake: Horton's crimes were the worst of the worst and
he should never have been released in the first place. But this
does not, by any stretch of the imagination, forgive the race-baiting and fear-mongering that followed. Lee Atwater and George
H.W. Bush's media consultant Roger Ailes (the current grand
wizard of FOX News Channel), along with producer Larry Mc-
Carthy, devised the Willie Horton commercial in order to scare
white voters. The script:

> Bush and Dukakis on crime. Bush supports the death
> penalty for first-degree murderers. Dukakis not only op-
> poses the death penalty, he allowed first-degree murder-
> ers to have weekend passes from prison. One was Willie
> Horton, who murdered a boy in a robbery, stabbing him
> nineteen times. Despite a life sentence, Horton received
> ten weekend passes from prison. Horton fled, kidnapped
> a young couple, stabbing the man and repeatedly rap-
> ing his girlfriend. Weekend prison passes. Dukakis on
> crime.

The commercial attempted to seize upon the prejudices of white
voters by convincing them that Democratic candidate Mike Du-
kakis, when elected, would release into the world black prisoners
who would all, like Willie Horton, go out and rape white women.
Be afraid, America.

Seriously, how different is this and, say, the election propaganda of the secessionist fire-eaters, or the exploitation of black

stereotypes in *Birth of a Nation?* The basic racial theme of *Birth of a Nation* is all there: *blacks can't be controlled and will eventually destroy America.*

In 1990, the notoriously racist Republican, the late Senator Jesse Helms of North Carolina, rolled out his famous "white hands" commercial which, some historians suggest, swung the entire election in Helms's favor and succeeded in re-electing him to his fourth term in the U.S. Senate. That year, Helms was running against an Africa-American candidate: Harvey Gantt, the mayor of Charlotte. The ad, which was masterminded by media consultant Alex Castellanos, showed a close-up of a pair of white, male hands crumpling an employment rejection letter. The narrator explains that "you" have just been passed over for a job because of "racial quotas" even though "you" were the most qualified. In other words, you're white and a black man just stole your job. And it's *so unfair.* The white man is always getting the shaft, isn't he?

Castellanos, by the way, went on to become Mitt Romney's media consultant and a political analyst for CNN—proving, by the way, that they'll hire anyone (see also the hiring of Glenn Beck). In an article on Politico.com, Castellanos commented about Senator Obama's race in light of the Reverend Wright controversy by suggesting that Senator Obama is one of *those* blacks:

> All the sudden you've got two dots, and two dots make a line... You start getting some sense of who he is, and it's not the Obama you thought. He's not the Tiger Woods of politics.[10]

---

10   http://www.politico.com/news/stories/0308/9116.html

Castellanos probably meant to say, *Obama is one of those Old Virginny types*. Any day now, I keep expecting to see a Republican cartoon in which Senator Obama is seated atop a stack of split rails with Reverend Wright—one of *those* angry, crazy blacks—hiding inside the woodpile.

In 2004, there was the "black hands" ad that aired in Oklahoma. Created by Republican race-baiter Scott Howell in support of Senator Tom Coburn and paid for by the National Republican Senatorial Committee, the ad showed, among other things, a pair of brown hands counting welfare money while the narrator claimed that Coburn's Democratic opponent, Congressman Brad Carson, would dole out free cash to Oklahoma City's urban poor. As for Scott Howell, you might remember his name from the 2002 Georgia senatorial race between Senator Saxby Chambliss and former-Senator Max Cleland, who lost three of his four limbs in Vietnam. Howell, it turns out, is responsible for the unforgivable ad claiming that Senator Cleland didn't have the "courage" to fight Saddam Hussein and Osama bin Laden. Chambliss, meanwhile, avoided the Vietnam draft. Bad knee.

A round of applause for the modern day "moral values" Republican Party.

Hello?

Anyone?

Paul Waldman, a senior fellow at Media Matters and columnist for the *America Prospect*, wrote in an article titled "Conservatives' Hate-Based Campaign Against Obama," that in light of the Reverend Wright videos, Republicans have been able to paint Senator Obama with their handy-dandy race-baiting brush. Waldman observes:

[Here is] the story as some conservatives are now telling

it: The comments of Obama's former pastor prove that deep down, Obama is just a black candidate. He may say he wants to transcend racial divisions, he may say he understands the concerns of white people, but when his mask comes off he'll be revealed as just another Sharpton or Malcom X, those blacks you've come to hate and fear.

And now, in the wake of Senator Obama's call for a national discussion about race in his Philadelphia Address, the Republican race-baiters don't even need to be implicit about their Southern Strategy. The speech has successfully drawn them out of the closet. Racists like Rush Limbaugh and Pat Buchanan deliberately misinterpreted the speech and thusly took it as a permission slip from a black leader to dust off their juke box of greatest bigotry hits, each ridiculous statement slyly presented as their "two cents" in the senator's race discussion when, in reality, it's just the same old bigotry and fear-mongering wrapped up in their disingenuous *Racist? Who me?* package.

As much as they'd love it if Senator Obama fit into their archaic Rastus frame, they know full well that Senator Obama isn't, as Waldman supposed, one of *those* blacks. But if they can freely and openly caricaturize him that way, it allows them to incite another Great Fear and appeal to the basest instincts of their listeners, viewers and readers. So it's all upside for the Limbaugh types: they get a bump in the ratings from an onslaught of racist white listeners and, as a bonus, maybe they can elect another fear-mongering Republican president in the process.

During a given week, racial fear-mongering can be heard on far-right talk radio and cable news. Maybe not with the same perspicuousness as its historical predecessors, but it's all there, and it's all well documented.

Paul Waldman, in his *American Prospect* column, quoted Rush Limbaugh two days after the Philadelphia Address: "It is clear that Senator Obama has disowned his white half—that he's decided he's got to go all in on the black side." Media Matters, several weeks later, quoted Limbaugh describing Senator Obama as, "a rookie, radical black guy who can't tell the time of day."[11] Again, far-right fear-mongering that reaches all the way back to those cartoons and movies and *Birth of a Nation* stereotypes: *radical yet stupid blacks who will take over the nation, subsequently destroying it.*

When Michelle Obama said, "For the first time in my adult life, I am proud of my country, because it feels like hope is making a comeback," Bill O'Reilly threatened to go on a lynching party against Mrs. Obama:

> And I don't want to go on a lynching party against Michelle Obama unless there's evidence, hard facts, that say this is how the woman really feels. If that's how she really feels—that America is a bad country or a flawed nation, whatever—then that's legit. We'll track it down.

Track it down? Seriously? With hounds and a posse, Bill? O'Reilly has a long history of racist remarks, including his famous Sylvia's restaurant iced-tea rant from 2007 (Sylvia's is a popular restaurant in Harlem):

> And I couldn't get over the fact that there was no difference between Sylvia's restaurant and any other restaurant in New York City. I mean, it was exactly the same, even though it's run by blacks, primarily black patronship... There wasn't one person in Sylvia's who was screaming,

---

11   http://mediamatters.org/items/200804010009?f=h_latest

"M-Fer, I want more iced tea."...

You know, I mean, everybody was—it was like going into an Italian restaurant in an all-white suburb in the sense of people were sitting there, and they were ordering and having fun. And there wasn't any kind of craziness at all.[12]

"THIS IS A WHITE MAN'S GOVERNMENT"
This cartoon depicts a black Union soldier reaching for a ballot box while the "white power structure" (as O'Reilly called it) tramples on his liberty and, thusly, American liberty (1868, Harper's Weekly).

Apart from being a racist, O'Reilly is entirely out of touch with white suburbia. Has he even *been* to a Buca di Beppo or an Olive Garden at 7 p.m. on a Friday night? It's like the fucking Thunderdome in there.

For the record, Bill O'Reilly has also been caught referring to Mexican immigrants as "wetbacks" and he's on record lamenting a multicultural tide while implying that the "white power structure" is a good thing:

---

12   http://mediamatters.org/items/200709210007

> That's because…many far-left thinkers believe the white
> power structure that controls America is bad, so a dras-
> tic change is needed. According to the lefty zealots, the
> white Christians who hold power must be swept out by a
> new multicultural tide, a rainbow coalition, if you will.[13]

I'm still trying to figure out what's wrong with multicultural-
ism in America. Is it just me or is it alarming to you that there's
only one African-American in the U.S. Senate (Senator Obama),
and, as of November, there will probably be *zero* African-Americans in the Senate (when, of course, Senator Obama wins the
presidential election and resigns from the Senate)?

The roster of grievous remarks is a mile long for O'Reilly
alone. But the record also includes FOX News radio talk-show
host John Gibson urging white viewers to have more babies in
order to counteract the growing minority population. It includes
late White House Press Secretary Tony Snow, in his first press
conference, using the offensive phrase "squeezing the tar baby."

Back in March, Geraldine Ferraro repeatedly suggested that
the only reason Senator Obama was the frontrunner was because he's black. In light of the historical record, we can clearly
understand the absurdity of her observations.

But before the Ferraro episode could really strike down hard
against the Clintons, the Reverend Wright videos magically appeared and became the big story. FOX News aired the clips of
Wright's fiery and controversial sermons around the clock. But it
wasn't just FOX News. Both MSNBC and CNN dedicated the
better part of a month to the story, while spending very little time
discussing the equally controversial remarks made by television

---

13   http://mediamatters.org/items/200605170006

evangelist and supporter of Senator McCain, Pastor John Hagee, who said that Hurricane Katrina was the result of God's wrath against New Orleans's gay population (see the chapter "The Atheist's Nightmare" for more about similar such fear-mongering remarks). Hagee is also responsible for anti-Semitic and anti-Catholic smears. Senator McCain has yet to be grilled with the same tenacity and fury as Senator Obama, mainly because white cable-news viewers are easily and irrationally frightened by black people who raise their voice in public. It's okay for Bill O'Reilly to scream "shut up" at his guests, and it's okay for O'Reilly to get up in the face of a kid whose father was killed in the World Trade Center (Google the words "O'Reilly and Jeremy Glick"). But if it's a black minister preaching with equal rage, forget it. Scary. And as we're aware, racial fear is FOX News Channel's bread and butter—their Southern Strategy. If their loudmouth white hosts are demonizing a black pastor, if they're proselytizing about immoral gays, if they're scaring their viewers about the subversive threats of evildoer Muslims and swarthy illegal immigrants—"wetbacks," as O'Reilly calls them—with the same volume and anger as exhibited by Reverend Wright, then their corporate conservative mission has been accomplished.

Regardless of his tone of voice, when Reverend Wright "damned" America, he was well within his rights to do so. When he suggested that on September 11, America's "chickens had come home to roost," he was really just repeating a similar observation made by many foreign policy experts, including Republican Congressman Ron Paul, who repeated this idea multiple times on national television during his presidential campaign. Or is the intelligence community's well-documented theory of blowback just the stuff of angry fringe rants? And considering the history of racial fear-mongering, not to mention the Southern Strategy, was Reverend Wright so wrong to conflate the United States and the KKK?

Nothing will ever quite absolve America from its ugliest chapters. And as far as I'm concerned, we should never be entirely absolved, no matter how many social policies for which Pat Buchanan (who opposed those programs anyway) is demanding gratitude.

My personal love of America comes from the knowledge that we're a tragically flawed nation, but also a nation that's willing to grow and evolve. In fact, we ought to be constantly reminded of the ugly chapters in our American narrative. Our flaws, as embarrassing and tragic as they are, serve a necessary purpose. Our flaws humble us, and they temper our penchant for arrogance. That's not to say that we ought to be proud of our litany of fuckups, nor should we ever repeat these episodes out of some kind of twisted nostalgia. This national humility forces us to constantly strive to form, as Senator Obama said, quoting the Preamble of the Constitution, "a more perfect union." The constant seeking of perfection is what makes this a great nation. It's not our wars or our rhetoric or our lapel pins. It's our imperfection that brings us together in this common effort to move forward.

This is why I recount all of these racial horror stories. Not as a sensationalized gimmick designed to guilt my fellow white people, but rather as a way to suggest that Americans are justified in asking God to both bless America *and* to damn it. As Senator Obama said in his Philadelphia Address:

> Understanding this reality requires a reminder of how we arrived at this point. As William Faulkner once wrote, "The past isn't dead and buried. In fact, it isn't even past."

Senator Obama didn't call for a national dialogue about race in order to give white people an excuse to say "nigger" or to bitch and moan about affirmative action or rap music. Nor was it necessarily a call for black people to continue to indict white Americans about slavery. I believe that Senator Obama was seeking to bring about a mutual understanding among us all, regardless of race. That is, I think it was about white people acknowledging the legacy of Jim Crow and slavery and accepting the horror of it all. At the same time, I think it was about black people understanding that white people might be exhausted with being held personally responsible for past sins. I believe that Senator Obama was saying that all of us, *We the People*, must, at long last, own these things, rather than battling over the exclusive rights to victimhood, blame and gratitude. And if we can do that, we can easily solve healthcare and jobs and Iraq and the climate crisis and all the rest of it.

So, given the profundity of Senator Obama's address, when I read Pat Buchanan's "Whitey" rant, the part that offended me the most as an American wasn't just the part about how blacks do more raping than whites, or any of Buchanan's other hacktastically resurrected ghosts of racist rhetoric past. The line that truly pissed me off was the line about Senator Obama attempting to deceive everyone. "It is the same old con, the same old shakedown that black hustlers have been running since the Kerner Commission blamed the riots [on white America]," Buchanan wrote. His willfully ignorant analysis of Senator Obama's address aside, it was Buchanan's inability to see beyond his own cynicism that was truly one of the most infuriating aspects of his "Whitey" column; it displayed a breed of cynicism that is commonplace in Washington. It suggests that anyone who speaks openly and honestly for the cause of change is automatically a flimflam artist running a scam. The implication being that only very serious, white, fear-mongering Washington hacks know what's good for America. It's this kind of fear-based establishment intransigence that's keeping our racial wounds open and bleeding, draining America of its strength to heal the wounds of history.

THE ATHEIST'S
NIGHTMARE

You'll get a kick out of this story. Paul Zachary "PZ" Myers is arguably one of the most popular science bloggers on the Internet.[1] He's also a professor of biology at the University of Minnesota, as well as being widely known among intelligent design (ID) and creationism true-believers as a scalawag—an evil-doer. His sharp, often hilarious science-based arguments against intelligent design and creationism have made him an unlikely hero among those of us struggling to keep actual science in, you know, science classes. In a 2005 interview, which he links from his Pharyngula blog[2], Myers lays out his position in no uncertain terms:

> I have nothing but contempt for ID... The old-school creationists were people who just didn't know much and were sincere in their belief in their Bible. Fine. But the new school is people who have had training, scientists who know a little bit about biology and molecular biol-

---

1 http://scienceblogs.com/pharyngula/ receives around 13,000-25,000 visitors per day, according to Professor Myers.

2 The pharyngula stage of embryonic development is the stage during which many species appear strikingly similar in form.

ogy and put on their lab coats and say all this ridiculous nonsense. I find that fundamentally dishonest.

Because he's a biologist, his blog combines all the snark of a typical left-leaning blog with actual scientific facts pulled from Myers's years of experience. In the same interview, the reporter describes Myers's blog like so: "Myers can write about whatever strikes his fancy—from the evolution of the mammalian vagina to Buffy the Vampire Slayer to the latest outrage from Pat Robertson—with the knowledge that his musings will be read." Here's PZ Myers on one of his favorite subjects. Squid sex:

> Just imagine it—great pelagic orgies, the males thrusting wantonly with their massive penile arms, promiscuously inseminating any nearby slickly molluscan body. Perhaps they end up sated and exhausted from their frenzied exertions and, oblivious and insensate, drift ashore to die content. Forget *March of the Penguins*. There's a great documentary to be made here: Squid Gone Wild. Cephalopod Sex Party. I want to see Michael Medved review it.[3]

Ewww.

I'm not, nor will I ever be, a scientist, but I read Pharyngula every day because I like to torture myself by attempting to learn about things that are astonishingly complicated. Evolutionary biology is obviously a vast and complex scientific discipline. To fully comprehend the basic notion of, say, *four and a half billion years* (the approximate age of the earth) requires some level of motivation to, you know, read and learn. It's not easy, but PZ

---

3   http://pharyngula.org/index/weblog/comments/great_pelagic_orgies/

Myers is one of those educators whose attitude and enthusiasm motivates me to want to learn more about this stuff, regardless of its complexity. Conversely, the euphemistic ideas proselytized by creationists and far-right fundamentalist Christians have experienced what I call the *Uh-doy!* Surge during the Bush years. (Author Chris Mooney called it "the Republican attack on science" in his appropriately titled book, *The Republican Attack on Science*.) The Bush administration surge in *Uh-doy!* is due mainly to the fact that too many allegedly educated and allegedly *adult* McBush Republicans, like Sean Hannity for instance, are content to go around as if they're ten years old, fresh out of Sunday school and, because of the fear of demons and God's wrath, are afraid to wrap their heads around a wide variety of complicated scientific facts. The surge in *Uh-doy!* has blurred the line between scientific *fact*, religious *faith* and political *opinion*.

Part and parcel of the far-right attacks on reality, rationality and free and fair elections, the McBush Republican "religious right" attack on science has been remarkably successful (in the pejorative sense) in terms of framing scientific fact as liberal bias. On PZ Myers's blog back in 2006, he blasted John Hinderaker of the conservative blog Powerline[4] when Hinderaker quoted and praised a ridiculous article by Michael Fumento.[5] Fumento, in this particular column, claimed that scientific journals had been taken over by liberals with a political agenda. PZ Myers responded in kind:

> Wow. So any science article that discusses, say, evolution, climate, energy, reproduction, conservation, petroleum geology, glaciers, pesticides, extinction, wetlands, mate-

---

4   http://powerlineblog.com/archives/013273.php

5   http://www.fumento.com/media/medjournals.html

rials science, transportation, agriculture, neurobiology, HIV/AIDS (shall I go on?), demographics, deforestation, habitat loss, human genetics (I could keep this up all day), influenza, psychiatry, ethanol production, sexually transmitted disease, medicine in general, stem cells, weather, sex (Okay, enough), all issues that have political implications, and which are therefore automatically suspect and tainted by <hiss> *liberals?* Jeez, John and Michael, why not just say, "Science is EVIL" and be done with it? When all the scientists are disagreeing with you, though, maybe instead you should wonder if you, people with no scientific competence at all, might just be wrong.[6]

And there you go. When, for example, science says that modern humans evolved over millions of years via a process of mutation and natural selection, creationists like Fumento leap to the conclusion that evil scientists are attempting to destroy the word of God by inventing scary elitist ideas that can only be understood by scientists.

And in response, creationists have invented what they perceive to be a strategy of counter-trickery: intelligent design. When the Supreme Court ruled in the late 1980s that creationism couldn't be taught in public schools due to the Establishment Clause of the First Amendment that separates church and state, creationists repackaged their dogma as intelligent design, or what amounts to a PR trick aimed at circumventing the Constitution. In the same way the Bush administration invented its interpretation of the Geneva Conventions in order to permit torture, the creationists simply invented a "science."

Then the creationists set about trying to redefine the very pa-

---

6   http://scienceblogs.com/pharyngula/2006/03/the_expected_powerline_slapdow.php

rameters of science by using intelligent design as a wedge. *Unless you want to vote against Christianity and God, you had better shove intelligent design (creationism) into public schools and call it a science—or else!* But it's not even a *pseudoscience.* In the words of PZ Myers, intelligent design is a "fundamentally dishonest" marketing ploy, which, in terms of its intended purpose to compete with the science of evolution, is nothing more than a metaphorical soap-box-derby racer competing in a flight test against the space shuttle.

The mortal fear of having their faith in biblical "creation" debunked by science has naturally given rise to the modern fear-mongering campaign against science. And intelligent design is one of the several duplicitous wedges in that effort.

If you "believe" in science (there's no such thing as "belief" in science) then you're denying God, they say, and therefore you can't be saved. Which is the worst possible outcome for a Christian. John Morris, the president of the Institute for Creation Research, writes that Christians really can't subscribe to evolution and also be saved by the risen Christ. Death, according to natural selection, is "good," but in the biblical sense, death was God's punishment for Adam's sin and to proclaim it as necessary for evolution is contrary to idea of conquering death through Christ's salvation:

> ...if evolution is right, if the earth is old, if fossils date
> from before man's sin, then Christianity is wrong! These
> ideas destroy the foundation for the Gospel and negate
> the work of Christ on the cross. Evolution and salvation
> are mutually exclusive concepts.[7]

So, by Morris's reasoning, unless you want to roll the dice and deny that Christ defeated metaphysical death by suffering

---

7   http://www.icr.org/article/336/

through some good old fashioned Mel Gibson torture-porn, you had better accept the biblical explanation for life as we known it.[8] And here comes intelligent design to save the day.

Let's be clear: if you choose to believe that earth is six thousand years old and that humans are sculpted by the invisible hands of an invisible supreme being, that's fine. If you buy into this marketing campaign called intelligent design, that's fine too. You're allowing yourself to be tricked, but fine. It's your call. This chapter isn't meant to suggest that religion is silly or wrong. Neither is it meant as an across-the-board indictment of all religions and people of faith. It's a mistake to indiscriminately attack religion across-the-board, unless, that is, it attacks first. That's an important distinction. Having been raised in a healthy and secure Catholic household and presently enjoying a comfortably non-religious adulthood, I can appreciate organized religion for some of its positive moralistic and communal qualities, while also thoroughly understanding and accepting how damaging, cruel and divisive it can be. So let me take advantage of this tangent to make myself perfectly clear: my beef is with far-right fundamentalist Christians who are attempting to legislate their specific interpretation of faith, an interpretation that is predominantly scripted by fear-mongers who preach judgment, discrimination, wrath and punishment while deceptively marketing their crusade as being all about "love" and "moral values." My argument herein is against those who try to pass off their faith as science, be it in the classroom or in the public square.

As PZ Myers notes, basic creationism, as opposed to intelligent design, is comparatively harmless because it doesn't really

---

8   "Torture-porn" is a slang term for mainstream movies that contain excessive torture and violence.

attempt to be anything more than it is: the literal interpretation of the Bible. But when it's wrapped inside this deceptive packaging—this infomercial called intelligent design—it comes off as insulting to those whom it's attempting to convince. Scientists, and even those of us with a general layman's understanding of science, can usually sniff out gimmicky pseudoscience like a fart in a car.

It's no wonder this debate is so volatile. When fundamentalist religious dogma is rammed down a person's gullet—especially with deceptive intentions—otherwise reasonable people tend to wretch, growl, then kick the religious proselytizer in the nuts for overstepping his or her bounds and attempting to trample personal liberty. To repeat: Faith is faith. Science is science. Politics is politics. When faith is crow-barred into our political discourse or into the scientific community, it tends to be confronted with all of the accompanying tenacity and ferocity associated with political debates and scientific research. It's impossible for faith to be subjected to any sort of scientific testing or any sort of mathematical proof or any sort of empirical analysis. So when creationists stick their Bibles where they don't belong, the debate tends to devolve into anger and divisiveness. The *Uh-doy!* Surge is a war that's been declared by people who fear science while attempting to fight actual scientists using bogus pseudoscience and cherry-picked, often-contradictory biblical references. This twisted and wholly subjective approach tends to make people like John Hinderaker of Powerline look like an idiot.[9] And Professor

---

9   Hinderaker, who used to be known by the anonymous internet handle Hindrocket (seriously—look it up), is really good at making himself look like an idiot. The *American Prospect*'s Ezra Klein once described Powerline with this beautiful simile: "Reading their site is like watching a blind child in a dog park—you keep trying to warn him not to step in the piles of shit, but you're never able to get there quite quick enough."

Myers doesn't miss a beat when exposing the idiocy.

Back to the story.

On Good Friday 2008, Professor Myers was waiting in line for a special screening of the intelligent design documentary, *Expelled! No Intelligence Allowed*, starring conservative actor Ben Stein. I tend to avoid movies with exclamation marks in the title. Enough people yell at me in real life and I'd rather not be yelled at by movie titles. Besides, movies with exclamation marks in the title usually suck. For example, *Stop! Or My Mom Will Shoot*. But that's just about all of the criticism I can throw at *Expelled!* or *Stop! Or My Mom Will Shoot* because, unlike Republicans, I don't make wild claims about movies I haven't seen.

However, here's something from the movie's official website claiming that evolution science somehow leads to becoming a Nazi:

> Many scenes are centered around the Berlin Wall, and Ben Stein being Jewish actually visits many death camps and death showers. In fact, Nazi Germany is the thread that ties everything in the movie together. Evolution leads to atheism leads to eugenics leads to Holocaust and Nazi Germany.[10]

Fact: you can also connect me to Kevin Bacon in six steps.[11] That doesn't mean I'm Kevin Bacon or even bacon-flavored. But you would expect that documentarians who were able construct such a circuitous and specious connection between the broad study of evolution and the Nazis would've taken a harder look

---

10   http://www.expelledthemovie.com/chronicle.php?article=11

11   My six degrees of Kevin Bacon: I write for the *Huffington Post*, founded by Arianna Huffington. Huffington ran for governor of California against Arnold Schwarzenegger. Arnold starred in the movie *Total Recall* with Sharon Stone (Quatto lives!). Sharon Stone starred in the movie *Casino* with Joe Pesci. Joe Pesci starred in the movie *JFK* with Kevin Bacon.

at PZ Myers's guests in line at the Mall of America multiplex for that screening of *Expelled!*

Accompanying Myers were his wife, his daughter and a close friend. The *Expelled!* crew must've recognized Myers from the photograph on his blog and ordered the police officer at the theater to pull Myers out of the line. The officer told Myers that the cowardly producers of the movie were forbidding him from entering that special screening of their intelligent-design-meets-*Schindler's List* film. As Myers tells it, the theater manager eventually instructed him that he would have to leave the premises of the theater. So even if Myers wanted to stay and watch *10,000 B.C.*, he wouldn't have been allowed. Now if Myers were a jackass like me, he would've made an obnoxious fuss about how the *Nazis* were known for separating men from their families, thus connecting the *Expelled!* producers with, well, you know. But Myers left the theater peacefully and then made a b-line to the mall's Apple Store so he could blog about this story.

In the process of freaking out over Myers and ordering him to be *expelled* from *Expelled!*, the producers totally overlooked Myers's friend who, while Myers blogged about what had happened down at the Apple Store, escorted Myers's wife and daughter into the movie.

The friend?

Richard Dawkins, the author of *The God Delusion* and quite possibly the world's most famous living evolutionary biologist and atheist. And Dawkins walked right on in and watched the movie with Myers's wife and daughter.

It took a while, but I promised that you'd get a kick out of the story. Paul Harvey's a lightweight next to Myers and Dawkins.

What makes the episode even more bizarre is that both Dawkins and Professor Myers are interviewed by Ben Stein *in the movie*. Dawkins reports that the duo was deceived into participating in a documentary with the working title *Crossroads*—most definitely not the kind of movie that ended up on screen. (Dawkins later called *Expelled!* "a shoddy, second-rate piece of work.") On his website, however, Dawkins treated the producers with modesty, fairness and magnanimity:

> Many people have wondered why, if PZ was expelled, I managed to get in. This has been adduced as further evidence of [Associate Producer Mark] Mathis's bungling incompetence, but I think that is unfair. It was easy for Mathis to spot PZ Myers's name on the list of those registering in advance. Like all guests, my name was not on any list, and therefore Mathis didn't spot me. So I think he can be absolved of stupidity in not spotting me. But convicted of extreme stupidity in expelling PZ when he spotted him. What was he afraid of? What did he think PZ would do, open fire with a Kalashnikov? Now that I think about it, that would have been all-of-a-piece with the overblown paranoia displayed throughout the film itself.[12]

"What was he afraid of?" Dawkins wrote. It was all about fear. Of course.

Fear and religious fundamentalism are inseparable. In the beginning, God told Adam: *don't eat from that fucking tree or the terrorists win.*[13] Adam disobeyed his authoritarian master and ate

12   http://richarddawkins.net/article,2394,Lying-for-Jesus,Richard-Dawkins

13   God didn't say "fucking." But He might have. We just don't know for sure. But if God invented everything, then He had to have also invented

the apple. Consequently, wrath and underpants entered the human experience.

Dawkins, in *The God Delusion*, writes about God's wrath and references the story of Noah. Being a scientist and a very smart man, Dawkins makes sure to note that the story of Noah was borrowed from other cultural myths, including the Babylonian myth of Uta-Napisthim and Gilgamesh. But who cares, Babylonian myth has a liberal bias.

From chapters six through nine in the book of Genesis, we're treated to the entire fear-mongering authoritarian epic about how God decided that human beings were evildoers, and how He opted to smoke 'em out with a global waterboarding experiment gone haywire. So everyone, including, we can only assume, perfectly healthy unborn babies at all stages of fetal development, were wiped out in a worldwide flood because, I don't know, humans suck. Except, that is, for Noah and his family, who constructed a boat large enough to somehow transport two of every animal species on the entire planet. Dawkins cites many theologians who agree that the Noah story isn't to be taken literally, and so Dawkins considers this to be a form of moral cherry-picking. *This* is real, but *that* isn't. And therefore, *this* morality is good, but *that* morality is bad. Personal interpretation, some theologians suggest, guides which parts of the Bible are to be accepted as truth and which aren't. Therefore, morality is open to personal interpretation. Hmm. Weird. That would seem to contradict the whole idea that the Bible is the infallible word of God, but okay.

---

the word "fucking." If *Expelled!* is allowed to connect evolution science to the Holocaust, then I can say God invented the word "fucking." And I'd like to add that the same reasoning dictates that God also invented the word "blumpkin." My Catholic mom is probably horrified enough by this chapter, so I won't make it worse by defining that word. You'll have to look it up.

Just so long as the upshot is fear, I suppose it doesn't really matter.

And then there are the Noah people here in America. Dawkins reminds us about a Gallup poll showing that around half of all Americans believe that the story of Noah is historical fact. So there are around 150 million Americans—some with licenses to carry firearms—who believe that God is responsible for a global genocide, save for a family of five and millions of stinky animals. Including dinosaurs, by the way. The Creationism Museum in Petersburg, Kentucky says that dinosaurs donned their Frank Costanza cabana-wear and hopped a ride aboard Noah's Carnival Cruise. Ken Ham, the founder of the museum, told *Australian News*, "What we've done here is to give people an opportunity to hear information that is not readily available."[14] Yeah, no one can get a copy of the Bible or find a church in America. Especially in no-Bible states like Kentucky. During a CNN-sponsored Republican debate in New Hampshire, three of the former Republican candidates for president, Mike Huckabee, Tom Tancredo and Sam Brownback, said that they subscribe to creationism and, thus, the Noah fable. In the same debate, Senator McCain said, "I admire [Huckabee's] description, because I hold that view."

It's no wonder why McBush Republican fear-mongering has been so effective. Fictitious, metaphorically based threats of wrath and retribution are built into the moral code of far-right fundamentalist Christians. Yep. The strategy is all right there in print and is being rapidly adapted to fit all sorts of present-day far-right conspiracies against science, civil liberties and freedom in general.

---

14   http://www.abc.net.au/news/newsitems/200705/s1934224.htm

After September 11, the late Jerry Falwell appeared on Pat Robertson's *700 Club* and made the following proclamation about the real reason for the September 11 terrorist attacks:

> I really believe that the pagans, and the abortionists, and the feminists, and the gays and the lesbians who are actively trying to make that an alternative lifestyle, the ACLU, People For the American Way, all of them who have tried to secularize America. I point the finger in their face and say, "you helped this happen."

Falwell's message was crystal clear. An echo of Noah. God was punishing America for its "fags" and civil liberties. And unless we want another similar attack—or worse—we had better renounce gays and civil liberties and pagans from America.

Uh-huh. Now who's being just a little too Holocaust-ish?

And then there was Pat Robertson's threat that God will forsake the town of Dover, Pennsylvania after voters there rose up in 2005 and voted out of office a gaggle of creationists who had previously commandeered their school board. When Dover voted to replace the creationist board members, Robertson said that God would ignore Dover if a disaster struck the town.

> I'd like to say to the good citizens of Dover, if there is a disaster in your area, don't turn to God. You just reject-ed him from your city, and don't wonder why he hasn't helped you when problems begin, if they do begin, and I'm not saying they will. But if they do, just remember you just voted God out of your city. And if that's the case, then don't ask for his help, because he might not be there.

If God doesn't understand the difference between voting

against creationism in science class and literally voting against God, then God is not only petulant and slow-on-the-uptake, but he couldn't possibly have created anything more complicated than, say, toast.

As evidenced by Robertson's comments, it's becoming clear that the real evildoer in America is God.

I'm not saying this myself, of course. His most famous ambassadors here in America appear to be suggesting that He is responsible for September 11, not to mention whatever future disasters are slated to hit Dover, Pennsylvania.

Back in June 2007, James Dobson, a spiritual advisor to President Bush and founder of Focus on the Family, hosted on his radio show an evangelical pastor named John MacArthur. MacArthur basically came right out and said that God was a terrorist, and rightfully so:

> I don't believe we're waiting for God's wrath in this society. We haven't had a massive calamity such as the destruction of an entire city. We certainly don't want that to happen—pray that does not happen—but it could happen. And God would be just in any calamity that he brought upon us. We have not entered into eschatological wrath; that comes in the end times. We are experiencing—all of us do—consequential wrath of sin. But this massive concept of the wrath of abandonment, I'm convinced, is now at work in our society. We like to talk about the fact that America was founded on Christian principles, God was at the center of it, and all of that—whatever it might have been in our founding, it's no longer the way it is, and I want to show you how you know that has happened. You know a society has been

abandoned by God when it celebrates lesbian sex.[15]

And Dobson agreed, "**I happen to agree with what John MacArthur was saying on this day,** and I want to thank him and his team and Woodman Valley Chapel for allowing us to share this message. It needs to be heard, especially at this time in our nation."

"God would be just in any calamity that he brought upon us." Unless MacArthur was drunk, he seemed to have been seriously implying that God would be justified in bringing about the destruction of an entire city—because of lesbian sex.[16] I'm reasonably sure he was attempting to repeat Falwell's remarks about how the gay community caused September 11, but the way MacArthur spelled it out, he was suggesting that lesbians are why God hates America. As the cranks and crackpots from Fred Phelps's Westboro Baptist Church say: "God hates fags." And He hates them so much that He's going to facilitate the destruction of an American city. In other words, God is the bin Laden. President Bush said that bin Laden hates us for our freedom; MacArthur is saying that God hates us for our lesbian sex. Freedom is to lesbian sex as bin Laden is to God. That sounds weird and sacrilegious, but *I'm not saying it.* Far-right Christian minister John MacArthur said it. God makes terrorist attacks because we have turned away from God and, instead, are paying too much attention to lesbian sex.

MacArthur's congregation is being brainwashed with the

---

15   http://mediamatters.org/items/200706070007

16   Question for Mr. Dobson and Mr. MacArthur: In the name of Wild Berry-Flavored Astroglide, have you guys ever actually seen lesbian sex? Clearly not, because if you gave it a chance, you'd celebrate it, too. For instance, I would encourage Dobson and MacArthur to screen a copy of Angelina Jolie's movie *Gia*. There's a lesbian sex scene in *Gia* featuring Jolie and Elizabeth Mitchell that's seriously worth celebrating.

idea that gays and lesbians—as well as their liberal, secular enablers—are just as guilty as the terrorists. They say we need to persecute the lesbians, the sodomites and the liberals because their perversions and liberties are begging God's wrath. MacArthur also said that God has abandoned our society. I still can't quite figure out, though, how God could bring a calamity down upon an entire city while having previously abandoned it. But, then again, it's God. He's crazy powerful like that.

Speaking of crazy, did you know that God designed the banana to fit perfectly inside the human hand? That's what TV's Kirk Cameron (the former teen heartthrob from the 1980s sitcom *Growing Pains*) and his sidekick, evangelical preacher Ray Comfort, told their congregation on their born-again Christian website called Way of the Master.[17] They also promised (in webvideo form) that they could "finish" the age-old debate between "intelligent design" and evolution "in just three minutes."

Their entire video argument against evolution, which turned out to be much longer than three minutes, is predicated upon treating evolution like a superstition or belief system.[18] So by simplifying and reducing the science of evolution to the level of faith, they're able to more easily attack it using their aggravatingly specious logic. They manage to achieve this by asking leading questions of ordinary, non-expert, anonymous young adults, rather than talking with actual scientists.

Comfort begins by asking his interviewees, "Do you believe in evolution?" Then we're supposed to be astonished when the interviewee answers by repeating Comfort's use of the word "be-

---

17   www.wayofthemaster.com

18   Choose item two from the animated menu on the main page. You can't miss it.

lieve," as in, "Yes, I believe in evolution." Comfort defines these reactions as the "language of speculation." In other words, just because his rundown of non-experts use words like "we believe" and "perhaps" and "possibly" means that evolution is merely speculative. The ultimate goal of this rhetorical trick is to prove that evolution (and, by proxy, science) is just like faith, so why can't faith and science be combined in the classroom? Clever.

Comfort continues with the falsely premised question: "Do you believe that man evolved from apes?" He conveniently ignores the fact that humans are apes. Gorillas, chimpanzees, orangutans and humans are all members of the same family known as Hominidae. But I wouldn't expect Comfort, who probably knows this, to be honest about it. (Later in the web video, Kirk Cameron hires an orangutan to imitate his facial expressions and explains that just because he and the orangutan can make similar faces, humans and orangutans are therefore no more biologically connected than a 747 and a biplane. Seriously. That's what he says.) And, once again, it's presented as proof that evolution is speculative when a random dude answers the ape question by saying, "Yes, I believe that." Whoa. That totally trumps the last century and a half of scientific study and experimentation in the field of evolutionary biology.

The interviews continue with more specific questioning.

Comfort asks, "How did life begin?" Some jock in his dorm room replies, "I don't know." Okay, scientists. Time to hang it up because an anonymous frat brother said, "I don't know." Comfort asks another dude on an airplane, "Do you think we were originally fish?" And—shockingly—the dude on the airplane also answers, "I don't know."

Skipping ahead to roughly the halfway mark of this way-longer-than-three-minutes debunking of evolution, Comfort and Cameron call an airline to see if they can book a seat on an airplane for their "relative." But get this—their "relative" is an orangutan. Get it? Naturally, the airline is confused when the duo calls the orangutan a "relative," so Comfort and Cameron use this as proof that primates and humans aren't "relatives." Seriously. Have you yanked your hair out yet? Yeah, I know. They're playing a semantic trick, mixing the familial use of the word "relative" with the general biological term "relative." See the earlier PZ Myers quote about intelligent design being "fundamentally deceptive."

And it gets crazier. Comfort and Cameron conduct an experiment to disprove the basic and verifiable scientific premise that, "primates are just about as intelligent as human beings" (Comfort's words). Of course this is generally true. Great Apes, especially the chimpanzee, are, in a relative sense, almost as intelligent as humans. Never mind that humans are Great Apes: members of the Hominidae family. Never mind that scientists around the world agree that chimps, orangutans and gorillas are the most intelligent non-human animals on the planet. But, nevertheless, for their informal experiment, Comfort and Cameron take their hired orangutan Bam-Bam to a restaurant for lunch and are delighted to discover that the orangutan is—gasp!—a sloppy eater, and therefore not very "intelligent." Heck, the orangutan even "covets" Ray Comfort's salad. Uh-oh. The orangutan doesn't understand the Ten Commandments. A-ha! Sinner. I don't need to tell you that they could've taken an undisciplined toddler to a restaurant and observed similar results. But whatever.

There are dozens of other equally nearsighted and deceptive arguments against evolutionary biology made by Comfort and Cameron. For instance, Cameron invokes the 747 gambit and asks whether an airplane is designed and constructed by people or if it just randomly assembles by accident. This fallacy is a modern relative of the most infamous creation argument: the two hundred-year-old Watchmaker gambit. If you find a pocket watch in the desert would you assume that the pocket watch evolved there by accident, or would you conclude that it was constructed and dropped there by a "designer" or "creator"? This argument is closely tied to the idea of irreducible complexity. That is, the intelligent design people claim that a complex organism couldn't possibly have evolved from less complex organisms. In the case of the pocket watch, it couldn't have directly evolved from a less complex watch. It had to have been constructed by a designer.

It goes without saying that anyone with a fifth-grade education would understand the vast differences between "organic life" and "inanimate objects" and how organic life mutates and adapts (or else becomes extinct) when confronted by environmental challenges. For a much more expert analysis, I would strongly recommend Richard Dawkins' book *The Blind Watchmaker*, which successfully dissects the Watchmaker fallacy.

But again, with modern science at our disposal, it's relatively easy to disprove the semantic trickery of intelligent design: this PR scam intended to deceive those who are more prone to believing anything described by an authority figure, especially authority figures who, audaciously enough, purport to speak as self-described messengers of God.

And Ray Comfort, who otherwise seems like a bright and articulate man sporting a crisp New Zealand accent, said that God designed the banana to fit perfectly in your hand. Just like a soda can.

He calls it the Atheist's Nightmare. And the nightmare is on YouTube.

> Behold the atheist's nightmare. Now if you study a well-made banana, you'll find on the far side, there are three ridges. On the close side, two ridges. If you get your hand ready to grip a banana, you'll find that on the far side, there are three grooves, and on the close side, two grooves. The banana and the hand are perfectly made, one for the other. You'll find the maker of the banana, Almighty God, has made the banana with a non-slip surface. It has outward indicators of inward contents. Green, too early. Yellow, just right. Black, too late. Now if you go to the top of the banana, you'll find as with the soda can makers who placed a tab at the top, so God has placed a tab at the top. When you pull the tab, the contents don't squirt in your face. You'll find that the wrapper is biodegradable and has perforations. Notice how gracefully it sits over the human hand. Notice it has a point at the top for ease of entry. Just the right shape for the human mouth. It's chewy, easy to digest. And is even curved toward the face to make the whole process so much easier. Seriously, Kirk, the whole of Creation testifies to the genius of God's creativity.

Where to begin. First of all, there are the obvious fellatio and masturbation jokes that I won't bother with because they're too easy. Suffice it to say that I thought of a few. Second of all, I checked my hand. If I make an "okay" gesture with my fingers as if I'm holding a banana, I count seven sides, including the bones of my thumb, index finger and that fleshy section between my thumb and index finger. Not five sides. And that's just the beginning of the all-too-easy debunking of this unintentionally farcical hoax. Several YouTube videos were created—errrrm, designed—to debunk Comfort's ridiculous flimflam. The best of the YouTube videos reminds us that the banana was, in reality, domesticated by the inhabitants of Papua, New Guinea around five thousand to eight thousand years ago. (Another source indicates seven thousand to ten thousand years ago.)[19] Over the years, the banana achieved its present form via selective breeding and harvesting. This is what a wild, undomesticated banana looks like:

Sorry, Mr. Comfort. No. The domesticated banana was not designed by the Almighty God to perfectly fit the human hand and mouth. But good job injecting this idea into the minds of those who don't know any better and who will repeat the idea as if a scientist told them about it.

And yet as ridiculous as Ray Comfort's banana theory

---

19   http://apscience.org.au/projects/PBF_02_3/pbf_02_3.htm

sounds, I can't help but to correlate its fiction with the fiction of any number of McBush Republican policies and actions throughout the last eight years. The *Uh-doy!* Surge is simply the banana theory applied to national policy. As easy as it was to debunk Comfort's made-up banana story, it similarly easy to slice through and expose the weaknesses and superficiality of the McBush Republican policies, not to mention its fear-mongering slogans. For example, "We don't torture." Or, "The insurgents will follow us home." Or, "You can't have civil liberties if you're dead." Simply put: *America's* Nightmare.

If these myopic slogans and theories are the best the modern Republican Party can do, then it's time to step off the stage for a while and reboot. Similarly, if a banana is the big intelligent design trump card—the atheist's nightmare—then it's time for Ray Comfort and Kirk Cameron to hand over the bananas to Bam-Bam and slowly step away from the science.

The rub, however, is that men like Ray Comfort and Kirk Cameron can't just walk away. They've permanently intertwined and scrambled their perception of science with their faith and morality, so their fear of God's wrath and their fear of hell—or the fear that their reward of heaven and eternal life might not be granted to them after they die—dictates that they continue down this road. (So much of religion, it seems to me, is focused on attaining a personal reward. This, of course, smacks of selfishness: the seeking of a prize or the avoidance of devilish pain, rather than the selflessness and altruism that Jesus often preached. So rather than morality for the sake morality, faith is too often bastardized and exploited as feigned morality "just to be on the safe side.")

This inability of faith—specifically the brand of faith held by those who practice fundamentalist Christianity or, for that matter, fundamentalist Islam—to concede a point or to compromise on a solution is what makes it so incompatible with secular democracy and liberty. No matter how airtight the scientific case for evolution; or the human influence upon global warming; or embryonic stem-cell research; or homosexuality; or any of the so-called "wedge" issues, there isn't any room for compromise from those who have been coerced through fear to believe that an almighty supreme being is judging their every move. Again, not to hedge too much, but this intransigence is fine if it's reserved to the private milieu of the home or church, synagogue or mosque. But when it bleeds into the public arena, it's inherently dangerous. Wars, crusades, inquisitions and genocides have been waged over similar inabilities to compromise or concede to the laws of reason. Beyond evolution, stem cells and all the rest, the bellicose extremism of religion is alive and well in the twenty-first century. Islamic jihad against the West. Israeli-Palestinian war-mongering. President Bush claiming that God told him to invade and occupy Iraq—an action that, of all things, has inaugurated a debate over the morality of waterboarding: a torture method used by the Spanish Inquisitition.

Intelligent design proponents will say that their pseudoscience is all about compromise when in fact it simply obfuscates a larger, more menacing goal of codifying religion as part of state curriculum, granting it the legitimacy of a science. From there, the goals of fundamentalism are gradually achieved. The former Republican presidential candidate Mike Huckabee said publicly that the Constitution ought to be amended to reflect God's law:

> [Some of my opponents] do not want to change the Constitution, but I believe it's a lot easier to change the Constitution than it would be to change the word of the living God, and that's what we need to do is to amend the Constitution so it's in God's standards rather than try to change God's standards.[20]

Huckabee was referring specifically to the issues of abortion and gay marriage. If Huckabee had his way, the former would of course result in the continued subjugation of women, and the latter would result in the continued subjugation of gay men and women. Regardless of any claims to the effect of "loving the sinner, but hating the sin," history has shown that hating the sin invariably leads to hating the sinner, too, especially when we're told, as Dobson, Falwell, MacArthur and so many others have, that lesbians and abortionists are the root cause of September-11-style destruction.

For these reasons, religion is constitutionally protected as a private expression of morality, yet it's expressly forbidden by the Establishment Clause of the First Amendment to the U.S. Constitution from interfering in the affairs of the state. This American government: founded upon the ideas of human liberty, democracy and compromise. If the Clause didn't exist, it would be all too easy for the government to be taken over by religious zealots who could freely write the "hating of the sinner" into law. For the record, here are some of the biblical laws that certain fundamentalist Christians would like to see added to our Constitution. Whenever a fundamentalist or a Bush Republican quotes biblical law in order to justify his or her homophobia, remind them about what *else* biblical law mandates:

20   http://firstread.msnbc.msn.com/archive/2008/01/15/579265.aspx

BAN ALL CLOTHING OF DIFFERENT FABRICS: Thou shalt not sow thy field with mingled seed: neither shall a garment mingled of linen and woolen come upon thee. —LEVITICUS 19:19

ADULTERERS EXECUTED: And the man that committeth adultery with another man's wife, even he that committeth adultery with his neighbour's wife, the adulterer and the adulteress shall surely be put to death. —LEVITICUS 20:10

GAYS AND LESBIANS EXECUTED: If a man also lie with mankind, as he lieth with a woman, both of them have committed an abomination: they shall surely be put to death; their blood shall be upon them. —LEVITICUS 20:13

ANYONE WHO TOUCHES A WOMAN ON HER PERIOD DEPORTED: And if a man shall lie with a woman having her [period], and shall uncover her nakedness; he hath discovered her fountain, and she hath uncovered the fountain of her blood: and both of them shall be cut off from among their people. —LEVITICUS 20:18

WOMEN WHO HAVE PRE-MARITAL SEX EXECUTED: And the daughter of any priest, if she profane herself by playing the whore, she profaneth her father: she shall be burnt with fire. —LEVITICUS 21:9

THE DISABLED BANNED FROM CHURCH: For whatsoever man he be that hath a blemish, he shall not approach [God]: a blind man, or a lame, or he that hath a flat nose, or any thing superfluous. —LEVITICUS 21:18

**RICHARD DAWKINS, PZ MYERS and BILL MA-
HER EXECUTED:** And he that blasphemeth the name
of the LORD, he shall surely be put to death, and all
the congregation shall certainly stone him: as well the
stranger, as he that is born in the land, when he blasphemeth the name of the Lord, shall be put to death.
—LEVITICUS 24:16

Yep. Leviticus is just dandy, isn't it? Deuteronomy, meanwhile,
dictates that anyone of a different religion ought to be killed
(17:2-7). This would have scary implications for people who
mistakenly believe that Senator Obama isn't a Christian. Also, if
your buddy sends you an e-mail suggesting that Buddhism looks
interesting, biblical law mandates that your buddy be stoned to
death (13:6-10).

And, of course, St. Paul had quite a bit to say in favor of
slavery:

Servants, be obedient to them that are your masters according to the flesh, with fear and trembling, in single-
ness of your heart, as unto Christ. —EPHESIANS 6:5

Let as many servants as are under the yoke count their
own masters worthy of all honor, that the name of God
and his doctrine be not blasphemed.
—I TIMOTHY 6:1

It goes without saying that not a single one of these biblical
laws has any place in the American constitutional form of government. In fact, I seriously doubt the ink would even stick to the
parchment. Men like Huckabee and Bill O'Reilly and too many
others, meanwhile, repeat this fallacy that America was founded
as a Judeo-Christian nation, even though the men of the En-

lightenment were all about natural law, rather than religious law. Thomas Jefferson, however, was vocally opposed to Christianity. For instance:

> The whole history of these books [the Gospels] is so defective and doubtful that it seems vain to attempt minute enquiry into it: and such tricks have been played with their text, and with the texts of other books relating to them, that we have a right, from that cause, to entertain much doubt what parts of them are genuine. In the New Testament there is internal evidence that parts of it have proceeded from an extraordinary man; and that other parts are of the fabric of very inferior minds. It is as easy to separate those parts, as to pick out diamonds from dunghills.[21]

Thomas Paine, whose writing inspired the Declaration of Independence, rejected all religions:

> I do not believe in the creed professed by the Jewish Church, by the Roman Church, by the Greek Church, by the Turkish Church, by the Protestant Church, nor by any church that I know of. My own mind is my own church.[22]

Arguably one of the more conservative and pious of the founders, John Adams, as president, signed the Treaty of Tripoli in 1796 in which he wrote unequivocally: "As the government of the United States of America is not in any sense founded on the Christian Religion." There's no gray area there.

Yet unless we stand against it, fundamentalist religion will

---

21   From a letter by Thomas Jefferson to John Adams dated January 24, 1814

22   *The Age of Reason*, 1794

continue to push its way into the realms of secular democracy, even though secular documents like the Constitution are tasked with magnanimously protecting religion from intrusion by the state.

And this insanely frustrating inability for fundamentalists to understand that our American Constitution affords for the peaceful coexistence of all sides can only be attributed to the hysterically blind fear-mongering, the deception and the cowardice of those on the religious far-right who will be unsatisfied until everyone is assimilated to their brand of faith. Whether it's the fear-mongering of James Dobson or President Bush; or the cowardice of the *Expelled!* producers; or the laughable deception of Ray Comfort and Kirk Cameron, not one of them seems willing to accept that by endeavoring to forcibly cram their faith into science and politics, they're opening themselves up to furious blowback. American government is a two-way road whereby we are taxed, yet protected; we're regulated, yet offered freedom; we're ruled by laws, yet we can influence the writing of those laws. So if fundamentalist Christian zealots insist upon having their biblically justified moral code written into the secular law, then they ought to hunker down and be ready to pay the price. Taxes and regulation. Just like a citizen or, hell, a corporation. Taxing the Catholic Church and the Southern Baptist Convention could single-handedly eliminate the federal budget deficit. This, of course, is an unthinkable option for all sides because when government is allowed to intrude upon your religion, there's nothing to keep it from intruding upon my speech. And this—all of it—is what's been happening during the Bush administration. It's all been mixed and mashed around and, consequently, liberty has been smothered.

So the only way to protect our liberty, our science and our democracy is to employ our secular ability to compromise: to guarantee religion all the latitude it requires, but to ensure its latitude remains secured within well-defined boundaries. Anything that crashes beyond those boundaries, whether innocuous or nightmarish, has to be met with tenacious opposition until the balance is restored. In a practical sense, the people of Dover, Pennsylvania set an example for us all by succeeding in their effort to roll back the dangerous convergence of church and state. And this 2008 election is the next best way for all of us to continue the reacquisition of American liberty, rationality and science.

PARURESIS

I thought I'd end with a somewhat embarrassing personal story about overcoming irrational fear and my standoff against a real-life fear-monger. Enjoy.

George Gordon Battle Liddy was one of the notorious Plumbers who worked inside the Nixon White House and was eventually convicted on multiple criminal charges surrounding his participation in the break-in at the Democratic National Committee headquarters inside the Watergate Hotel in Washington, D.C.

An FBI agent, Korean War veteran, lawyer, failed politician, and a childhood fan of Adolf Hitler, G. Gordon Liddy was involved in the arrest of Timothy Leary in 1966 and eventually worked on the campaign staff of President Nixon in 1968. Throughout the 1960s and early 1970s, Liddy ran with a circle of shady villains including CIA agent E. Howard Hunt, who also eventually rose to infamy with the Plumbers.

Drawing operating cash from a White House slush fund, the Plumbers were organized after Daniel Ellsberg leaked the Pentagon Papers to the *New York Times*. A top-secret Defense Department document, seven thousand pages long, publicly revealed massive government malfeasance and deception during the Vietnam War, including illegal bombings and secret orders to escalate the war. If the Watergate investigation was the main course in the demystification of the presidency, the Pentagon Papers were the naiveté-obliterating appetizers.

Authorized by West Wing operatives at the highest levels of the Nixon White House, including chief of staff H.R. "Bob" Haldemann, and special counsel to the president, Charles Colson, the White House Special Investigative Unit was formed and nicknamed the Plumbers.

CIA veteran E. Howard Hunt and Hunt's sometimes-sidekick G. Gordon Liddy were hired to do what plumbers do. Plug leaks. This involved ratfuckings[1] and various degrees of political espionage against potential and known leakers within the executive branch. As a way to categorize leaks and threats within the Nixon White House, Liddy invented ODESSA: the Organization Directed to Eliminate the Subversion of the Secrets of the Administration. Given Liddy's obsession with all things Hitler, it's no coincidence that it shares its name with the Nazi ODESSA apparatus tasked with smuggling SS fugitives out of Germany towards the end of World War II.

It's also no coincidence that Liddy was regarded to be more than a little batshit.

Liddy personally masterminded a break-in at the office of Daniel Ellsberg's psychiatrist's office in order to attain Ellsberg's psychiatric records. The idea was to discredit the leaker of the Pentagon Papers by proving he was nuts. In those days, merely

---

1   "Ratfucking" is a political term used to describe double-crosses and dirty tricks orchestrated against Democrats. "Rat" being derived from Demo-cRATs. The term was popularized in Bob Woodward and Carl Bernstein's Watergate tome *All The President's Men* and attributed therein to Donald Segretti and other Republican operatives.

visiting a psychiatrist was cause enough to prove a man's mental instability and would've convicted Ellsberg in the court of public opinion. Although the medical file wasn't removed from the office, the psychiatrist Dr. Lewis Fielding reported that Ellsberg's files were opened and appeared to have been examined during the break-in. It's likely that the pages were photographed by one of the burglars.

After the Fielding break-in, White House counsel (and current anti-McBush Republican hero) John Dean hired Liddy to serve as a special counsel for the Committee to Re-Elect the President—CREEP, for short. Mr. Liddy accepted the job and joined Hunt, former Nixon Attorney General John Mitchell, and other power-drunk white guys who, when listed, read like the screenplay for the movie adaptation of Woodward and Bernstein's *All The President's Men*: McCord, Segretti, Sloan, Stans, MacGruder and so on.

Even though CREEP had a legitimate purpose, it was more or less a front for some of the darkest, most sinister political operations in modern presidential history: wiretaps, eavesdropping, sabotage, ratfucking, smear-mongering, nefarious tax audits, intimidation and what could be defined as forms of political terrorism. Sound familiar? And it all ended at the Watergate Hotel on the morning of June 17, 1972 when, at the command of G. Gordon Liddy and E. Howard Hunt and with authorization from President Nixon and his inner circle, Frank Sturgis and a gaggle of sinister characters, including CREEP member and former CIA associate James McCord, were arrested during an aborted burglary inside the Democratic National Committee headquarters at the Watergate. This led to a series events that destroyed the Nixon presidency.

Mr. Liddy, Howard Hunt and the five burglars were convicted in 1973—Liddy on charges of wiretapping, burglary and criminal conspiracy. One of Liddy's proudest claims is that he never ratted on his cohorts, unlike, he says, his nemesis John Dean who eventually and famously testified to the Senate Watergate Committee that there existed a "cancer on the presidency." Liddy and John Dean? They're not friends.

But the Watergate story only scratches the surface of the whole Liddy *Wow! He's Fucking Crazy!* Legend. In his autobiography *Will*, published in 1980, Liddy details some truly batshit stories from his personal timeline.

For example, Liddy learned to build up his willpower by burning himself with lit cigarettes and candle flames, not unlike that Gary Busey "Mr. Joshua, your arm, please!" scene in *Lethal Weapon*. Naturally, most of us would agree that there are better ways to increase our willpower. Quitting smoking. Dieting. Exercise. Staying awake during a John McCain speech. Painful but non-mutilating things.

But if you choose to burn yourself like an idiot, well okay. Knock yourself out. Maybe just open a window for ventilation and for heaven's sake, wear eye protection. And I should also caution you: please, only burn *yourself*. Burning other people is frowned upon by law enforcement.

Liddy eventually became really good at, you know, torturing himself with fire. Like a close-up magician, he would occasionally burn himself upon request at parties. I imagine people inviting him over to a backyard barbeque just to witness his crowd-pleasing self-immolation routine. *Gather around, kids! Crazy Mr. Liddy's gonna burn himself for our shock and delight. Yay!*

Here's the really psychotic part.

In *All the President's Men*, Bob Woodward recounts a deep background conversation he had with Mark Felt, then known simply as Deep Throat. Felt told Woodward about the time he witnessed Liddy burning himself at a party until the skin on his hand was charred. Someone asked Liddy, "What's the trick?" and Liddy famously replied, "The trick is not minding."

"Not minding."

This man worked in the White House.

Somewhat recently.

When President Carter magnanimously commuted Liddy's prison sentence in 1977, television cameras surrounded the gates of the federal penitentiary in Danbury, Connecticut where Liddy was being held. In debt and in need of something new and exciting with which to repulse and frighten the nation, Liddy reached into his weirdo basket of crazy and didn't disappoint.

Accompanied by his wife, Frances, the grim-faced Liddy strode through the crowd to a waiting Pinto... Asked how he felt, he responded, this time in German, "What does not destroy me makes me stronger." His destination, he said, was "east of the sun and west of the moon."[2]

Liddy loaded up the trunk of the Pinto with his belongings from prison: a pair of rubber pants, his collection of shivs made from human genitals, his mustache collection.[3] Then he closed the trunk and, I'm not making this up, karate chopped the goddamn car.

It's on videotape. I've seen it. Liddy inexplicably karate chopped the ass-end of a Ford Pinto. Now, many of us who were around when people drove Pintos know that it was best to handle

2   *TIME* Magazine. Monday, September 19, 1977.

3   I'm guessing on this.

Pintos with kid gloves, mainly because a sudden blow to the vehicle could cause them to, well, burst into flames. Seriously. Ford Pintos would occasionally explode due to a flaw in the placement of the fuel tank. So when a Pinto was involved in a rear-end collision, they would sometimes blow up.[4]

The thing is I wonder if Liddy *wanted* the Pinto to explode. Can you guess where I'm going with this? If the Pinto exploded, he could dazzle the press with his awesomely crazy self-immolation trick, only this time using the explosive power of a gasoline-fueled fireball.

Karate chop. Boom! "The trick is not minding." Round of applause.

The most batshit story from Liddy's book, however, spotlights a rat. Have you noticed, it's always rats with this group? *Ratfucking.* Don't *rat* on your fellow Watergate conspirators. "Democrat Party." And now this: the most famous story about Liddy involves rats and fear and more crazy.

In *Will*, Liddy writes that when he was little boy, he was scrawny and weak. With the exception of his full, bushy mustache by age six,[5] Liddy described himself as "frightened, small and a coward," "frequently ill" and "self-loathing." He was also terrified of rats.

Some people have rats as pets, but most of us would rather

---

4   Ford was reportedly deceptive about the incendiary tendencies of their Pintos. Remember that scene in *Fight Club* in which Edward Norton describes his major car company employer's mathematical equation for determining whether a recall or lawsuit would be more costly? That was based on the "Ford Pinto Memo," which outlined just that. In the memo, the cost of a recall and replacing the defective fuel tank was calculated to be $121 million, while allowing people to die in fiery infernos was a steal at only $49 million. Naturally, the recall never happened.

5   Again, guessing.

this species of rapidly multiplying, plague-like giant rodent stay the hell out of our houses and restaurants. People, by in large, don't like rats—what with all the biting and the filth and the diseases and the living in the sewers and such. But few of us have sought to overcome our fear and loathing of rats… the Liddy way.

Liddy tells of a day in 1941 when his cat, Tommy,[6] killed a rat and presented it, as cats do, on the front step of the Liddy home. Rather than disposing of the rat in the rubbish can using a shovel or a rake, Liddy decided that it was time for him to overcome his unnatural and inhuman fear of rats. It was time. No more fear of rats. So he forced himself to pick up the rat using both hands. He carried the dead beast into his backyard where he constructed a small Hibachi with some bricks and proceeded to cook the rat.

> For the next hour, I roasted the dead rat. Then I removed the burned carcass with a stick and let it cool *[he hadn't yet overcome his fear of heat and fire]*. With a scout knife I skinned, then cut off and ate the roasted haunches of the rat. The meat was tasteless and stringy *[coincidentally, so is his radio show]*. Finished, I dismantled the little fireplace and buried the rest of the carcass. As I stamped down the earth over the remnants of my meal, I spotted the cat, Tommy *[Run, Tommy! Run for your goddamn life!]*. I smiled as the thought occurred to me: from now on rats could fear me as they feared cats; after all, I ate them too.[7]

First, I'd like to think that by "I ate them too" Liddy meant to imply that he eats rats like cats eat rats, and not, "I ate [cats]

---

6   Primus rules!

7   *Will*, pg. 24

too." But it wouldn't shock me if scrawny pre-pubescent Liddy ran around eating all varieties of cats and other vermin like some sort of hairless, inner-city Gollum. I suppose he opted to be patient until he could graduate up to human prey. Secondly, do rats have some sort of underground network through which they dispatch threat levels and the identities of known predators? Like a rat version of Homeland Security? If not, how would *all* rats fear him?

For the postscript to Liddy's rat-eating story, he writes in *Will* about an incident in prison when "a big black man" (whose dialogue Liddy wrote phonetically) challenged Liddy's manhood by placing a dead rat on the ground at his feet while the inmates were having recess or whatever they do in the outdoor prison courtyard. Not one to be intimidated—after all, he burns himself—Liddy decided to leap up like Spider-Man and stomp down on the rat's head. The book describes in detail about how the rat's "putrefied" guts erupted from rat's anus. Quoting Jeff Spicoli: *Oh! Gnarly!*

Liddy picked up the rat and said to the "big black man," "I think I fucked up your rat."[8] Then Liddy swung it around like a lasso—spraying rat guts everywhere—and hurled it over the fence.

When the break-in at the DNC headquarters took place, my parents and I lived in Pentagon City at the River House apartments, just across Shirley Highway from the Pentagon. I was eleven months old. From their apartment window, my parents could see the White House and the Watergate Hotel itself.

Twenty years later, in 1993, I ended up working ten feet away

---

8   Ibid. pg. 317

from G. Gordon Liddy every damn day. The only thing physically separating us was a large pane of broadcast-quality plate glass.

In 1993, I was hired to be a college intern for the *Don & Mike Show*, a nationally syndicated afternoon radio talk show hosted by Don Geronimo and Mike O'Meara. The show broadcast from WJFK-FM in Fairfax, Virginia, which was about ten minutes from Annandale, where, after my parents moved us further into the suburbs, I grew up listening to *Don & Mike* every day. This was a really big deal for me since my career aspiration at the time was to be a talk-radio host. The novelty being that there weren't many liberal talk shows at that time and maybe I could use that as a hook to get noticed by program directors. Even though I went on to host my own talk shows from various stations in Virginia and Pennsylvania, I was ultimately about ten years too early on the liberal-talk thing.

After a couple of months of learning about radio by fetching Don's salad and Diet Cherry Coke Big Gulp every day, I was appropriated by the show's news anchor, Buzz Burbank and was assigned to monitor and organize Associated Press wire-service reports, which were printed on an oversized dot-matrix printer in the newsroom.[9] During the morning hours, I would sort through all of the pages and prioritize the stories that Buzz was actively following in his newscasts. From there, Buzz would narrow down his final selections, and then he would write-up original versions of the news items in his own style and with the show's sense of humor in mind.

Almost immediately, Buzz and I developed a mentor/stu-

---

9   This was before the Internet. In the olden days, AP would upload their news to a satellite, which, in turn, beamed—as if by magic—the news down to newsroom printers around the world.

dent relationship and, due partly to our similar politics and mutual admiration of David Letterman, we eventually formed a comradery that has gratefully endured to this day. Buzz's small newsroom, where he and I lived for eight hours a day, looked directly into the main broadcast studio through a five-by-five-foot triple-paned soundproof glass window that allowed Buzz to make eye contact with Don and Mike during the show and, at the same time, allowed him to assemble his newscasts without disrupting the wacky on-air goings-on, which often included strippers, circus freaks, hobbits, mentally challenged callers and the occasional Van Patten.

The *Don & Mike Show* broadcast from 3 p.m. to 7 p.m. every afternoon, so much of what I did in the newsroom happened before the show. And, via that glass broadcast window, I worked in plain view of the program that aired in the timeslot immediately preceding *Don & Mike*. While I sorted through Buzz's AP items and prepared news audio clips, I was able to observe G. Gordon Liddy hosting his psychonaut, right-wing, nationally syndicated show from 11 a.m. to 2:30 p.m. every damn day. Convicted Watergate conspirator G. Gordon Liddy. Right *there*.

When I was first hired, I knew about the Liddy show and how it originated from the same building, so I took the opportunity to refresh myself on Watergate. I read *All The President's Men* for a second time and watched the brilliant movie adaptation for the third time and read *Will* for the first time. Which was a mistake. The result was that I was immediately intimidated by Liddy. And when I began to work in the newsroom on the other side of the glass, I was especially terrified. After all, I was a long-haired liberal college elitist who worked for an obscene radio talk show hosted by a deejay who challenged Liddy's claim to have the largest testicles in the building.[10] I also learned that while Liddy couldn't legally carry a firearm, he did in fact carry some sort of bladed ninja weapon in an ankle sheath; and it's important to note that he was some kind of expert in handling this weapon. The prevailing wisdom around the building was essentially that Liddy was a doddering old man... who could strike and kill anyone at any moment.

So in other words, the scariest co-worker imaginable. I unapologetically feared this guy and with good reason. He ate a goddamn rat. He burned himself at parties. He was a player in the most notorious and sinister political operation of the twentieth century. And he made it clear that he wasn't a fan of President Clinton in a very scary way: one day he described how he instructed his grandchildren to use a photo of the president on their firing range targets. Mainly, though, Liddy was completely unhinged.

---

10   I'm not making this up. Liddy and Don Geronimo had a feud over who had the largest balls. Don was doing it as a bit. I think Liddy was serious. Ten years later, Liddy appeared on *Hardball with Chris Matthews* shortly after President Bush sported his ball-hugging flight suit aboard the USS Abraham Lincoln and declared "major combat operations have ended" in Iraq. Liddy described the scene as such:

MATTHEWS: What do you make of this broadside against the USS Abraham Lincoln and its chief visitor last week?
LIDDY: Well, I—in the first place, I think it's envy. I mean, after all, Al Gore had to go get some woman to tell him how to be a man. And here comes George Bush. You know, he's in his flight suit, he's striding across the deck, and he's wearing his parachute harness, you know—and I've worn those because I parachute—and it makes the best of his manly characteristic. You go run those—run that stuff again of him walking across there with the parachute. He has just won every woman's vote in the United States of America. You know, all those women who say size doesn't count—they're all liars. Check that out. I hope the Democrats keep ratting on him and all of this stuff so that they keep showing that tape. (*Source*: http://mediamatters.org/items/200604270005)

Also, did you spot it? "The Democrats keep *ratting* on him..."

Liddy's radio show is and was ridiculous. For instance, after pretending to deliver a ship-to-shore SOS from outside the Beltway ("the eight-lane death strip," as he called it) to the so-called liberal elites inside the Beltway over a recording of Jan Hammer's *Miami Vice* theme song, the first hour of the show was G. Gordon Liddy reading from various newspapers.[11] Literally. He didn't paraphrase or discuss the headlines. He read the articles. Word for word. On the air. For the longest hour of radio ever. Then, for the next two hours, he would take calls from white bigots and far-right militia crazies who would ask him about his favorite Nazi aircraft (he loved to say "Messerschmitt!"). It was like watching the History Channel without the Hitler footage but hosted by, you know, Hitler.

And wouldn't you know it; Hitler—I mean, Liddy—nicknamed me High Pockets. One morning during my first week in the newsroom, Liddy was reading from the *Washington Post* on the air, like always. On this day, Liddy was reading aloud about Federal Reserve Chairman Alan Greenspan. Now, everyone pronounces the name Greenspan exactly the same way. But for some reason, Liddy pronounced it Green-shpun. And while he was reading the article, he kept saying it that way. Over and over. *Greenshpun.* He was entirely serious, too. By the twentieth mention of Alan *Greenshpun*, it struck me as oddly hilarious and I began to laugh. It was one of those uncontrollable and uncomfortable church laughters—the more I tried to stop, the harder it was to contain.

My laughing increased with each repeated pronunciation of

---

11   Liddy's resume includes a guest-starring role on *Miami Vice* in which he played a doddering old man who could kill anyone at any moment.

Greenshpun, and it must've eventually caught Liddy's attention because, on the air, he wrapped up his story time and said, "High Pockets in the newsroom thinks this is funny!"

Yes, I was High Pockets.

I suppose it was because I'm a tall guy and Mr. Liddy is approximately the same height as a G.I Joe action figure. Low Pockets, if you will. But I'll take High Pockets over death by ninja ankle blade any day.

An hour or so later, I entered the lobby restroom and stepped up to the urinal. Just as I unzipped, in walked G. Gordon Liddy.

"Hello there, High Pockets," he blurted out in his nasally rasp.

"Oh, hey, Mr. Liddy," I replied as he stepped up to the urinal next to mine. Of course I continued to be terrified of his historically accurate penchant for crazy, but now he had caught me laughing at him and his horrible radio program. And there we were side by side, standing next to each other at those public urinals, my genitals within striking distance of his ninja blade.

And so I couldn't urinate.

They say it's a social anxiety disorder called paruresis. Bashful bladder. Pee shyness. Stage fright. The inability to urinate in public. There's even an International Paruresis Association for people who have a serious on-going problem with this disorder.[12] G. Gordon Liddy—or more appropriately, my *Irrational Fear of G. Gordon Liddy*—gave me stage fright. For a week or so, I couldn't urinate in the public restroom at WJFK regardless of whether G. Gordon Liddy was in there or not. If he was in the restroom when I walked in, I would wash my hands and leave. If I was in there and he walked in, my urinary tract would seize up mid-stream, which,

12   www.paruresis.org

if you're a guy, is extraordinarily painful for reasons I'll never fully understand. If he wasn't in the restroom or even if he had gone home for day, I feared that he would burst in, kill me and dispose of my gutted carcass using some kind of untraceable vivisection process he learned from his creepy CREEP friends.

Clearly this terrible case of stage fright was caused by a psychological accumulation of everything I knew about Liddy's morbid personal history along with an over-thought self-evaluation that I was the embodiment of everything he found to be loathsome and dangerous in America. In the 1960s, Liddy would have considered someone like me to be a radical left-wing subversive, a socialist, a threat to decent Republican society, dangerous to America and therefore someone who ought to be marginalized and targeted by him and his underground network of authoritarian black-operatives. I had built up in my head an entire syllabus of justifications for Liddy one day killing me that I lost the ability to relieve my bladder in that building.

The *Irrational Fear of G. Gordon Liddy*. It's very likely that I'm the first person to have experienced this phobia since, maybe, John Dean and Daniel Ellsberg in the early and middle 1970s. But even they haven't to date revealed any such disorder. For the first time since his days as a White House Plumber, it can be said that G. Gordon Liddy successfully plugged a leak.

As the subsequent few weeks rolled on by, I eventually got over my pee shyness but not my fear of Liddy. Meanwhile, Buzz had received as a birthday gift from a fan: a framed, autographed eight-by-ten photograph of David Letterman. Buzz chose a spot on the newsroom wall and hung the photograph using a push-pin. Innocuous enough. David Letterman is universally considered a national treasure. He's not as mainstream as Jay Leno, but he's certainly not a freakish ne'er-do-well worthy of hatred or attack based strictly on his photographed image.

Except in G. Gordon Liddy's twisted little craptastic world of madness.

During a commercial break one afternoon, I was dubbing some news audio from a reel-to-reel tape deck onto several broadcast cartridges, which, before computers took their place, were a kind of looped audio tape not unlike 8-track cassettes and were ubiquitously used in radio for quick access to sound effects and audio clips.

So I had my back turned away from the newsroom door when I heard from behind, "High Pockets!"

This was Liddy. And he was pissed off.

"High Pockets! I want you to take down this photo of this asshole here!"

"The David Letterman photo? Why?" I asked, stalling while quickly scanning the room for a weapon with which I could defend myself. My mind raced, *A Sharpie marker? It might claim to be sharp, but will it protect me from his berserker blade? Nope. The stapler, then! Yes! I'll staple his bald head!*

"It's distracting me and I can't do my show with this asshole staring at me!" Oh man, he was really angry and even though he's a little man, I was sitting, so he seemed to be, in my distorted emotional state, a *ten-foot-tall* hairless, doddering old man who could kill anyone at any moment.

My voice cracked as I began, "Well, it's Buzz's photo," then I somehow mustered the wherewithal to speak his authoritarian language, "and I don't have the *authorization* to remove anything from Buzz's newsroom."

Liddy stared at me for a brief moment. He appeared to be

temporarily confused by my defiance. Then he made a series of noises that, in print, would probably look like, "Mrr-ruh-ruh-ruh-rrrrr." He turned and stormed off.

Was he serious? An eight-by-ten photograph hung on a wall at least ten feet away from him, through a soundproof glass window and barely within his peripheral vision... was distracting?

When I mentioned this to Buzz, he immediately called Don Geronimo and relayed the story. I could hear Don laughing on the phone, then screaming something about Liddy being a doddering old man. Buzz grinned from ear to ear, and then hung up. He turned to me and answered Liddy's demand with a simple two-word phrase: "Fuck Liddy." Fuck Liddy. After this unpleasantness had dissipated, I arranged for the printing of a Fuck Liddy bumper sticker as a thank you gift for Buzz. This beautifully perfect Fuck Liddy response to Liddy's persnickety jihad against the Letterman photograph inspired me. I felt empowered by Don and Buzz. After all, I was exhausted with being afraid of this guy. And besides, he had ultimately revealed himself to be a coward by not bringing this up with Buzz or Don. Instead, he opted to bully an unpaid intern. Why? Was he afraid to face the unkempt, liberal freaks who hosted the show after his, so much so that he had to resort to going after the new guy? High Pockets?

Fuck Liddy.

So I teamed up with Robb Spewak, one of Don's producers, and we decided to strike back against Liddy's megalomania. We decided, in a manner of speaking, to eat the rat. To hold our arms over the open flame. For me, that which came next was all about facing my *Irrational Fear of G. Gordon Liddy*.

With permission from Buzz, the next morning before Liddy arrived at the station, Robb and I acquiesced to Liddy's demand

and removed the Letterman photograph from the newsroom wall. We removed it from the wall, and then removed the photo from the frame. We photocopied Letterman's face and printed what must have been hundreds of copies at various sizes. A batch of full-page Letterman faces and dozens of smaller ones. Then we cut out all of the faces and grabbed several rolls of Scotch Tape.

What happened next was one of those things I wish I had documented on videotape. Robb and I decorated the entire goddamn building with Letterman faces. We taped Letterman faces on the restroom mirror. We wallpapered the hallway near Liddy's office with Letterman faces. We taped tiny dozens of Letterman faces on each of the leaves of the ficus tree in the lobby. We taped Letterman faces over the heads of people pictured inside his copy of the *Washington Times* and *Wall Street Journal*. We taped Letterman faces to the salt and pepper shakers in the lunchroom. In the elevator Liddy rode every morning, we cut one of the large Letterman faces in half down the middle and taped each half to the inside of the elevator doors. So when Liddy stepped into the elevator and the doors closed, the two halves would come together and form a giant Letterman face staring right back at him.

I would venture a guess that for years WJFK employees discovered Letterman faces hidden in unexpected places.

When Liddy arrived for his show that day, Letterman's face was there to greet—and distract him—around every corner. It was inescapable. On the studio ceiling tiles, on cartridges stacked along the wall, on individual paper towels in the restroom, on doorknobs and on computer screens. That night, he would discover Letterman's face staring back at him through his windshield, tucked under his windshield wiper blades.

But Letterman's face wasn't on the newsroom wall.

Just as he had requested the day before.

Liddy, despite his over-the-top reputation, turned out to be fairly typical of our present-day McBush Republican fear-mongers. The most common trait is relatively clear: Liddy was, and still is, a coward. Throughout his life, he overcompensated for his self-admitted cowardice by engaging in feats of unhinged madness and attack, not unlike what we've witnessed for the last eight years of McBush Republicanism: knee-jerk, reactionary fits of irrational madness.

It only took a little defiance, some creativity and a lot of Letterman heads to shut him down. In a strange way, the lesson I learned out of this ridiculous episode came from Liddy himself, and I hasten to note that this is the only life lesson I've taken away from the crazy bastard. When confronted by the far-right's predictions of doom and terror and death—the fire-eyed warnings of fear-mongers of all forms, from the very serious to the self-satirical to the menacingly powerful—the secret to enduring these hyped and often fictitious dangers is, as Liddy once said... *not minding.*

CONCLUSION

ANOTHER HERO GENERATION

Now we can make it, Mac. I feel big as a damn mountain.

–Chief Bromden
One Flew Over the Cuckoo's Nest

The American spirit of liberty and resiliency has been systematically whipped out of us. Regardless of your personal political or ideological affiliation, there can be no denying that the McBush Republican fear-mongers have twisted and manipulated and contorted our collective emotions for far too long, and for the most cynical, maniacal and destructive reasons. This nonstop assault has broken too many of us. It's given way to complacency and ambivalence, a resignation to accept the same tired old script. It's the hack script that says: Republicans are presidential; Democrats are effete elitists; opposing the occupation means opposing the troops; lapel pins equal patriotism; a black man with a different-sounding name can't be trusted; and you can't have a Bill of Rights if you're dead. This is the script that, once we were all tricked into embracing it, bought us an expensive national ticket aboard this dark ride.

Half of America—at *least* half of it—has been scared into submission, into supporting the wrong things while ignoring the right things. Despite all of the crap, there continue to be blood-red states across the Middle West populated by Americans who have yet to fully grasp that George W. Bush or Dick Cheney or John McCain won't save their homes or rescue their jobs or preserve their liberty. To wit: after eight years of Bush Republicanism—six of those years supported by a Republican Congress, all of those years supported by FOX News Channel and by far-right talk radio, and with five of those years providing the president with high approval numbers—there's still a painful recession, a massive deficit, mortgage foreclosures, terrorism, rape, condoms, abortion, disproportionately high middle-class taxes, a communist nation grabbing chunks of our economy and all of those things that the McBush Republicans were supposed to be against. All of this after a decade of near-single-party Republican control. But on the upside, gay men can't get married in Kansas. So that's something. But the truth is that the red states were good for a scare, and then a pile of electoral votes, and then they were forgotten along with the rest of us.

And as you and I have seen, the one thing we should have feared was, as President Roosevelt famously said, fear itself. The infrastructure upon which the McBush Republicans have built their power has been carved entirely out of fear and cowardice. In other words, it's been fear that has prevented us from moving forward, and certainly *not* all of those exaggerated or wholly falsified "threats" with which they have been pummeling us for too many years.

Naturally, FDR's inaugural warning didn't preclude fear, but instead, a particular brand of fear. He defined this destructive brand of fear as "nameless, unreasoning, unjustified terror which paralyzes needed efforts to convert retreat into advance." The fear of terrorism in Zanesville succeeded in scaring up some votes for President Bush and Bob Ney, but this "unjustified, paralyzing" fear has prevented Zanesville from doing anything about the politicians and the corporations that are polluting the air and water with deadly toxic chemicals. The fear of black people might succeed in electing or re-electing white Republican bigots, but this "unreasoning" fear is standing in the way of a new direction that we so desperately need after eight years of truly menacing conspiracies.

There was a time there, after September 11, when we could've achieved something heroic. From Tehran to Beijing, from red states to blue states, everyone was an "American." There was a seldom seen unity among humans and an opportunity to harness that energy to create for ourselves a truly awesome future. It was right there on the tips of everyone's tongues. Once we shook off the initial trauma of the attacks, Americans of all ideologies looked to our leaders for instructions. *What do we do? We feel really damn unified—we should do something great!*

But instead of pointing the way towards new and terrific horizons, the Bush administration didn't even try. They patted us on the head and asked us to go shopping. They asked us to do...nothing. And anyone who was still paying attention became the target of a massive conspiracy. Through carefully constructed lies and propaganda Americans were frightened into behaving like semi-catatonic drones whose votes were about as independently motivated as the ones cast by Diebold. Americans were frightened into complacency and acquiescence and much of that attitude endures today, even after Hurricane Katrina helped to pull back the curtain on the McBushies. The pendulum has swung too far to one side that oftentimes it doesn't seem as if it will ever fully swing back the other way. And irrespective of the crimes perpetrated at the top, our post-September-11 hysterical blindness is partly to blame for this stuck pendulum. We either allowed it to happen or we didn't do enough to stop it. Too many otherwise decent liberals stood with the president in those night-marish days of late 2001. Too many Americans gave the admin-istration the benefit of the doubt leading up to the invasion of Iraq. Too many voters were frightened into being "fooled again" in the election of 2004 only to witness more death and disaster less than a year later when the levees broke.

So what do we do now? How do we, at this critical stage in American history, succeed in countermanding some of the stink and awfulness for which our generation has been responsible?

What we have witnessed and endured all these years makes the challenges we face even more daunting because we're starting from a place of zero national morale. At this moment in Amer-ican history, we each have just enough motivation to keep our credit-card interest rates from spiraling out of control and our homes from being foreclosed upon. Ceaseless fear-mongering has dulled our ability to separate the truth from the trickery, to separate that which is irrelevant from that which is truly vital to our survival as a nation and as a species.

Because we have been forced to start from this place of disil-lusionment and dismally low motivation, the accomplishing of our next great achievement will be all the more sweet. A coura-geous American once said:

> What we need is another hero generation. We—those
> of us who are alive in the United States of America to-

day especially, but also the rest of the world—have to somehow understand that history has presented us with a choice... I believe we have the capacity at moments of great challenge to set aside the causes of distraction and rise to the challenge that history is presenting us... How many generations in all of human history have had the opportunity to rise to a challenge that is worthy of our best efforts? A challenge that can pull from us more than we knew we could do. I think we ought to approach this challenge with a sense of profound joy and gratitude that we are the generation about which a thousand years from now philharmonic orchestras and poets and singers will celebrate by saying, They were the ones that found it within themselves to solve this crisis and lay the basis for a bright and optimistic human future. Let's do that.[13]

This call to action was written and delivered by Al Gore in February 2008 at a presentation in Monterey, California. And he was, of course, talking about the climate crisis.

The World Health Organization estimates that 150,000 people die each year worldwide as the result of the present-day effects of global warming, and an additional five million people are suffering from various illnesses as the result of the climate crisis.[14] Those figures are expected to double by the year 2030 unless there are significant changes.

Some people (fewer by the day) will suggest that Gore uses fear with the same deceptive intentions as President Bush. Of course, these are the same people who tend to deny that the climate crisis even exists while continuing to cling to the notions

---

13   http://www.ted.com/talks

14   http://environment.about.com/od/globalwarmingandhealth/a/gw_deaths.htm

that Iraq has WMD, Senator Obama is a Muslim and the Noah's Ark story really happened. Nevertheless, while Gore discusses scary aspects of the climate crisis—each of which is based on nearly unanimous scientific evidence—he does so in a way that's intended to motivate positive, proactive solutions that will benefit everyone on the planet in every way. On the other hand, President Bush and Senator McCain, as we have seen repeatedly in this book, exploit our human tendencies for irrational, knee-jerk vengeance and fear in order to consolidate political and financial power, and, subsequently, as a catalyst for fighting an endless, expensive and ultimately self-defeating war against what FDR called, a "nameless terror." Gore asks us to rise to a historically significant challenge: one that will create jobs, one that will create economic opportunity, one that will create social unity and prosperity. President Bush, on the other hand, asked us to go shopping and to pardon corporations that violated our constitutional rights. There's no similarity whatsoever.

In order to confront the climate crisis and to ensure, as Gore said, a "bright and optimistic human future," we have to find it within ourselves to cast off the fear and the complacency of the Bush years. America's most significant achievements have come when we've reached beyond our limitations, when we refused to say *this can't be done*, or *that's too hard*. Becoming, as Chief Bromden says in *One Flew Over the Cuckoo's Nest*, "big as a mountain" requires us to break free of the McBush Republican fear. To achieve that unwritten human right: *freedom from fear*. To convince ourselves that we're Americans and we won't be coerced into laying down our constitutional rights and liberties. We're Americans and we won't be told that protecting a corporation is more important than protecting our right to be "secure in our persons, houses, papers and effects." We won't be told that, as former Bush White House press secretary Ari Fleischer warned, "We need to watch what we say and watch what we do." We won't be frightened into voting against our economic and social interests. We're Americans, and you know what? We can solve this thing called the climate crisis. America was, after all, founded by human beings who saw beyond their immediate predicament, and envisioned something unprecedented in modern history. Their goal wasn't for war, and it wasn't merely for their own personal liberties, but for the liberty and rights of all people.

As such, solving the climate crisis is about more than saving polar bears. Solving the climate crisis is also about preserving liberty. If we make this fourth American century the time in which we gave rise to what I like to call a Green Industrial Revolution, we will have successfully secured our place in history. The Green Industrial Revolution, like the Industrial Revolution of the late nineteenth century, could build an entirely new American economy including jobs for everyone from service workers to engineers to scientists to programmers to laborers. All sectors of the economy, all tasked with the goal of producing and manufacturing clean, renewable energy and products. This would, first and foremost, help to bring about the slowing and perhaps the reversal of global warming. But it would also make us safer and more secure by ending our dependence on the Saudis and other state sponsors of Islamic terrorism. By confronting terrorism through economic growth, our liberty is both preserved and safeguarded. And ultimately, the economic prosperity of such an endeavor would guarantee our sovereignty by loosening the oppressive grip of our national debt and the foreign governments who own most of it. All of this can easily be achieved without scary 24-style web videos and without fear-mongering and without risking a single American life. Solving the climate crisis is about saving humanity, but it's also about saving and strengthening America. Nothing, short of sacrificing your life for your nation, is more patriotic.

Here at the beginning of the fourth American century, we can be that next great Hero Generation worthy of our national legacy. But we won't achieve a thing if we allow ridiculous fear-mongers in cowboy (or maverick) disguises to dupe us into believing they seek any goal nobler than fear itself.

ACKNOWLEGMENTS

I wouldn't be writing about politics if it wasn't for my friend, boss and captain, Roy Sekoff, the founding editor of *The Huffington Post*. You might not know his name, but suffice it to say, he's absolutely one of the unsung heroes of the liberal blogosphere. I salute you, Captain!

On that note, a big thank-you hug for Arianna Huffington. In the middle of her own book tour for *The Right is Wrong*, she was kind enough to take the time to write my foreword. I'm honored and humbled to share space on the cover and in these pages with such a legend and visionary. I genuflect before her awesomeness.

There's a maxim a colleague of mine invented: "Does this edit make it better, or just different?" Thanks to Drew Nederpelt, Rachel Trusheim and Michael Axon at Sterling & Ross for making this book better.

An enormous h/t to my blogotubing friends including (in no particular order) Paddy, GottaLaff, John Amato, Cenk Uygur, Elvis Dingledein at Clustedouche!, Mark Crispin Miller, Eric Boehlert, Jamie at Intoxination, Lacey at Earwig & His Fearsome Critters, Steven Weber, TRex, Cliff Schecter (author of *The Real McCain*), Lee Stranahan, Martin Longman (BooMan), Steve Young, RJ Eskow, Rachel Sklar, Andy Borowitz, Rude Pundit, Paul Abrams and Big Jonny at Drunk Cyclist.

Thanks to the entire gang of commenters and readers of my personal blog (www.bobcesca.com). I'm fortunate to have the smartest, funniest and most insightful group of readers on the intertubes. America would be a better place if they were all members of Congress. Only, it'd be known as The Goddamn Awesome Congress! Go! A bashful thank you to Sunita Pillay and the members of the (blush) Facebook "Bob Cesca Fan Club." Aw shucks, guys.

Terrorist fist jabs all around for my parents, brothers, my mother-in-law, my sister-in-law and my niece. And all my love and thanks to my beautiful wife, Tara, and my daughter, Lauren (a future president of the United States—trust me). I wouldn't have been able to do this without their unconditional support—especially during the days when I was writing the Fear Bomb chapter and ended up climbing onto the roof of my house while screaming obscene derivations of the name "Glenn Beck." I love my two ladies more than anything in the world.